The Promise of Greatness

The
Promise
of
Greatness

Sar A. Levitan
and
Robert Taggart

Harvard University Press
Cambridge, Massachusetts
London, England

HN65
L44

Copyright © 1976 by the President and Fellows of Harvard College
Second Printing 1977
All rights reserved
Printed in the United States of America

Library of Congress Cataloging in Publication Data
Levitan, Sar A
  The promise of greatness.
  Includes index.
  1. United States—Social policy. 2. United States
—Economic policy—1961–   3. Economic assistance,
Domestic—United States. 4. Public welfare—United
States—Finances. 5. Public welfare administration.
I. Taggart, Robert, 1945–   joint author.
II. Title.
HN65.L44   362.9′73   75–40422
ISBN 0–674–71455–5

Contents

65145

Preface

The Great Society's strategy of "throwing money at problems" was ill conceived and ineffectual, exaggerating the capacity of the government to change institutions and individuals.

The nation was pushed too far, too fast, and was unable to afford or digest the overly ambitious agenda of the Great Society; its legacy was inflation, worker alienation, racial tension, and other lingering ills.

The growth of social welfare efforts begun under the Johnson administration has sapped our resources and vitality and the advance of the welfare state must be halted.

Today, a large proportion of our policy makers and a majority of voters would probably agree with these statements. There is growing doubt over the government's capacity to change institutions or individuals, to design and operate efficient programs, or to solve basic and persistent domestic problems.

Like many others who have attempted an evaluation of the last decade, we too have been critical of the Great Society and its efforts. In the belief that improvements were needed, we pointed out inefficiencies and inequities, mismanagement and misdirection, questioning the worth of some policies and suggesting changes in others. Our assumption, however, was that the value of these undertakings was generally accepted and that the only question was how government activities could be made more effective and resources better allocated. In the 1970s the burden of proof shifted. The need for improvement in federal programs and the lack of conclusive proof of their effectiveness were taken as evidence of ineffectuality; constructive criticism was reinterpreted as indictment. The guarded support of evaluators like ourselves was dismissed as the ranks of the gainsayers were swollen by discouraged liberals as well as by traditional conservative opponents of the welfare state.

In this book the major programmatic components of the Great

Society as well as their combined effects on the primary target groups and their success in achieving the broader aims will be examined.

Information on many questions is totally inadequate. The tools of measurement and evaluation are very crude, and the latitude for normative judgment is very wide. A completely comprehensive or objective study of anything so diverse and complicated as social reform in the 1960s and early 1970s is unattainable.

This book was written to defend our belief that the 1960s programs and policies and their continuation had a massive, overwhelmingly beneficial impact and that the weight of evidence convincingly supports this view. It seeks to draw from, rather than repudiate, the past, arguing for renewed governmental activism and continuing efforts to realize a greater society.

This is not intended as a polemic. The analysis is based on a vast array of data and studies which have been used or can be used to judge the impacts of government activities. While the interpretation emphasizes the half-full rather than half-empty cup, and the positive rather than the negative, no attempt is made to bend the facts. Our underlying assumptions and standards of judgment are spelled out to be accepted or rejected by the reader. In brief, the case stands or falls on the data and information that are readily available (even if frequently ignored).

Such a synthesis and analysis cannot be simple. The domestic programs of the 1960s encompassed almost every aspect of our lives and nearly all institutions in our society. The underlying normative and political issues are diverse. The range of relevant data and information is staggering. To put all this together in some understandable form is a formidable challenge.

We believe, however, that it was worth the risk, despite the inevitability of coming up short in many dimensions. The sweeping and erroneous conclusion that the Great Society failed continues to hold sway over decision makers and the public, generating a timidity and negativism which has retarded needed and possible progress. The issues are not merely of passing intellectual interest but rather of vital present and future importance. Whatever the cogency of our arguments to others, we remain convinced that there are grounds for hope and potentials for action, and that a better society can be realized.

The study was prepared under a grant from the Ford Foundation to the George Washington University's Center for Manpower Policy Studies. In accordance with the Foundation's practice, complete responsibility for the content was left to the authors.

SAL
RT

September 12, 1975

Part One The 1960s, the Great Society, and the Legacy

1 Perspectives and Retrospectives

> We stand at the edge of the greatest era in the life of
> any nation. For the first time in world history, we have
> the abundance and the ability to free every man from
> hopeless want, and to free every person to find fulfillment
> in the works of his mind or the labor of his hands.
>
> Even the greatest of all past civilizations existed on
> the exploitation of the misery of the many.
>
> This nation, this people, this generation, has man's first
> chance to create a Great Society: a society of success
> without squalor, beauty without barrenness, works of
> genius without the wretchedness of poverty. We can open
> the doors of learning. We can open the doors of fruitful
> labor and rewarding leisure, of open opportunity and
> close community—not just to the privileged few, but to
> everyone.
> ————Lyndon B. Johnson, June 26, 1964

Contrasting Visions

President Johnson's vision of a Great Society, contrasting so
markedly with the phlegmatic ideology of the preceding decade,
stirred the nation. Under the banner of the Great Society, there
was a dramatic acceleration of governmental efforts to insure the
well-being of all citizens, to equalize opportunity for minorities
and the disadvantaged, to eliminate, or at least mitigate, the social,
economic, and legal foundations of inequality and deprivation.
Congress moved ahead on a vast range of long-debated social
welfare measures and pushed on into uncharted seas. In its 1,866
days the Johnson administration moved vigorously to implement
these new laws and to fully utilize existing authority. The Warren
Court aided this dynamism with sweeping, precedent-setting decisions on a number of critical issues. The public supported this
activism, giving Lyndon Johnson the largest plurality in history,
his Democratic party an overwhelming majority in both Houses of
Congress, and his administration high public approval ratings as
action got underway.

Just four years later, a very different mood prevailed in the
nation—one of fear, distrust, anger, and alienation. Presidential
nominee Richard Nixon, claiming to speak for the "forgotten
American," put it succinctly: "For the past five years we have

been deluged by government programs for the unemployed, programs for cities, programs for the poor, and we have reaped from these programs an ugly harvest of frustration, violence and failure across the land." Urging return to normalcy and promising to correct the many mistakes of the Great Society but also bolstered by discontent with the Vietnam war, President Nixon eked out a narrow victory. But four years later with essentially the same platform he almost matched the Johnson landslide, garnering more than three of every five ballots. While voters returned a Democratic Congress, the 1972 victory was interpreted, at least by the administration, as a repudiation of the Great Society and its vision.

Within another three years, there was a new President and an embittered nation had substantially increased the Democratic majority in Congress. Yet this represented more an indictment of President Nixon's leadership than a negation of his philosophy. The criticism of the Great Society had become firmly rooted, and if anything, the distressing economic, political, and international events of the 1970s intensified the general sense of dissatisfaction.

Economic traumas, the Vietnam war, urban unrest, and Watergate had had a major impact on social philosophy and policy. The war undermined the moral authority of the Great Society and drained the resources needed for the full implementation of its agenda. Even more fundamentally, the activism of the 1960s was nurtured by a booming economy providing the resources for expanded governmental efforts. As growth slowed and then reversed in the 1970s, the price tag of previous commitments became more onerous and opposition more strident. Yet throughout our nation's history, military, political, and economic changes have resulted in sweeping turns in philosophy and policy. Values and hopes tend to move dialectically; institutions and groups threatened by change gradually reassert themselves while the have-nots are coopted. That the Great Society's vision was subsequently rejected was neither a historically unique nor an unexpected pattern.

Facts and Fads

There was, however, at least one important difference in these recent developments. Before the 1960s there was very little interest in, and very little basis for, assessing the impact of governmental activities. The concern with program performance and effectiveness is a recent development. New techniques of evaluation and decision making have been developed and applied during the Great Society years, such as the much heralded planning-programing-budgeting system (PPBS) and cost-benefit analysis. Data have increased exponentially to meet the needs of evaluators and policy makers. Able to influence decisions and to be well rewarded in the process, legions of social scientists have enlisted in the effort to assess government programs and advise on public policy.

For the first time, then, programs and policies have been tested on the basis of performance. The repudiation of the Great Society in the late 1960s was based on a tide of analyses alleging to demonstrate the failures of the Johnson administration's domestic endeavors. Public and national conditions change, but presumably the facts are the facts. The "proof" of the Great Society's shortcomings, which probably has been accepted as a given by a majority of the public and its policy makers, remains a primary obstacle to renewed social welfare activism. It is a matter of current and future, as well as historical, importance whether a valid judgment has been reached on the basis of the available evidence. Is the proof convincing that the social welfare programs of the Johnson administration were failures? By the same token, are there reasons to foreswear similar approaches to present and emerging problems?

Surprisingly little careful consideration has been devoted to these broad questions. Researchers and social scientists have done their individual pieces of work but have largely ignored the task of synthesis and integration. Prestige in the new discipline of assessing government activity usually has come from thinking small rather than big, specializing in narrow disciplines and using sophisticated methodologies. While there has been bitter debate about the fine points, the total picture has been largely ignored. It has been left to politicians and the media to pick from among the usually wide-ranging views of experts the facts and conclusions that meshed with their own views.

Academics were, like others, willing to applaud their Caesars, especially since the government footed most of the bill for evaluation. In the early days of the Great Society there was a surfeit of social thinkers proposing new or refined approaches to social problems, and of evaluators documenting the early success of the new ventures. A few years later when gainsaying had become fashionable and profitable, there was an equal number of pundits, some of them disenchanted proponents, who proclaimed the failure of the same programs and policies.

Presumably sophisticated, usually quantitative, techniques yielded seemingly rigorous answers highly valued by decision makers. Discussions of important assumptions and their implications (frequently placed in notes and appendices) were ignored, and social scientists were usually willing to go along with the uncritical acceptance of their work. In the late 1960s, the reservations were reread with more care, revealing that most findings were neither rigorous nor clearcut. Ironically, the discovery that the emperor was naked did not damage the reputation of social scientists and their techniques as much as it did the subjects of their evaluation: if evaluations could not conclusively prove the value of governmental programs, then the programs must not have been worthwhile.

In the 1970s, there were a few scattered attempts to review the Great Society experience in totality. Some analysts set out to document popular notions of failure. Others tried to cull the positive lessons. The generalized conclusions resulting from these reviews provide a good starting point for more detailed analysis.

First, the inflated rhetoric of the Great Society was largely to blame for the subsequent sense of failure. Measured against the grandiloquent promises, nothing could have succeeded.

Second, the apparent consensus of failure was deceiving. Some criticized the Great Society for not doing enough, or for creating inequity by helping only a small segment of the needy. Others challenged the effectiveness of governmental efforts with a view to making improvements. Still others condemned the programs on philosophical grounds for interfering with natural processes. The critics were strange bedfellows, differing fundamentally in viewpoints and prescriptions.

Third, assessment is an art rather than a science, built on normative as much as technical foundations. For instance, success or failure is relative. Compared to the promises, most efforts fell short, but the promises were clearly unrealistic. Yet what is reasonable? Differing judgments have resulted from analyzing the same facts from different perspectives.

Fourth, the Great Society experience was mixed. Some ventures were unquestionably successful, and others were justifiably condemned as failures. Sweeping judgments based on a few cases could be, and frequently were, misleading.

These general assessments, while valid, did not confront the really fundamental issue of whether the Great Society failed. This cannot be resolved by conceptualization, rhetoric, and assertion. Only by carefully reassessing the volumes of data and analytical studies in a detailed yet broad-ranging way can meaningful perspective be gained. And only by demonstrating a fair measure of success can the assumption of failure be discounted.

Leading Themes

Before delving into the volumes of evidence concerning the Great Society's achievements and failures, it is worthwhile to articulate at the outset the major conclusions which emerge from or are supported by the analysis so that the reader will be forewarned of any possible bias.

1. *The goals of the Great Society were realistic, if steadily moving, targets for the improvement of the nation.* Few would argue against "success without squalor, beauty without barrenness, works of genius without the wretchedness of poverty." Many, however, question the realism of these aims. By concentrating on the small minority of welfare recipients who are cheaters, persons who shun work, youths who squander their educational opportunities, or others who may "bite the hand that feeds them," critics have chipped away at the ambitions of the Great Society, and have suggested that those in need somehow deserve their fate. This view ignores the overwhelming majority of welfare recipients who have no other alternatives, workers who either cannot find employment or are locked in low-wage jobs, the millions of disenfranchised who are seeking only their constitutionally guaranteed rights, or youths who are striving to make the best of their lives in a confusing world.

Other less strident critics emphasize the difficulties in changing institutions and socioeconomic patterns. No matter how desirable a change, it is likely to have some unwanted side-effects, and the process itself can be an ordeal. Where opportunities and rewards are distributed unequally and unjustifiably, redistribution will obviously affect the previously chosen people. Improvements cannot be accomplished without effort and sacrifice, and the existence of impediments is not proof of unrealistic or unattainable goals.

A related argument is that there are natural processes at work which cannot be altered—fundamental racial differences, a minimum unemployment equilibrium, or a persisting poverty floor. The proof for such relationships is that they have always existed, and from this it is reasoned that they must always continue. The fundamental hypothesis of the Great Society is that such conditions are not foreordained but are rather supported by public policies and private actions which can and should be changed. The test should be in the outcome of efforts toward change rather than merely presupposing their ineffectiveness.

2. *The social welfare efforts initiated and accelerated in the 1960s moved the nation toward a more just and equitable society, mitigating the problems of the disadvantaged and disenfranchised.* The claims that these programs were uselessly "throwing dollars at problems," that government intervention cannot change institutions or individuals, or that problems remain intractable are glib rhetoric. The results of government intervention varied, undesirable spillover effects occurred, and the adopted intervention strategies were sometimes ill designed; but progress was almost always made in the desired directions. The gains of blacks and the poor, the two primary target groups of federal efforts, offer the most striking evidence. Government programs significantly reduced poverty and alleviated its deprivations. Blacks made very significant strides in education, employment, income, and rights in the 1960s.

3. *The Great Society's social welfare programs were reasonably efficient, and though improvements need to be made, there is no proof that government endeavors are inherently wasteful or that there is any alternative to active intervention.* Retrenchment of housing, manpower, and compensatory education programs in the 1970s was supported by claims of poor performance. Reforms in health, community development, and other areas were proposed on the same grounds. More often than not, these criticisms were based on unreasonable criteria or mistaken, if not purposely dis-

torted, judgments. Many critics confused high cost with inefficiency, charging that any solution that was expensive was wasteful.
In buying cosmetics, or medical care, or automobiles, the consumer usually associates high price with high quality, but this does
not apply to government activities where parsimony is considered
a virtue. The government also operates in a fishbowl, so that all its
mistakes and excesses are laid bare to the public; similar problems
in the private sector are hidden away, leaving the impression of
greater efficiency. Little allowance is made for the problems inherent in rapid expansion and experimentation. Criticism of programs
is part of the process by which needed or desired changes are
engineered, and the discovery of failure is part of a continuing
process of improvement.

4. *The negative spillovers of social welfare efforts were too
frequently overstated and were usually the unavoidable concomitants of the desired changes.* Examples are legion. Medical care
programs were blamed for the inflation in medical costs, beyond
the reasonable assumption that shortages did drive up costs. Housing programs were criticized for deteriorating property values if the
assistance dispersed subsidized units or for contributing to segregation if they concentrated in low-income neighborhoods. Busing
was heatedly opposed as inconveniencing the many to help the
few. And welfare was blamed for breaking up stable families. In
fact, however, medical costs rose largely because demand was increased suddenly while supply could respond only slowly. Inflation
was unavoidable if reliance were placed on the price mechanism to
expand and redistribute resources. Busing to achieve racial balance
involves difficulties but critics have not offered alternatives to integrate the schools. Every program generates problems, but these
have usually been manageable.

5. *The benefits of the Great Society programs are more than the
sum of their parts, and more than the impact on immediate participants and beneficiaries.* If anything has been learned from the last
decade of social intervention, it is the interrelationship of seemingly disparate actions. In attacking a specific problem such as
unemployment, for instance, there is a whole nexus of variables.
On the supply side, consideration must be given to the education
and vocational training of the unemployed, their access to jobs,
their knowledge of the labor market, and their work attitudes,

impediments, and alternatives. On the demand side, the quality and location of jobs must be considered along with their number. Discrimination and hiring standards are also crucial factors. Unemployment might be combated by education and training, better transportation, improved placement services, sticks and carrots to force the unemployed to take jobs, provision of child care, economic development in depressed areas, equal opportunity enforcement, and a variety of other measures. None of these alone is likely to have much impact, but together they can contribute to change, not only in the labor market, but in all those dimensions of life so intimately related to work.

6. *The nation has continued moving toward a better society, despite efforts to check the growth of the welfare state.* It was consistent with the social philosophy of the Johnson administration to take credit for every new program and expenditure just as the rhetoric of the Nixon administration focused on restraint and retrenchment. In fact, however, there were cases where President Nixon's initiatives were more innovative and expansionary than those of his predecessor, and many more cases where the actions of the administrations differed little. Even if overkill was sometimes exercised in setting the stage for reform, there is no doubt that a considerable "shaking out" was needed after a period of rapid experimentation and expansion. Reform was usually based on claims of ineffectiveness, but more often it was part of the process of growth and change in the welfare state. As one set of problems was solved, new ones could be addressed, or as problems were alleviated piecemeal, comprehensive efforts became more feasible. The landmark laws passed in the mid-1960s had a momentum of their own, and this carried through most of the Nixon years.

7. *By the mid-1970s, however, a plateau had been reached and new initiatives were required if the previous momentum were to be renewed.* Many of the Great Society's goals had been largely achieved, such as medical care for the aged or voting rights for blacks, and the issue was whether to extend aid to others or to broaden the scope of governmental action. Other efforts had stalled in the face of mounting public opposition, and the question was whether to press on or to ease off. Instead of boldly addressing new problems and thus supplementing the social agenda, the

nation despaired of its ability to find solutions and moved cautiously in the 1970s. This inaction reflected overly pessimistic judgments of past efforts. A judicious review of the Great Society and its legacy not only provides grounds for optimism about the potential of governmental intervention but contains lessons for future action if progress is to continue toward a greater society.

These conclusions are obviously controversial, and they cannot be proven unequivocally. Social and economic relationships are too complex, our knowledge too limited, and the normative issues too basic. The wide ranging evidence can only provide the framework for informed individual judgments. Yet the weight of the evidence is positive rather than negative, and if the above conclusions cannot be proved, they can be documented convincingly.

The Analytical Framework

Many critics of the Great Society have focused on the least successful attempts at social improvement with their attendant horror stories. There is an opposite temptation to concentrate on and generalize from the areas of accomplishment. The only valid approach is to consider the successes and failures within the entire range of social welfare activities. The Great Society is usually identified in terms of specific programs. These include income supplement efforts such as social security and public assistance, programs providing in-kind aid such as health care and housing, others offering services such as education and manpower training, and finally those seeking to change the rules of the game or to organize the powerless. The myriad programs in each of these separate categories need to be examined carefully to determine what they sought to do and what they accomplished.

But reality is not compartmentalized, and programmatic analysis can yield only part of the story. Two of the major aims of the Great Society were to alleviate poverty and to improve the lot of the nation's blacks. Welfare and social insurance, health care, housing assistance, education, and manpower programs all played a role in achieving these goals. What was their combined impact? Was poverty reduced and a greater measure of equality achieved? By the same token, the war on poverty was only one dimension of the broader effort to redistribute the nation's bounty. The implicit aim of the welfare state is to take from the haves and give to the have nots. Did such a redistribution occur? The health of the economy determines the wherewithal of society to provide for those in need, as well as the number who must rely on its assistance. Full employment was an end and a means of the Great Society, and the low levels of unemployment achieved in the late 1960s are a documented fact and could have been achieved without a war. There is debate, however, over the role of government policies and the long-run economic consequences of trying to maintain a tight labor market. Were good times an aberration and is full employment achievable over the long run?

Having analyzed the various programs as well as the broader goals of the Great Society, it is possible to sum up the evidence to determine whether it supports the conventional wisdom that the vision of greatness was myopic. This determination and the supporting evidence have implications for the future.

Yet, the specifics of the Great Society are not as crucial as its underlying thrust. The social welfare efforts begun in the 1960s were based on the belief that the future is not predetermined but can be molded by our energies and resources, that our nation is not condemned to passive acceptance of inequality of opportunity, poverty, hunger, urban blight, high unemployment, and other ills. This faith has been challenged and blunted by the criticism of the 1970s. As the nation enters its third century, there is need for the positivism, commitment, and compassion that were and still remain indispensable in the quest for a better society.

2 Programs and Policies

A Legislative Fountainhead

The essence of the Great Society was increased federal intervention to assist the disadvantaged and disenfranchised by providing needed goods, services, and income and by changing the socioeconomic system. Government action begins with legislation. Perhaps the most characteristic scene of the Great Society years was President Lyndon B. Johnson signing important new laws and with rhetorical flourish promising to wipe out poverty, urban and rural blights, and age-old inequities in education, civil rights, health, and housing. Whatever the effectiveness of the legislation, there is no debate about its scale and scope. In almost every area of social welfare policy, the federal government shouldered new responsibilities.

Poverty and Income Support Initiatives

In his first State of the Union message, President Johnson declared an unconditional war on poverty. The Economic Opportunity Act, passed in 1964, was the first offensive, spawning a wide array of programs to mitigate the consequences and to eliminate the causes of poverty. The Community Action Program established community based agencies to mobilize the poor and to give them a voice in decision making. Legal services, adult education, neighborhood health centers, and a number of other approaches were developed under this umbrella. The Job Corps sought to alter the lives of disadvantaged youths through intensive training and education in a residential setting away from their poverty environments. The Neighborhood Youth Corps was to provide work experience and needed income to teenagers in and out of school. VISTA sought to mobilize volunteer workers to go out among the poor and help them. Head Start aimed to equalize opportunity at the starting gate through improved early education, while Upward Bound was to provide talented but disadvantaged students a chance for higher education. The Office of Economic Opportunity was created to administer these diverse efforts, to represent the interests of the poor in the federal establishment, and to serve as a catalyst for mobilizing government and private resources. While the commitments never matched the promise, the war on poverty was significant in moving beyond simple care for the poor in an attempt to alter the economic and social causes of poverty.

If the antipoverty effort was the favorite child of the Great Society, it was the whipping boy of the Nixon administration. One by one, poverty programs were transferred from the Office of Economic Opportunity to other agencies until only the umbrella was left; and in 1974 it was closed. Yet the poverty activities themselves took root, gaining a firm foothold in the galaxy of federal responsibilities.

When it came to caring for the needy, as opposed to alleviating the causes of need, the contrasts between the Johnson and Nixon legislative records were not as marked. The Great Society is frequently blamed or credited for the welfare explosion which occurred in the late 1960s and continued through the early 1970s, but this development was not the direct product of federal legislative initiatives. The only major changes in the welfare system were the 1967 Social Security amendments, which sought to halt expansion by providing incentives for recipients of Aid to Families with Dependent Children to work their way off relief. The welfare reforms proposed by the Nixon administration also sought to slow growth but were, in some ways, more liberal than previous policies in that they would have guaranteed an income for all poor families.

Health Programs

The passage of Medicare and Medicaid in 1965 was probably the foremost legislative achievement of the Johnson administration. Federally operated health insurance for the aged had first been proposed and actively pushed by President Truman. Vehemently opposed by the American Medical Association as a step on the road to socialized medicine, the issue was debated for the next two decades. President Kennedy advocated a modest system covering hospital costs, but President Johnson was firmly committed to a more ambitious measure. His first special message to Congress in 1965 dealt with health. What resulted was not only a comprehensive insurance program for the aged but a major expansion of previous aid programs for public assistance recipients. These two programs went far toward delivering health care as a right and a reality for the aged and poor.

More health care resources were needed to meet this expanded demand, and the Johnson administration followed through with a number of legislative measures to expand supply. In 1964 a nurses' training program was initiated, and in 1965 and 1968 aid was increased for medical schools and needy medical students. In 1966 and 1968 similar assistance was given for the training of allied health manpower. Funds were provided for the staffing of mental retardation facilities, for the expansion of birth control programs, and for the establishment of treatment facilities for narcotics addicts and alcoholics. The Partnership for Health program, launched in 1966, was aimed at rationalizing the delivery system through better areawide planning, as well as improving public health, migrant, and immigrant programs.

One of the six great goals of the Nixon administration was to improve and increase the availability of health care, but its approach was markedly different. "We must recognize," President Nixon said, "that we cannot simply buy our way to better medicine. We have already been trying that too long . . . It must be our goal not merely to finance a more expensive medical system, but to organize a more efficient one." The major aim was thus to cut back and reform the Great Society initiatives. Besides vetoing three HEW appropriations bills in his first term, in part because of excess health funding, the President vetoed an extension of the longstanding grant program for hospital construction and modernization and sought to reduce maternal and child health programs. In 1971 the administration effectively stalled a $60 billion proposal for a comprehensive health insurance program with a counterproposal involving annual federal outlays one twentieth as great. The only other legislation pushed by the Nixon administration (other than a $100 million fight against cancer and heart disease) was reform of the medical delivery system to establish prepaid group practices as well as professional standards review organizations to monitor doctors serving Medicare and Medicaid patients. Medicare and Medicaid were also amended in hopes of cutting down on their rapid growth.

Federal Aid for Education

There were no general federal programs of aid for elementary, secondary, or higher education before the 1960s. While the needs of the expanding public schools were apparent, action had stalled for more than two decades over the school segregation and church-state questions. Federal aid was opposed by segregationists who saw it as an instrument to force integration and inhibited by clashes between opponents and advocates of aid to parochial schools. The Civil Rights Act of 1964 reduced the first roadblock, while the second was circumvented by emphasizing aid to needy children regardless of the school in which they were located. The result was the swift passage in 1965 of the Elementary and Secondary Education Act, which provided funds to support programs "designed to meet the special educational needs of educationally deprived children," including experimentation with new teaching methods, bilingual instruction, and special offerings for the mentally and physically handicapped.

The Higher Education Act of 1965 was equally significant. It authorized scholarships and low interest loans for undergraduate students based only on need, and it expanded the work-study program begun the year before under the Economic Opportunity Act. In addition, the antipoverty law initiated the Upward Bound program aimed to help talented disadvantaged youth to prepare for college.

The education record of the Nixon administration paled in comparison. Four vetoes in the first term involved "excessive" congressional appropriations for education. The President was in office more than three years before he proposed his first major education legislation to expand grants for needy college students. As it turned out, however, this program was funded at modest levels and did not much increase education financing for students from poor families. The Nixon administration favored federal aid for de-segregating school districts and a moratorium on busing. The latter was enacted but ruled unconstitutional by the Supreme Court.

Shelter and Subsidies

The Johnson administration initiated the first major low-income housing programs since the New Deal. The longstanding public housing program had promised "a decent home and suitable living environment for every American family," but its performance fell far short of the rhetoric, and construction was relatively dormant over the 1950s and early 1960s. The Great Society, therefore, intro-duced a whole range of new tools to stimulate production and to subsidize the costs of housing for the needy.

The Housing and Urban Development Act of 1965 reduced interest rates on loans for rental units built for the poor and the elderly. Public housing agencies were authorized to lease private dwellings. Rent supplements were introduced for low-income tenants in specified units. The Housing and Urban Development Act of 1968 established programs to subsidize interest rates on private loans for units renting or being sold to low-income families.

The Nixon administration actively applied these new tools in its first few years. Production of assisted units reached an all-time high. But there were no new legislative initiatives other than some minor reforms to correct observed deficiencies. As costs mounted, administrative support wavered and in 1973 all construction was halted in order to study alternatives to the Great Society programs that were pronounced failures.

Employment and Training

Until the 1960s little was done to help the millions of Ameri-cans failing in or being failed by the labor market. This was changed under the Johnson administration. The Manpower Devel-opment and Training Act, passed in 1962 to train the technologi-cally displaced, was expanded and redirected to the hard core unemployed. The Economic Opportunity Act of 1964 created the

Neighborhood Youth Corps and the Job Corps, as well as Work Experience and Training to help public assistance recipients and other needy persons, Operation Mainstream to employ primarily older workers in rural settings, and New Careers to fund paraprofessional training and employment opportunities for the disadvantaged. The 1967 Concentrated Employment Program provided block grants to community groups for comprehensive attacks on employment problems, and in the same year the Work Incentive program was implemented to train and place welfare recipients. Private firms were subsidized to hire and train the disadvantaged the next year, and vocational rehabilitation was extended to the socioeconomically handicapped.

There were also some important legislative initiatives in the 1970s. The Emergency Employment Act of 1971, providing funds to state and local governments to hire the unemployed, was the first general public employment effort since the New Deal. Congress passed this legislation over the President's opposition and despite a veto of a similar bill in 1970. On the other hand, the administration favored the Comprehensive Employment and Training Act of 1973, which combined many of the Great Society's categorical programs into a block grant to state and local governments. Public employment programs were expanded somewhat under the Ford administration to deal with the massive joblessness in 1974 and 1975, but endorsement was far from enthusiastic and a large job creation bill was vetoed in 1975.

Civil Rights

The civil rights record of the Johnson administration was certainly one of its greatest achievements, and some have characterized the 1960s as a Second Reconstruction. There was no general civil rights legislation in the twentieth century until 1957 when a limited measure was passed to protect registered voters from threats and intimidation. In rapid succession during the Johnson years, laws were passed to make discrimination illegal in almost all public realms. The Civil Rights Act of 1964 was the cornerstone, guaranteeing voting rights, access to public accommodations, equal employment, and educational opportunity. The Voting Rights Act of 1965 strengthened the federal government's hand in registering minorities. Housing discrimination was barred three years later.

This left the Nixon administration with the sometimes thankless and certainly less glamorous task of applying and refining these laws. In 1972 new powers were provided for the enforcement of equal employment opportunity, though stronger measures were opposed by the administration. The Equal Rights Amendment of 1971, guaranteeing equal status for women, had not achieved ratification by the end of 1975.

Social Welfare Spending

New laws inevitably require new outlays, and the legislative activism of the Great Society was reflected in the rapid growth of federal social welfare expenditures which continued through the Nixon years. Many undertakings begun with relatively small initial expenditures for research, planning, and experimentation developed into massive obligations as more eligible persons participated. Reorganization and reform usually increased rather than reduced outlays. Once begun, spending was difficult to stop as recipients and beneficiaries defended their newly acquired benefits. The expansionary process begun by the Johnson administration continued under its successors despite their aim of restraint and retrenchment. Measured by spending, the contrasts between the Johnson and the Nixon–Ford administrations are far less significant than the differences between the entire 1965–75 decade and the two preceding ones.

A Decade of Growth

Social welfare change seems to come in cycles. In 1929 federal social outlays totaled less than one billion dollars (in 1975 dollars this equals about $3 billion, still less than is currently spent on railroad retirement alone). The New Deal initiatives resulted in a tenfold real expansion by 1950. Then for the next fifteen years the rate of growth slowed. Real outlays rose 22 percent in the first half of the 1950s, 55 percent in the second half, and another 43 percent in the first five years of the 1960s (Figure 2-1). During the Great Society years through fiscal 1970, expenditures accelerated

Figure 2–1. Federal social welfare expenditures

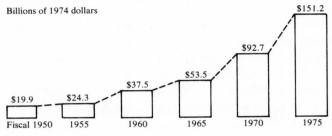

Billions of 1974 dollars

$19.9　$24.3　$37.5　$53.5　$92.7　$151.2

Fiscal 1950　1955　1960　1965　1970　1975

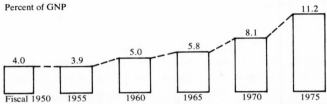

Percent of GNP

4.0　3.9　5.0　5.8　8.1　11.2

Fiscal 1950　1955　1960　1965　1970　1975

Source: Alfred Skolnik and Sophie R. Dales, "Social Welfare Expenditures, Fiscal Year 1974," *Social Security Bulletin,* January 1975, pp. 7–11; and *The United States Budget in Brief, 1976* (Washington: Government Printing Office, 1975), p. 49.

75 percent in constant dollars and then rose almost two thirds over the first half of the 1970s. Put another way, the real increase in social welfare expenditures between fiscal 1965 and 1975 was almost double the total spending at the outset of this period and four times the level in 1955. Federal social welfare expenditures were 4.0 percent of GNP in fiscal 1950, 5.8 percent in 1965, but 11.2 percent by fiscal 1975. They increased from 26 percent of the federal budget in fiscal 1955 to 33 percent in 1965, then to 52 percent by fiscal 1974.[1]

The federal government has become an increasingly important factor in everyone's lives. In 1965 only three of every ten dollars spent for medical care, education, retirement plans, charity, and other social welfare purposes came from the federal coffers. By the middle 1970s the feds were accounting for two of every five dollars of social welfare spending. Federal outlays rose by 121 percent in the decade prior to 1965, while private outlays rose 133 percent and state and local outlays increased 87 percent. In the next ten years federal spending skyrocketed 161 percent, while private expenditures rose 63 percent and state and local outlays 94 percent.

Viewed from a longer-run perspective, then, the differences between the Johnson administration and its two successors in the 1965–75 decade were less significant than the consistencies. Whether it was the momentum of extravagance, as President Nixon labeled it, or a reasoned response to what President Johnson called "a challenge constantly renewed beckoning us toward . . . destiny," the growth process begun in the Great Society continued through the middle 1970s. Spending grew massively in absolute terms and as a proportion of GNP; public spending accounted for a rapidly increasing share; and the federal role grew most of all.

Slicing the Pie

It is only when aggregate expenditures are broken down by year and by type that significant differences are noticeable between the Great Society and its successors. Fiscal 1965–67 were the years of most dramatic expansion (Table 2-1). By fiscal 1968 the Vietnam war forced domestic belt-tightening, and inflation thwarted budget

Table 2-1. Annual growth of federal social welfare expenditures, 1965–75

Fiscal year	Expenditures (billions)	Rate of increase (percent)	Expenditures (in 1973 billions)	Rate of increase (percent)
1965	$ 37.7		$ 49.0	
		20		18
1966	45.4	17	58.0	14
1967	53.3	13	66.3	10
1968	60.3	13	72.9	9
1969	68.4	13	79.8	8
1970	77.3	20	85.9	15
1971	92.5	15	98.5	11
1972	106.2	15	109.6	12
1973	122.3	14	122.3	5
1974	139.6	21	128.3	8
1975 (est.)	168.3	–	139.0	–

Source: Alfred Skolnik and Sophie R. Dales, "Social Welfare Expenditures, Fiscal Year 1974," *Social Security Bulletin* (January 1975), 7–11; and "Social Welfare Expenditures 1969–70," *Social Security Bulletin* (December 1970), 5–9; and *The United States Budget in Brief, 1976* (Washington: Government Printing Office, 1975), p. 49.

increases. The recession and the winding down of the war in the first year of the Nixon administration pushed up social spending, but gradually momentum was slowed, as inflation cut back real spending. By fiscal 1974 the rate of expenditure increase in constant dollars had been reduced to 5 percent. In the face of the worst economic downturn since the Great Depression, federal action was limited with greater reliance on the tax cuts than social welfare increases to stimulate the economy.

It is not so much in the size or growth, but in the slicing of the social welfare pie, that the contrasts between the Great Society and its successors are most apparent. The Johnson years were characterized by a rapid expansion of service and in-kind programs. In fiscal 1965 three fourths of all federal social welfare expenditures were cash payment to social security beneficiaries, welfare recipients, and veterans (Table 2-2). By fiscal 1969 the proportion had declined to 63 percent as medical and other aid programs grew rapidly. It remained at this level as service programs became the target of the Nixon administration's budget cutting. In real terms, federal education expenditures rose six times faster in the late 1960s than the early 1970s. Growth in outlays for health insurance and medical care for welfare recipients also slowed. Housing programs grew rapidly until an abrupt leveling off in fiscal 1973 when new commitments were halted. The food stamp program was the only in-kind program that continued to expand as outlays more than doubled between fiscal 1970 and 1974.

While the antipoverty efforts during the Johnson years fell short of an all-out "war," the real value of social welfare expenditures for the poor increased by three fourths, rising slightly from 20.2 to 21.6 percent of all social welfare expenditures according to estimates from the Office of Management and Budget. Between fiscal 1970 and 1974, antipoverty real spending increased less than two fifths, declining from 21.7 to 20.1 percent of all outlays though the number of persons in poverty rose.[2]

Yet, the decline in the real growth rate of antipoverty expenditures hardly supports the view that the Nixon administration reversed the Great Society's initiatives. Rather, there was a gradual slowing of momentum and a reshuffling of priorities within the social welfare sector resulting in a leveling off by the time Presi-

Table 2-2. Changes in the components of federal social welfare spending, fiscal 1965-74 (constant fiscal 1974 dollars in millions)

Benefit	1965	1969	Percent change	1970	1974	Percent change
Total	*$53,492*	*$86,558*	*62*	*$93,738*	*$139,580*	*49*
Social insurance	*30,932*	*51,779*	*67*	*54,843*	*82,508*	*50*
OASDI	24,110	33,956	41	35,983	54,952	53
Health insurance	0	8,362	–	8,666	11,322	31
Unemployment insurance, employment services, and workers' compensation	1,103	1,329	20	1,435	2,936	105
Railroad and public employee programs	5,719	8,133	42	8,759	13,298	52
Public assistance	*5,079*	*9,643*	*90*	*11,695*	*21,237*	*82*
Cash benefits	3,731	5,206	40	5,412	8,023	48
Medical care	787	2,798	256	3,160	5,824	84
Social services	10	511	5,010	633	2,000	216
Food stamps and other aid	579	1,647	184	2,490	5,390	116
General health and medical	*3,944*	*5,751*	*46*	*5,788*	*8,005*	*38*
Hospital and medical care	1,524	2,462	62	2,479	3,742	51
Maternal and child health	104	240	131	238	236	−1
Research and construction	2,316	3,048	32	3,071	4,027	31
Veterans' programs	*8,526*	*10,005*	*17*	*10,850*	*13,878*	*28*
Pensions and compensation	5,874	6,297	7	6,538	6,823	4
Health and medical aid	1,743	1,952	12	2,162	2,988	38
Educational and other	909	1,756	93	2,150	4,067	89
General education	*3,503*	*6,386*	*82*	*7,119*	*8,046*	*13*
Elementary and secondary	1,102	3,276	197	3,584	4,126	15
Higher	1,726	2,245	30	2,613	2,727	4
Vocational and adult	695	865	24	922	1,193	29
Housing	*338*	*524*	*55*	*705*	*2,132*	*202*
Other social welfare including food	*1,152*	*2,470*	*114*	*2,738*	*3,764*	*37*

Source: Alfred Skolnik and Sophie R. Dales, "Social Welfare Expenditures, Fiscal Year 1974," *Social Security Bulletin,* January 1975, pp. 7-11; and "Social Welfare Expenditures, 1969-70," *Social Security Bulletin,* December 1970, pp. 5-9.

dent Ford assumed office. The entire decade ending in 1975 must be viewed as a growth period of the welfare state.

The Whip and the Reins

A multitude of forces affect legislation and spending in a checks and balances system. An activist president, a Congress with a large and liberal Democratic majority, and a dynamic Supreme Court, were all responsible for the dramatic changes of the 1960s. Conflicts between a conservative Republican president, a Congress with an opposition majority, and a changing Supreme Court, retarded action in the 1970s. Events were less a manifestation of any consistent social philosophy than of a constantly shifting balance of power. Yet in the actions of the Executive Office, the contrasts between the Johnson and Nixon–Ford administrations—between the Great Society and free market philosophies—are more readily observable. The Johnson administration used all its energy and power to whip the government and the public into action while the Nixon and Ford administrations pulled tenaciously on the reins to slow what they considered the Great Society's runaway spending.

Presidential Vetoes

The President can thwart congressional action with the veto. Lyndon Johnson vetoed 13 bills during his years in office and none of these vetoes was primarily to reduce federal spending. During his first five years in office President Nixon vetoed 38 bills. In January 1970 he turned back the $20 billion appropriation for the Departments of Labor and Health, Education, and Welfare, and the Office of Economic Opportunity, explaining to the nation that "these increases are excessive in a period of serious inflationary pressures. We must draw the line and stick to it if we are to stabilize the economy." Reacting to the "profligacy" of the 91st Congress, the president also vetoed a $2.8 billion hospital construction program, a $4.4 billion appropriation for the Office of Education, $18 billion in appropriations for the Department of Housing and Urban Development, a $9.5 billion authorization for federal manpower programs, plus several other measures. The succeeding Congress proved to be equally excessive in the President's view, and he vetoed appropriation bills for accelerated public works and regional development, the Office of Economic Opportunity, Labor and HEW (twice), water pollution control, vocational rehabilitation, health care for veterans, and a variety of lesser spending measures. In 1973 a vocational rehabilitation bill was vetoed, another for rural water and sewer construction, and a minimum wage law. President Ford was even more vigorous, going so far as to veto a highly popular job creation bill in the face of the worst unemployment in more than three decades. In only five cases during the Nixon administration were the vetoes overridden, and in most of the others Congress was forced to reduce authorization and appropriation levels in order to achieve presidential approval. There is no exact way to measure the impact of the veto, but it probably held down social welfare spending by many billions of dollars.

Budgeting

The federal budget is a central mechanism for expressing and achieving administrative policy. It spells out the executive's priorities and goals and it stakes out a bargaining position that is the framework for congressional fiscal deliberations.

All budget messages bear a superficial resemblance, claiming to meet macroeconomic goals and basic national needs while squeezing out the fat from the federal bureaucracy. Underlying the rhetoric and the sometimes confusing statistics, however, are some basic differences.

The first budget message of the Johnson administration for fiscal 1965 set the tenor for others.

> I have been guided by the principle that spending by the Federal Government, in and of itself, is neither bad nor good. It can be bad when it involves overstaffing of government agencies, or needless duplication of functions or poor management, or public services which cost more than they are worth, or the intrusion of government into areas where it does not belong. It can be good when it is put to work efficiently in the interests of our national strength, economic progress, and human compassion.
>
> I have been guided by the principle that an austere budget need not be and should not be a standstill budget. When budgeting restraint leads the government to turn its back on new needs and new problems, economy becomes but another word for stagnation.[3]

In marked contrast, the Nixon administration's budgets emphasized the evils of federal spending and the need for restraint:

> There will be those who contend in this [1973] budget their favorite programs are not financed as much as they want them to be. They will be absolutely right.
> . . . It is essential to preserve the private enterprise system, with its competitive spirit and its work ethic, which has

done so much to inspire the independent and help the dependent and which has made this nation the economic example to the rest of the world.

I do not wish it said of my administration that we furthered or encouraged the process of discarding that heritage. So I have emphasized fiscal responsibility and downward pressure on federal expenditures . . . In this way, every citizen will have a larger share of the fruits of his labor to spend the way he or she freely chooses.[4]

These differing views were manifested in the detailed requests for social welfare programs from year to year. In the Johnson budgets, the tendency was to hide the full extent of expenditures. One way was to shift the reporting basis of the budget and the means of accounting for trust funds. Another was to rely on financing techniques such as interest subsidies rather than on direct loans because of the less visible budget impact. Some items were also underbudgeted with the knowledge that the needed funds would be later provided through supplemental appropriations. Another approach was reshuffling resources to start programs promising or requiring larger future investments. Altogether, the major social welfare programs inaugurated or substantially modified and expanded by the Great Society equaled only 2 percent of the budget in 1963 but grew to 11 percent in 1970.[5]

Nixon budgeters constantly lamented the uncontrollability of federal expenditures and this was more than buck passing. Despite retrenchment efforts, Great Society programs grew to 14 percent of the 1973 budget, while new initiatives of the Nixon administration accounted for only between 1 and 2 percent. President Nixon was loath to start undertakings that would lead to future commitments, and where the Johnson administration budgets frequently hid costs, the Nixon accounts more often disguised cutbacks. Inflation was a way to cut real outlays quietly while pointing to increased dollar expenditures. Funds carried over from one year to the next were used to fill budget needs. Reforms consolidating programs such as revenue sharing promised extra services through greater efficiency but resulted in lower outlays.

Budget Enforcement

Once a budget has been approved and appropriations made, there is still some leeway to prevent expenditures. The Nixon administration resorted to these tactics repeatedly in its search for economy. The surest way to cut costs is to simply refuse to spend congressional appropriations. Impoundment, though of questionable legal foundation, has been used by most presidents. In 1966, for instance, President Johnson withheld $1.1 billion in funds for housing, urban development, and education to counteract the inflationary pressures of Vietnam spending. The Nixon administration, however, expanded and regularized this procedure. In fiscal 1973 nearly $15 billion was impounded including $6 billion for water pollution control, $2.9 billion for the Department of Transportation, $2.5 billion for highway construction, and appropriations for a variety of other programs. Through the use of the veto, the President also forced Congress to allow the impoundment of $1.2 billion out of the fiscal 1974 Labor–HEW appropriation.

Congress and the courts balked at these presidential initiatives. In 1973, a measure was passed to temporarily restrict impoundment. The same year, a circuit court held that highway funds were not to be withheld from obligation for reasons totally unrelated to the highway programs, and subsequently the administration lost in most impoundment decisions. By this time, however, Congress had been forced into action on budget control, establishing the principle of restraint.

Where the Johnson approach was to budget low and then come back for supplements after giving the appearance of frugality, the Nixon administration tended to stick closer to its budgets, despite unforeseen inflation and severe economic problems which would normally contribute to large overruns. From 1965 through 1969, actual obligations for social welfare efforts averaged 12 percent above the budget authority requests for each year; from 1970 through 1974, despite problems of unexpected severity, overruns exceeded requested authority by only 6 percent.[6]

Aims, Assumptions, and Approaches

The Johnson administration pressed Congress to enact measures in health care, civil rights, and education which were debated for years without result. Legislation dealing with poverty, manpower training, and housing pushed into new areas or ventured totally new approaches. The first half of the 1970s was mostly spent digesting these measures, with no legislative initiatives of comparable scale or scope.

New and expanded social welfare efforts required dramatically increased spending and the growth momentum begun in the Great Society continued through the early 1970s. From a historical perspective, the entire decade beginning in 1965 represented an acceleration of the long-run trend toward greater federal responsibilities. There was, however, a leveling off in the later years and this would have been more marked if two recessions had not intensified needs.

The response to the active braking efforts by the Nixon administration was sluggish. Through vetoes, impoundment, and zealous interpretations of executive privilege, the momentum of the Great Society was gradually dissipated. In the absence of new laws and initiatives, which the Nixon and Ford administrations tried to avoid, the impetus for future social welfare expansion was also reduced.

The laws, expenditures, and administrative actions were only the outward manifestations of an underlying set of aims, assumptions, and approaches. While the underlying philosophies can only be inferred, the following generalizations seem to square with the facts and give some better understanding of the essence of the Great Society.

First, its fundamental aim was to use the federal government's power to correct societal inequities as well as to guarantee a minimal standard of welfare for every citizen. While the term welfare state has a pejorative connotation to many—and President Johnson was no more in favor of handouts than President Nixon—the Great Society's activism clearly expanded the jurisdiction of the government in protecting the welfare of its citizens. The alternative was to rely on market processes to improve the welfare of all citizens on the assumption that tampering with the engines of economic betterment would be self-defeating. As society and the economy have grown more complex, government intervention has necessarily increased. The Great Society's thrust was to speed up this trend to achieve goals immediately rather than waiting for slower, more conventional processes. The Nixon and Ford administrations sought to "leave well enough alone" or even to try to reverse the momentum of governmental growth.

Second, the Johnson administration was willing, and indeed tried, to commit the nation to future actions. The rapid growth of the AFDC caseload and some other developments were not engineered and came as unpleasant surprises to policy makers, but in most other instances the clear intent was to build a groundwork and to generate momentum for change. The mortgages came due in the Nixon administration, and there was less latitude for new initiatives. But potentials for action were not realized. The preoccupation with retrenchment and reform in the 1970s laid the groundwork for future inaction.

Third, the Great Society was posited on the assumption that the nation's resources would be constantly expanding and that by redirecting a portion of this growth, social problems could be overcome while still allowing for expanded private activity and consumption. The anticipation of a fiscal dividend was basic to the Great Society architects, who, while firm believers in the private enterprise system, felt that government activities could be expanded out of growth. It is ironic that a less optimistic view was held by those claiming to defend the "great motor" of progress—the free market economy—by reducing government activity. Just as it is possible to overestimate the resource dividend and to overcommit the nation, it is equally possible to underestimate and to undercommit. The problem is to reach a balanced appraisal of the long term, not to get overly enthusiastic about rapid growth nor overly disturbed by temporary stagnation.

Fourth, the Great Society viewed the federal government as a lever of institutional change. Its power in the product and labor markets as a buyer and employer was used to alter private sector practices and to compensate for their effects. There was no hesitancy to push forward with new regulations such as civil rights laws to alter private sector institutions. Federal grants to state and local governments were given with many strings attached, and even more, state and local agencies were bypassed in order to create competing delivery systems and to test alternative approaches. In contrast, the subsequent administrations have relied upon established institutions to achieve social goals and emphasized the direct impacts of government programs.

Fifth, the Great Society relied on the categorical approach, specifying exactly how funds were to be spent and initiating separate programs for separate problems. The result was an active, federal, centralized system of government. The next two administrations challenged the categorical programs as duplicative, wasteful, and ill-considered, preferring revenue sharing as an alternative, "comprehensive" solution. Implicit was a decentralization of authority to the state and local level under the auspices of elected officials.

Sixth, the Great Society believed in compensatory efforts to alter the lives of disadvantaged individuals. Human resources development programs from preschool education to vocational training were emphasized. The paradigm was the Job Corps, which created a completely structured environment with the aim of dramatically changing the future of disadvantaged youth. The subsequent attack on the Job Corps was symbolic of the administration's opposition to "meddling" with individual lives and its belief that it was enough to open doors without helping people through.

Seventh, the Great Society was willing to take bold steps to experiment with different approaches on a large scale. Efforts to change institutions and individuals are inherently uncertain, high risk ventures. It would have been much safer and much less wasteful to use tried and true approaches, but change may be good for its own sake and new approaches may work more efficiently after the learning curve period. The Johnson administration, influenced by social thinkers and tinkerers, was willing to take the risks, hoping for the best. It refused to neglect needs or to rely on the "filtering-down" of overall gains. President Johnson's view was, in his own words, that "We have the power to shape the civilization that we want."

Part Two   Social Welfare Efforts

3 Income Support

The 1960s in Perspective

In scale and impact, the most important social welfare development during the Great Society was the expansion of income support. Public cash transfers rose by two thirds between fiscal 1964 and 1969, with the preponderance of benefits going to persons and families with below average income.

This rapid growth of outlays and the Great Society's antipoverty rhetoric have left the impression that the Johnson administration dramatically changed the income maintenance system and was responsible for its growth. Yet the major components were initiated, not in the 1960s, but in the 1930s and before. From the beginning of the nation, the government had aided disabled veterans and their survivors. Veterans programs, rarely in the public spotlight, have grown steadily over the decades to the point where they support millions of low-income households. Workmen's compensation, initiated under state laws mostly dating back to the early 1900s, also grew steadily to the point where over $4 billion is expended to defray medical costs and to compensate for lost earnings due to job injuries. The Social Security Act of 1935 was the legislative source of the welfare state. It established an old age insurance program, which was subsequently expanded to survivors and the disabled. Coverage was initially limited in scope; benefits and contributions were low, and eligibility was restricted. By the 1960s, however, the system had become firmly established, nearly universal, and much more generous.

The risk of forced idleness was alleviated by the unemployment compensation program also established in 1935 under the Social Security Act. Over the years, there were significant extensions in coverage, and benefit levels were raised to replace an increasing proportion of lost earnings. Again, however, most of this occurred before the Great Society. With states setting eligibility standards and benefit levels, and with the number of beneficiaries determined chiefly by economic conditions, the federal government played a minor role in the 1960s.

The Social Security Act distinguished between these work-based programs, largely financed out of payroll taxes, and needs-based public assistance efforts, financed out of general revenues. Separate public assistance programs were established for the poor, the aged, the blind, and the disabled, as well as for female-headed families. In the 1930s, when few women with children worked or were expected to, and when most female family heads were widows, there was little difference in substance or in public perception between Aid to Families with Dependent Children (AFDC) and the other three categorical programs—Old Age Assistance (OAA), Aid to the Blind (AB), and Aid to the Permanently and Totally Disabled (APTD). Over the years as AFDC expanded rapidly and as attitudes toward work by mothers changed, the program was viewed with less favor. Benefits were distributed in a niggardly fashion, while aid to the "deserving" poor was given, if not graciously or generously, at least without constant complaint.

The Great society made no substantial changes in OA, AB, and APTD. Under AFDC, the major federal initiative was an effort to combine the stick and the carrot to get more mothers to work and to halt welfare growth. The food stamp program was a product of the Kennedy administration and did not experience its major growth until the Nixon and Ford administrations. The Great Society's welfare as well as social insurance programs were thus inherited, not created.

The growth of income support over the 1960s was an acceleration rather than a redirection of secular trends. There had been a continuing rise in social insurance and welfare outlays for many decades as America prospered. In fact, during the Eisenhower decade, public outlays for social insurance, veterans and public assistance programs, adjusted for inflation, rose 119 percent compared with 87 percent during the 1960s. Alternately, public income support expenditures increased from 3.7 to 5.3 percent of GNP, or by 1.6 percentage points over the 1950s, then to 6.4 percent of GNP, or by only 1.1 percentage points in the next ten years (Table 3-1).

The real difference from the past was in the changing composition of aid. In the 1950s only 3 percent of the increase in real expenditures came under the various public assistance components compared with one seventh during the 1960s. Social insurance was the major factor in growth.

The 1970s rhetoric suggested an aggressive effort to check the advance of the welfare state. Yet in the four years from fiscal 1970 to 1974, public outlays rose by 45 percent, or more than in the preceding five years. Public assistance growth was somewhat slowed, but social security expanded at a rapid pace, accounting for nine tenths of overall expansion. The food stamp program also

Table 3-1. Public income support expenditures, fiscal 1950-74

Expenditure	Public expenditures (billions of fiscal 1974 dollars)					
	1950	1955	1960	1965	1970	1974
Total	*$17.2*	*$24.4*	*$37.9*	*$49.5*	*$70.9*	*$103.0*
Social insurance	8.4	15.1	27.3	37.5	54.3	83.1
Veterans	4.6	5.1	5.7	6.4	7.1	7.3
Public assistance	4.3	4.1	4.8	5.6	9.4	12.6
	As percent of GNP					
Total	3.7	4.1	5.3	5.6	6.4	7.9
Percentage change in real expenditures	1950– 55	1955– 60	1960– 65	1965– 70	1970– 74	
Total	*42*	*55*	*31*	*43*	*45*	
Social insurance	81	80	38	45	53	
Veterans	12	12	12	10	3	
Public assistance	−3	16	15	69	34	

Source: Alfred M. Skolnik and Sophie R. Dales, "Social Welfare Expenditures, Fiscal Year 1974,' *Social Security Bulletin* (January 1975), pp. 10, 18, and 19.

experienced a tenfold growth between fiscal 1969 and 1974. Total expenditures for food stamps and cash transfers rose by 49 percent between fiscal 1970 and 1974, and the needs-based segment accounted for an even larger share of growth than during the Johnson years.

Was this the delayed impact of the Great Society's liberal policies? The evidence suggests that it was not, despite the widespread belief to the contrary. It was under the Johnson administration that a work incentive program was first implemented to substitute "workfare for welfare." In 1967 Congress tried to cut off the spigot altogether by placing a cap on welfare rolls. In contrast, the Nixon administration proposed a family assistance plan which would have added millions of recipients, including male-headed families, and billions of dollars to costs. Public assistance programs for the aged, blind, and disabled were significantly expanded and liberalized under the Nixon administration. The Ford administration then supported the expansion of unemployment insurance into a comprehensive transfer program.

The goals of providing for the needy and insuring everyone against the risks of age, disability, joblessness, injury, and death are fundamental to a compassionate affluent society. Every administration has sought with varying degrees of commitment and success to achieve these ends. While policies and priorities have fluctuated, and different components of the income maintenance system have grown at different rates in different periods, the result has been a secular expansion of the welfare state.

The fundamental question is not who is to blame or praise, but whether the implemented measures and committed resources have achieved their proposed aims. Have income support programs protected the needy and improved their well being, or have these efforts been found wanting as so many critics charge on grounds of equity, efficiency, and adequacy?

The Foundation

In signing the Social Security Act in 1935, President Roosevelt characterized it as "the cornerstone of a structure which is being built but is by no means complete." After forty years of growth and change, and some important finishing work over the last decade, the structure is much closer to completion.

At the outset, social security was a straightforward retirement program, with benefits to be based on covered earnings and taxes paid equally by employers and employees. In 1939 Congress added benefits for the dependents of retirees and for the survivors of insured workers. Coverage was extended significantly in 1950, and in 1954 insurance was added for totally disabled workers. Two years later the dependents of disabled beneficiaries were also brought under the umbrella.

By the time President Johnson assumed office, nine out of ten wage earners were covered, and only state and local government employees and domestic workers were left out. Seven out of every ten aged persons were receiving social security, which represented 30 percent of their aggregate income.[1] Adding survivors, dependents, and the disabled, 19 million persons received social security benefits in 1963.

Despite this rapid development over the first three decades, and its massive impact, there were some important shortcomings. With no provision for medical care, the aged were left with the haunting fear that their carefully husbanded resources could be wiped out by illness and hospitalization. The average retirement benefit received by married couples with one eligible recipient was only half of the poverty threshold income for a nonfarm aged family of two. There was no assured protection against the ravages of inflation, and while benefit increases came every few years, living standards were eroded in the interim. Eligibility criteria were restrictive in an attempt to maintain the insurance base. Work was discouraged by the reduction of benefits for earnings above a low level.

In the 1960s and 1970s these shortcomings were largely corrected. Medicare's implementation in 1965 was a major step, lifting "the specter of catastrophic hospital bills . . . from the lives of our older citizens." Financed through the traditional social security payroll tax, it covered the bulk of costs for in-patient hospital care as well as providing for post-hospitalization needs, out-patient diagnostic services, and home health visits. A supple-

mentary program financed by subscribers' contributions and direct
government subsidies was established to pay doctors' bills and the
costs of medicine.

The provisions for retirement, survivors, and disability were
also changed in 1965. Qualifying requirements were lowered for
the disabled and for persons age 72 years and over. A minimum
payment of $35 monthly for a single worker was established.
Work was encouraged by raising the earnings exemption from
$1,200 to $1,500 with further earnings up to $2,700 offset by 50
percent benefit reductions.

Similar amendments followed in 1967. Benefits were raised
across the board by 13 percent, and the monthly minimum for
single persons 72 years and over was increased to $40. The defini-
tion of blindness was liberalized, additional benefits were provided
for the dependent children of mothers covered by old age, survivors, and disability insurance (OASDI), and eligibility requirements for younger disabled workers were reduced. The earnings
exemption level was raised to $1,680. Along with a number of
detailed changes in Medicare, a "lifetime reserve" of 60 days of
hospital coverage was added to regular benefits.

The changeover to a Republican administration effected few
changes in social security policies. Benefits were raised more than
enough to compensate for accelerating inflation, with a 15 percent
increase in 1969, a 10 percent rise in 1971, 20 percent in 1972,
and another 11 percent in 1973. Recognizing that inflation was
here to stay, Congress authorized an automatic cost-of-living ad-
justment beginning in 1975. In 1972 the earnings exemption was
raised, and the upper threshold beyond which earnings were offset
dollar for dollar by benefit reductions was eliminated. Benefits for
widows were increased, Medicare was extended to disabled social
security beneficiaries, and a minimum benefit of $170 monthly for
an individual and $225 for a couple was guaranteed for those
working at least 30 years in covered employment. Amendments in
1973 further raised the earnings exemption to $2,400.

As a result of these numerous adjustments, the minimum benefit
for a fully insured single recipient rose 135 percent between 1963
and 1973, while the cost of living went up 45 percent. The maximum benefit was increased 270 percent.[2] A worker who in every
year had earned the average for all private industry would have

received a monthly benefit of $121 if he or she retired in 1963. A comparable worker in 1972 would have received $210. The earlier benefit would have been 29 percent of the last year's earnings, compared to 32 percent in January 1972.[3] The hikes in subsequent years raised this ratio even higher.

With the maturation of the system, newly retiring workers also tended to have more quarters of covered employment at higher wages, and with the reduction in earnings offsets working recipients were allowed to keep more of their benefits. On the other hand, as eligibility restrictions were eased, more low-wage workers qualified. Average benefits, therefore, rose substantially but by somewhat less than the maximum benefit limit.

	Average monthly benefits		
	1963	1974	Percent increase
Single retired persons	$77	$188	144
Wives and husbands	40	96	140
Children of deceased workers	54	127	135
Disabled workers	91	206	126
Widowed mothers	59	134	127
Persons with special age 72 benefits	–	64	–

Eligibility liberalizations and extensions, combined with the maturation of the system, resulted in a very dramatic growth in beneficiaries. With more persons qualifying for disability and retiring early, the proportion of persons age 62 through 64 years receiving benefits rose from two fifths in 1963 to 53 percent a decade later. Where three fourths of the aged 65 years and over were beneficiaries in the earlier year, more than nine out of ten received aid in 1974. The proportion of youths receiving benefits rose from 4 to 6 percent.[4]

	Millions receiving benefits		
	1963	1974	Percent increase
Total	*19.0*	*30.9*	*63*
Persons age 62–64 years	1.7	3.0	76
Persons age 65 years and over	13.2	20.0	52
Persons under age 62	4.1	7.9	93

Insurance versus Redistribution

While formally an insurance program, social security has redistributive features because low earners and low contributors get disproportionately high benefits. In 1974 a fully covered single retiree with $750 in average monthly insured earnings would have received monthly benefits 53 percent of this amount; one with $400 insured earnings would have received 65 percent in benefits; a worker with only $100 average monthly covered earnings would have received 121 percent.[5] With insured earnings and tax contributions more than six times as great, the highest paid worker would have qualified for a benefit three times that of the lowest paid.

In terms of replacing final earnings, highly paid construction workers retiring in 1972 who had average earnings for their industry in every previous year would have qualified for a benefit equal to only 24 percent of their last year's earnings. Lower paid retail employees would have received benefits equal to 42 percent of the final salary.[6] Changes in the system increased these redistributive features in the 1960s and 1970s.[7]

Social security is funded on a pay-as-you-go basis, with current receipts covering current benefits. The increased number of beneficiaries and benefit levels demanded increased contributions as total taxes rose from $13.3 billion in 1963, or 4.2 percent of wages and salaries, to $48.5 billion in 1974, representing 6.8 percent of earnings.[8] The extra funds could have been raised by increasing the tax rate, extending the tax base, or supplementing payroll taxes from general revenues, the first approach being the most regressive and the last the most progressive. Congress chose the middle road. While the employee tax was raised from 3.625 percent in 1963 to 5.85 percent in 1975, the maximum taxable income was raised from $4,800 to $14,100. As estimated four fifths of the growth in contributions between 1963 and 1972 resulted from the latter increases. If the taxable limit had kept pace only with the rise in the cost of living, the 1972 tax rate would have been on about $6,500 of annual earnings and would have produced only one third the revenues which were actually received.[9] Since the benefit/contribution ratio declines at higher levels of income, raising the maximum taxable income also has the effect of increasing the redistribution of income.

Does this mean that social insurance has become a "bad buy" for the high earner? It is difficult to evaluate this claim because there are no private insurance policies covering such diverse and comprehensive risks. Unquestionably, past social security recipients at all income levels have done quite well, since as the system expanded and became more generous, they were given benefits far exceeding the actuarial value of their previous contributions. This "transitional" transfer should diminish in importance as more of those with long work histories in covered employment become beneficiaries and as real benefit increases slow down. Yet social security can and probably will always pay out more than the actuarial equivalent of contributions as money wages rise and the economy grows.

There is also room for a great deal of redistribution. For every two dollars of private insurance benefits paid in 1973, the companies took a dollar in dividends, taxes, administrative, advertising, and sales costs.[10] In comparison, total administrative costs of the OASDI system in 1972 were only 1.8 percent of benefits paid.[11] Being universal and mandatory, the social security system has economies of scale and does not have to sell itself. It is also apparently run more efficiently than the private system.

To the extent society has an obligation to maintain income standards for the needy, the transfers under social security serve as an acceptable substitute for welfare programs. The value of the social security investment for an individual or group cannot be considered without recognizing the extra costs which would have to be paid in some other way to support the poor. Thus, social security remains a good insurance buy for most Americans though it has shouldered noninsurance transfer responsibilities.

How Secure Is Social Security?

Granted the effectiveness of the social security system in the past, the issue is whether similar performance can be expected in the future. The 1974 report of the Board of Trustees of the OASDI Trust Fund raised disturbing questions about the long-term outlook for social security. The trustees estimated that the tax rate would have to be raised to 17.7 percent by the year 2045 to finance currently slated benefits. Their report also emphasized the precarious dependence of social security financing on a number of long-term factors such as population growth rates, inflation, rising productivity and real wages.

Under the pay-as-you-go system, it is the children born today who must support their parents and grandparents a generation or two hence. Between 1960 and 1974 the total fertility rate fell from 3.6 to 1.9 per hundred married women of childbearing age. If this "birth dearth" were to continue the number of elderly would climb from 10 percent of the population in 1974 to 15 percent in 2045. There are now four social security beneficiaries for each ten contributors. Zero population growth would result in six for every ten by the year 2045.[12]

If population does not grow, benefits can only be expanded as a result of earnings increases. Real wage gains of 3 percent (coupled with 3 percent inflation) would require 12 percent of payroll to provide currently promised benefits in 2045; if real growth were at only 2 percent, 18 percent of wages and salaries would have to be set aside. The Board of Trustees assumed that 2 percent real growth was the most realistic, despite the 3 percent average from 1947 through 1974. Its argument was that the productivity gains in the service sector would be slow, and that resource scarcities would exert a drag on economic growth. Given this pessimistic forecast, financing difficulties were foreseen.

The trustees' report was important in setting forth the alternative long-term scenarios and their implications for the social security system. Unfortunately, there was a rash of publicity which highlighted the negative and questioned the solvency of the entire system—raising the specter of bankruptcy a generation hence. This threat of insolvency was clearly exaggerated, and there are a number of reasons for believing that the social security system will remain secure.

First, any dangers to the social security system are very long range. According to the statistical simulations, demographic trends will not start raising costs significantly until 2030, leaving ample time for corrective action. Projecting so far into the future increases the weight of the underlying assumptions and assumes predictive accuracy, which is impossible even in the short run.

Second, the assumptions of the trustees' report were purposefully conservative to emphasize what could happen at the worst. A decade ago, the crisis noted by demographers was the population explosion. Values and circumstances changed, birth rates dropped precipitously, and projections proved grossly in error. Values and circumstances could change again over several decades, with the joys of children and childbearing rediscovered. The assumed stagnation of real wages is not inevitable. Resource scarcities may be a factor, but the potentials for improved productivity in our increasingly service-oriented economy may not be as limited as some have claimed. Automatic check-out systems, pocket calculators, health maintenance organizations, and a variety of other technical and organizational changes are drastically altering industries and occupations. Moreover, the movement of the highly educated postwar babies into the prime working years may give a dramatic boost to the nation's productivity. Finally, work force projections, from which the number of future contributors is estimated, may also be understated. Female labor force participation has tended to exceed previous predictions. There is also a possibility that increased immigration (or simply the coverage of immigrants who are already working illegally) could greatly expand the work force.

Third, the projected tax rate increase from 12 to 18 percent over seventy years may not be unbearable. From 1955 to 1974 the tax rate more than doubled, yet private pension plan contributions also expanded, rising from 2.2 to 3.2 percent of wages and salaries between 1955 and 1971. This suggests the percentage of compensation deferred for retirement, voluntarily as well as under mandatory programs, rises with income. Cross-sectional data support this conclusion. Low wage industries tend to spend a substantially smaller proportion of compensation on retirement and welfare benefits than high wage ones.[13] As average wages and salaries rise, it is to be expected that the proportion available and desired for retirement purposes will increase.

It is also important that if zero population growth continues the working age population in the future would be better able to afford social security taxes than the current generation, since there would be fewer youngsters to feed and shelter.

Finally, neither the current OASDI benefit formula nor the rapid pace of improvements in recent years is sacrosanct. The formula could be changed to maintain the present absolute standards, and simulations have demonstrated that with zero population growth and a reduction in the age of retirement to 60, it would be possible to hold tax rates constant and keep real benefits fixed as long as the growth in real wages is over 1 percent.[14] Thus, even if the nation decides that it cannot afford significant improvements in the social security replacement rate, it can almost certainly afford to maintain current standards.

Adjustments may well be needed in the social security system as conditions change. Social security benefits clearly cannot expand at the same real rate as in the past, but progress since 1935 has resulted in a fairly mature and comprehensive system which provides minimally adequate benefits, and the need for further rapid increases is not evident. If society can afford to do more in the future, that is all to the good; but if the dire predictions come true and growth stagnates, then the improvements will have to be less ambitious. Nevertheless, there is no basic threat to the system as it is currently constructed. Social security has worked extremely well to date, and there is every reason to believe that with some foresight it will continue not only to function but to improve for future generations.

Aid for the Deserving Poor

While social insurance protections were improved over the years, many persons only qualified for minimal or no benefits because of limited work experience and low earnings. Aid to the Blind (AB), Aid to the Permanently and Totally Disabled (APTD), and Old Age Assistance (OAA) were the safety nets for the needy blind, aged, and disabled. While growing more slowly than other income support components, these programs paid $3.5 billion in benefits to 3.2 million recipients in 1973.

	Recipients (in thousands)		Benefits (in millions)	
	December 1960	December 1973	December 1960	December 1973
Total	*2,681*	*3,173*	*$1,948*	*$3,457*
Old Age Assistance	2,305	1,820	1,626	1,743
Aid to the Permanently and Totally Disabled	269	1,275	236	1,610
Aid to the Blind	107	78	86	104

Serving a low-income, handicapped clientele, OAA, AB, and

APTD were rarely questioned. The target groups could be defined rather specifically by age, medical, and income criteria. Since the clients were either physically handicapped or old, there was little concern about creating work disincentives by the provision of welfare. Given the obvious difficulties and impairments of these individuals, relatively generous benefits were provided. The federal contribution was increased in 1965 and the earnings exemption liberalized in 1965 and 1967. The states, determining benefit levels as well as eligibility criteria, gradually increased payment levels. The average AB and APTD payments rose 67 and 96 percent respectively between December 1960 and 1973. OAA's increased by less, 29 percent, because expanded social security and veterans' benefits more generously supplemented public assistance.

The Shortcomings

Despite increasing benefits, moderate growth, and an absence of controversy, OAA, AB, and APTD had some shortcomings similar to, though much less serious than, those so controversial under AFDC. One problem was marked geographic variations. In August 1973 the average monthly OAA payment was $78, ranging from $54 in Texas and Mississippi to $118 in Alaska and $112 in New York. There were 50 separate formulas for counting income and allowing for rent and homeownership expenditures, assets, and living arrangements. There were also some differences in eligibility rules.

Integration with other welfare and in-kind programs was minimal. For the more than three fifths of OAA recipients also aided by OASDI, increases in social security would have been offset dollar for dollar by decreases in public assistance if Congress had not stipulated pass-throughs as it did in 1969 and 1972. According to the Joint Economic Committee's 1972 survey, 28 percent of aged, blind, and disabled public assistance recipients also received food stamps, and another 18 percent were given commodities directly.[15] These beneficiaries, as well as the lucky minority in subsidized housing, were much better off than others.

The 1970 Nixon administration reform proposals were aimed at alleviating these problems of benefit and eligibility variations and program overlaps through the welfare system. While most of the debate focused on the proposed income guarantee for families with children, the family assistance plan also called for changes in OAA, AB, and APTD, including the federalization of administration and the standardization of eligibility regulations, the establishment of a national benefit floor, and the "cashing out" of food stamps. The guaranteed income idea was scrapped because of the high cost of bringing many state AFDC payments up to reasonable standards, the concern over work disincentives for family heads, and the difficulties of agreeing on benefit levels and earnings offset rates. These issues were less imposing obstacles to the reform of aid for the aged, blind, and disabled. Consequently, tax rates could be placed at low levels and basic benefits at high ones without massively increasing costs. Despite this advantage, reform proved neither easy nor complete.

Supplemental Security Income

The 1972 Social Security amendments replaced the three separate public assistance categories with a single federally funded program, Supplemental Security Income (SSI), and established a uniform monthly basic benefit of $140 in 1974 for an individual and $210 for a couple. Under nationally uniform criteria, an individual was eligible for benefits if countable income were no more than $420 a quarter; for a couple the limit was $630. The first $20 per month of income and up to $85 of earnings plus work-related expenses and one half of earnings above this were excluded from income. Uniform asset limits as well as blindness and disability definitions were established which were more liberal than those existing in some states.

The new federal floor was below the level of payments in more than half of the states so that some previous recipients would have been either ineligible or would have received a reduced benefit unless states made supplemental contributions.[16] The law required the high benefit states to supplement federal payments to maintain pre-SSI levels for all pre-SSI recipients but permitted them to pay only the federal floors for new beneficiaries.

As originally designed, SSI would have "cashed out" the food stamp program. This would have adversely affected beneficiaries in states paying cash or combined cash and in-kind benefits above the SSI levels. Congress amended the law providing that recipients would be eligible for food stamps unless their cash payments at least equaled the total of the state welfare payment and the food stamp bonus they would have been eligible to receive in December 1973. These complex arrangements were necessary to insure that some of those in need would not be made worse off by federally instituted reforms.

SSI also sought to reduce the administrative overhead in having three separate programs run differently by each state. The law provided for federal payment and record keeping in the distribution of the basic SSI benefits. States could elect to administer their supplemental payments above the federal floor but would stand to lose some federal subsidies. However, through fiscal 1974, two thirds of the states retained some administrative responsibility, requiring the maintenance of separate state bureaucracies.[17]

The Limits of Reform

The Supplemental Security Income program only partially realized its reform goals of reducing the complexity and raising the level of benefits, improving administration, and better integrating public assistance with in-kind programs.

First, while benefits were raised in a number of states, it is likely that the more liberal ones will build on the federal payment while the more conservative states will reduce their own outlays by letting the federal government foot an increasing portion of the bill. The continuance of food stamp eligibility affects the previously high benefit states. Their recipients will qualify for both SSI and food stamps while others in low benefit states will get only SSI. The federal floor reduced the range in benefits but left wide differentials, which are likely to increase with time.

Second, the administrative savings achieved under SSI are debatable. The majority of states continued to maintain certification and bookkeeping staffs to administer supplementals, while HEW added several thousand employees to administer the federal part of the program.[18] The discovery of large overpayments in 1975 resulting from federal computer errors reflected the problems inherent in changing administrative arrangements.

Finally, integration with other social welfare programs remains a problem. SSI recipients are still eligible for food stamps, and procedures for determining eligibility and benefit levels are more complex than in the past. The raising of the public assistance floor also increased the overlap with social insurance. In February 1973 only 1.2 million aged persons received both OAA and social security, while in January 1974, 3.7 million received both.[19] Under the SSI benefit formula, OASDI recipients earning a pension after years of payroll deductions from their meager wages may receive little more than would a person with no previous earnings. Furthermore, increases in social security are offset dollar for dollar by reductions in SSI unless specifically excepted.

Even these modest reforms had a steep price tag. In December 1973 there were 3.2 million recipients under the three separate programs receiving annualized monthly benefits of $3.5 billion. A year later there were 4.0 million recipients, receiving $5.6 billion annually—a 26 percent increase in the number of beneficiaries and a 63 percent increase in benefits.

The SSI experience provides a sobering demonstration of the limits of welfare reform. Because of the nature of the clients, the programs for the deserving poor were the most amenable to modification, yet the improvements which could be engineered were less than revolutionary. Benefits were raised in a number of states, and eligibility standards liberalized, but wide variations remained. Costs were raised by three fifths within a year and further equalization would be even more expensive. Moreover, the narrowing of benefit variations may only be temporary as parsimonious states rely exclusively on the federal contribution, while more generous ones use federal payments as a foundation for improving aid. Federal policy makers do not want the responsibility of cutting back benefits, and the protection of current benefit levels causes distortions. The SSI provisions for continued participation in food stamps and the requirements for state supplementation confused the situation and undermined potential administrative gains possible through federalization. The overlap of welfare and social insurance programs continues to complicate reform. If social security benefits had been exempted as liberally as earnings in calculating SSI benefits many more OASDI recipients would have been eligible, reducing the target efficiency of public assistance. Even with the low exemption, the number of dual recipients rose substantially. In-kind benefits are difficult to convert to cash payments without hurting many recipients.

In brief, sweeping improvements in the welfare system do not seem likely or particularly feasible based on the SSI experience. Rather, progress must be incremental. The Supplemental Security Income program has raised benefits, standardized eligibility, and partially cashed out food stamps; not much more could have been done given political realities and budget constraints.

The Eye of the Storm: AFDC

In his August 1969 message on welfare reform President Nixon voiced what was, or has since become, a view widely shared by conservatives, liberals, and moderates. "The present welfare system," he stated, "has to be judged a colossal failure . . . failing to meet the elementary human, social and financial needs of the poor. It breaks up homes. It often penalizes work. It robs recipients of dignity. And it grows." Although the welfare system included a wide range of programs, there was no doubt that the criticism focused on Aid to Families with Dependent Children. AFDC rolls had more than doubled during the 1960s while costs quadrupled. Since able-bodied fathers were only rarely helped, AFDC was assumed to provide financial incentives to split up low-income homes and deter marriage. High benefits, in some areas exceeding wages available to the unskilled, were believed to discourage work. There was continuing debate also over the manner of giving, with measures to protect the privacy and dignity of recipients in conflict with those aiming to cut down on abuse of the system. AFDC was thus the major culprit in the alleged welfare mess.

A Brief History

AFDC was a source of little concern until the 1960s. The number of recipients had grown from 1.2 to 2.2 million over the 1940s and to 3.1 million over the 1950s, but the percentage of all children on the rolls had remained stable at 3.3 percent. The majority of family heads on AFDC were widows left to support their families. The average monthly payment in 1960 was $108 for a family of four, and there was little doubt that those with an alternative to relief would use it.

In the early 1960s, however, AFDC rolls began their exponen-

Figure 3–1. AFDC payments and recipients, 1940–1974

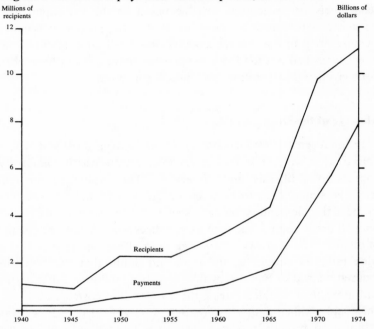

Source: Social Security Bulletin, August 1975, pp. 63–64.

tial expansion (Figure 3-1). Amendments in 1961 authorized aid to families with unemployed fathers. While only half the states ultimately instituted such aid and though fewer than one in twenty AFDC families in 1972 were headed by an able-bodied male, the presence of employable men on relief spurred public concern. Initiating rhetoric that became popular a decade later, President Kennedy called for rehabilitation instead of relief and established a Community Work and Training program to allow recipients the opportunity to work for their welfare payments in publicly created jobs. CWT never grew, and its jobs proved neither useful to recipients nor very productive, but congressional hopes endured. The Economic Opportunity Act initiated the Work Experience and Training program, a work relief effort with somewhat greater emphasis on training and placement. WET was also a disappointment to those who anticipated that dependency could be reduced through rehabilitation. Three out of every four participants departed without completing their assignments, only one fifth of these to take a job. Among completers, less than one half obtained employment immediately.

The failure of the war on poverty and a booming economy to arrest welfare growth was an embarrassment to the Johnson administration and it took action. The 1967 social security amendments set a ceiling on federal contributions, covering costs only for the proportion of children on state rolls in January 1968. A Work Incentive (WIN) program was also initiated providing placement services to employable recipients, training to those with handicaps, special works projects for the jobless, plus day care and other assistance. As an incentive, the law exempted work-connected expenses and the first $30 of monthly earnings plus one third of the remainder in calculating benefits, in contrast to the previous formula which had frequently reduced benefits dollar for dollar with net earnings.

Despite these measures 1967 was a take-off point rather than a plateau in the growth of AFDC. The number of recipients doubled during the next four years. When President Johnson left office, he pinpointed this welfare explosion as one of the nation's chief domestic problems, and the subsequent administration heated up the rhetoric, blaming the situation on the Great Society. Unquestionably, the war on poverty and its offshoots such as the National Welfare Rights Organization, community action agencies, and neighborhood legal services heightened awareness and acceptability of welfare among the poor, advancing the notion that welfare was a right of families living in poverty. Changes in the federal contribution formula in 1965 provided increased subsidies to roughly a dozen high benefit states and may have encouraged them to be more liberal. But other factors beyond the control of the Johnson administration were more crucial. The number of children in need increased. Supreme Court decisions outlawing the man-in-the-house rule in 1968 and state residency requirements in 1969 reduced state authority to discourage potential applicants. The states themselves were more responsible than anyone, significantly raising benefit levels and loosening eligibility standards. Over the 1950s and early 1960s, benefits had risen in proportion to average earnings; but from the beginning of 1965 through 1968 the average benefit went up by a third, or more than double the rise in annual average spendable earnings of a worker with three dependents. At the same time, states became less restrictive in determining eligibility. Where only 54 percent of all welfare applications had been accepted in 1953, 81 percent were approved in 1970.

Rhetoric aside, the Nixon administration's proposed policies were more liberal than those of its predecessor. While proclaiming the colossal failure of the system, President Nixon proposed major reforms which would have added millions to the welfare rolls and billions of dollars to relief costs. His family assistance plan guaranteed a family of four persons, whether headed by a male or a female, $2,400 annually. The first $720 of earnings and one third of anything above that were to be disregarded in calculating benefits. The conservatively estimated price tag for such a program was $6 billion, or double the outlays for AFDC.

Congress rejected this plan. Conservatives opposed the extension of aid to male-headed families, liberals found the proposed benefits too skimpy, and Congress balked at the price tag of reform. While legislative action stalled, the AFDC rolls continued to grow. The ceiling imposed in 1967 was postponed and then scrapped. It was not feasible (and probably unconstitutional) to limit aid when new applicants were eligible by the same criteria applied to existing recipients. In response to rising inflation, Congress required states to make cost-of-living adjustments in their AFDC needs standards beginning in July 1969. This added to costs. Liberalization of the food stamp program at about the same time raised the benefit package and the propensity of low-income family heads to opt for welfare in preference to a job. These factors were compounded by the recession, and between 1969 and 1972 the number of recipients rose by 3.7 million, an increase exceeding the total number of AFDC at the beginning of the 1960s.

In the face of this massive expansion and upcoming elections, the Nixon administration wavered in its support of welfare reform, acquiescing to more spartan congressional measures. The Talmadge amendments in 1971 mandated work registration for most adults, emphasizing direct placement over training. In the same spirit, some states reduced their benefit levels and most held the line despite inflation, raising needs standards with living costs but failing to raise benefits commensurately. The real average monthly payment declined 2 percent between January 1970 and 1975. More restrictive application procedures were also adopted, doubling the rejection rate between 1970 and 1973.

Coincident with these steps, the number of recipients declined from 11.1 million in December 1972 to 10.7 million in July 1974. Then the recession pushed the number upwards again to 11.4 million by April 1975. Even though this increase was modest relative to earlier growth, especially in light of the worst economic slump since the Great Depression, it was enough to keep alive the attacks on AFDC and the charges of its basic failure. The Ford administration reiterated the need for welfare reform, making this its major domestic thrust.

Putting Mothers to Work

It is a fundamental tenet of our society that those who can support themselves should do so. The income maintenance system was structured on the premise that social insurance would provide for the employables while welfare would be confined to those unable to work. As more and more mothers have entered the labor force, the implicit assumption of AFDC that women could not or should not leave the home has been increasingly questioned. In fact, the major criticism of AFDC, as well as the chief focus of proposed reforms, has been its failure to encourage work. Studies suggested that recipients had no more negative attitudes about employment than other women, yet only a small minority were in the labor force and an even fewer worked their way off assistance rolls. Placement, training, and job creation programs met with limited success. Economists argued about high marginal tax rates and their work disincentive effects, while policy makers struggled with the tradeoffs between increased work incentives, higher costs and possible harm to recipients unable to work. "Workfare versus welfare" was one of the major national issues of the late 1960s and early 1970s. Yet it was never resolved, and more confusion than insight resulted from the thousands of pages of analysis and argument that were generated.

The fact stands out that the average welfare recipient faces extremely limited prospects in the labor market. Employability is a complex balance of economic, social, and psychological factors, and attempts at precise measurement are elusive, but there are clearly a number of overlapping problems besetting the average recipient. Sixteen percent of AFDC mothers were currently employed in 1973, and 12 percent were actively seeking work but unable to find a job, yielding an unemployment rate, by conventional definitions, of 43 percent. Two thirds of all welfare mothers in 1973 were high school dropouts with fully a fourth having an eighth grade education or less.[20] Two in five were restricted from some types of jobs because of their health, and one in five could not work at all because of physical problems.[21] Five out of eight had children under six, so that more than half of the recipients in 1973 required child care facilities or were needed in the home full time.

In light of these facts, the limited reliance upon work by AFDC mothers is neither surprising nor cause for alarm. Among the 45 percent not incapacitated and not restricted by child care responsibilities in 1973, over a third were working, a fourth were unemployed, and a twelfth were in training or awaiting placement, leaving less than a third (or 15 percent of all welfare mothers) not actively seeking work. Of these, three fifths had not held a job for a year and two fifths for three years, perhaps because of limited work experience and employability.[22]

The difficulty of overcoming the disadvantages of welfare clients is suggested by the modest success of training and placement efforts. The Work Incentive program was designed to provide individualized assessment of needs, on-the-job or institutional training, placement assistance, child care, other supportive services, and even subsidized employment. The aim was to restore to economic independence all employable adults on AFDC rolls; HEW estimated that as many as a million families could work their way off welfare.

Only one in ten recipients ever enrolled, of whom less than a fifth completed a course of training. One of seven participants ended up being placed in jobs where they stayed for 90 days or more. Since one sixth of welfare recipients find employment on their own, the successful placement of such a small proportion of the most employable hardly justifies the program. There are many reasons for this limited achievement. Participants had many personal and family problems which caused them to drop out. WIN experienced start-up difficulties. Most critically, however, jobs proved difficult to find for welfare mothers.

Job creation efforts for welfare recipients did not materialize. Initially, plans called for a fifth of WIN enrollees to be employed in special work projects with public or private nonprofit employers, but few openings were created. The tax law amendments in 1971 authorized a 20 percent tax credit to private employers on the wages paid to AFDC recipients, and these could be combined with training subsidies. Public service employment was also to be expanded. Yet employers did not leap at these bonuses. In fiscal 1973 there were only 29,000 WIN participants in supported work positions and 33,000 in OJT. The reason was simple: welfare recipients were so disadvantaged that employers could not be induced to hire them even with substantial subsidies.

Neither the stick nor the carrot has done much to increase work by welfare recipients. There was mandatory referral of certain classes of employables under WIN, and the Talmadge amendments required work registration and acceptance of jobs if available. But in a slack labor market, a work requirement for those at the end of the labor queue has little meaning; and even under the best of circumstances, it is difficult to mandate work. If welfare benefits for an entire family are cut off, its dependent members will suffer, and it is difficult to distinguish between the person who is voluntarily unemployed and another who seeks but cannot find work. States have, therefore, rarely refused aid because of nonemployment.

Work incentives were not any more successful. Critics of AFDC went to great lengths to document how welfare benefit reductions offset a substantial portion of wages and salaries and create a high marginal tax rate on earnings. Yet these same critics largely ignored the evidence that lowering tax rates and earnings offsets had little impact on work propensities. The WIN program, which allowed AFDC recipients to retain $30 and one third of monthly earnings before losing any public assistance payments, substantially increased the payoff of work, lowering the marginal tax rate from 100 to 67 percent and the average tax rate even more. As an example, the General Accounting Office estimated in 1971 that an AFDC mother in Los Angeles with three children earning $433 monthly would have lost only $3 of her welfare payments because WIN permitted her to disregard $54 in payroll deductions, $212 in work related expenses, plus $30 and one third of gross wages.[23]

Not all areas were as liberal, yet there was no doubt that the 1967 law improved the payoff for work.

The impact on work patterns was very little. In 1967, 15 percent of welfare recipients worked; in 1971, 15 percent; and in 1973, 16 percent. The proportion working full time rose from 7.2 to 9.8 percent over the six years, but this was explained, in part, by the increased eligibility of fully employed workers. It must be questioned whether a further reduction in the tax rate, say to 50 percent, would have any greater impact, especially in a slack labor market.

Any such reduction would increase the welfare universe by raising the maximum eligibility level. If there is a basic guarantee of $2,000, a marginal tax rate of 100 percent means that anyone earning over this amount would be ineligible; a 67 percent tax rate raises the eligibility point to $3,000, while a rate of 50 percent increases it to $4,000. It was estimated that the use of a 50 percent rather than 67 percent tax rate under the family assistance plan would have increased the number of beneficiaries by more than half.[24] If lowering tax rates has little effect on work by existing AFDC clients, and leads to increased eligibility for benefits, the effect is to increase rather than decrease welfare costs.

If the incentive of lower tax rates is not the answer, the goad of lower basic benefits is questionable. Admittedly, low or no benefits would induce some AFDC recipients to seek employment. In states paying 100 percent of their needs standards in 1971, only 17 percent of AFDC mothers were labor force participants; in those paying three fifths or less of needs, nearly two fifths were working or looking for work. According to two different estimates, raising the annual income guarantee from $500 to $1,500 leads to a decrease in employment rates of between 15 and 40 percent. Presumably, then, a two thirds cut in a $1,500 annual benefit might increase employment from 16 percent to between 18 and 23 percent of recipients. But this would be achieved at the cost of increased deprivation for the other three fourths of recipients whose benefits would also be reduced.

In summary, then, training and employment programs for welfare clients have had limited success. Reform measures aiming to substitute workfare for welfare through improved incentives or coercion are destined to modest success at best. Some persons can be trained and helped permanently; some can be encouraged to make it on their own; some new opportunities can be opened; but this will not be enough to significantly change the AFDC population or its well-being. Work and welfare can go together, but attempts to force the marriage have shown limited success. Adult persons on welfare might be encouraged to supplement their public assistance payments with earnings. But recent experience has shown that relatively few welfare recipients can "make it" without support.

Impacts on the Family

The accelerated deterioration of family structure in recent years has been a source of deep concern. Between 1960 and 1973 the percentage of families headed by a woman rose more than a third and the number of poor living in households with a female head rose from one in five to one in three. The changes were particularly severe among blacks. In 1960, less than a fifth of nonwhite families were headed by a female; a decade and a half later more than a third had a woman as their head.

These family changes were a factor in the growth of dependency. It is more than coincidence that the 2.1 million rise in the number of female-headed families between 1960 and 1973 was accompanied by a 2.2 million increase in the number of female-headed families on relief. The 1.0 million net increase in nonwhite female family heads was matched by a caseload growth of 1.1 million.

Since more than two fifths of all female-headed families are poor prior to receipt of transfers and since AFDC is directed specifically to low-income female-headed units, the increasing incidence of female heads would be expected to increase the caseload. The uncertain issue is whether causality runs in the opposite direction as well—whether the greater availability and attractiveness of welfare increased the number of female-headed families and thus the number of potential recipients. With limited aid for male-headed families, it might make financial sense to avoid marriage or for the husband to absent himself in order to make his family eligible for public assistance.

It was generally agreed in the early 1970s that the destabilizing effect of welfare on black families was significant. Some critics went so far as to say that because of these family impacts, welfare was doing more harm than good. Yet the evidence was never as unequivocal as the consensus.

Changes in marital patterns—whatever their cause—were of secondary importance in AFDC's growth. During the 1960s the proportion of nonwhite women 14 years and over who were heads of families or subfamilies with children under 18 rose from 8.2 to 11.4 percent. If the proportion on welfare had not changed, there would have been 292,000 fewer nonwhite female heads on relief in 1970. Since the number of nonwhite mothers on AFDC rose by 723,000 over the decade, the increased propensity to head families with children could account, therefore, for two fifths of the caseload expansion, at most.

Factors other than the availability of welfare explain a large part of the increase in female-headed families. Census figures reveal that 8 percent of the net growth in nonwhite female-headed families resulted from the increased propensity of mothers without husbands to form their own households; 15 percent was related to the increase in marital disruption; and 21 percent was due to the rising proportion of unmarried women with children. Some portion of this 44 percent could have been related to welfare. Greater frequency of children in split families (24 percent), population growth (16 percent), and a combination (17 percent) of the above factors accounted for the balance of the increase.[26]

A cross-sectional analysis of 44 metropolitan areas found that the proportion of nonwhite women heading families in 1970 rose roughly 2 percent for each 10 percent increase in the AFDC stipend. Yet 10 percent higher wage levels for males and females were related to 9 percent lower and 7 percent higher incidence respectively.[27] Expanding job opportunities for black women as well as the slow rise of wages of black males have apparently been the major causes of the increase in the number of families headed by females.

The relationship between welfare and the birth of children out of wedlock is tenuous. Illegitimacy declined during the past decade and this was not just the effect of the pill. Between 1960 and 1964, before the large rise in AFDC caseloads, "shotgun" marriages legitimized less than a fifth of live births conceived out of wedlock. The proportion actually rose slightly in the last half of the decade.[28] There is no evidence that the greater availability of welfare reduced the propensity to marry after conception.

Finally, there is little cross-sectional relationship between illegitimacy rates and AFDC monthly benefit levels. The 1970 nonwhite illegitimacy rate in the seven states paying the highest AFDC benefits was the same as that in the seven with the lowest benefits.[29]

The consequences of illegitimacy and the formation of families headed by females are uncertain. The controversial claim of the mid-1960s that black society suffered from the deterioration of the family was based on sketchy evidence concerning lower school achievement, higher crime among children raised without a male influence, and the lower income of female-headed families. Yet data from the Survey of Equal Educational Opportunity suggest the father's absence has a negligible impact on the school achievement of black youths.[30] Where marriages are broken or avoided in order to qualify for welfare and to increase per capita income, well-being is improved rather than undermined.

The preceding analysis does not disprove the conventional wisdom that AFDC has disrupted marital and family patterns, especially among blacks. Clearly, however, this relationship is not as serious in scale or consequence as many critics have claimed. The notion that the welfare system is feeding its own rapid growth is an exaggeration. Economic factors explain only a part of the changes in marital and family patterns; welfare is only one of these economic factors, and it is probably not the most important. Family deterioration may have positive as well as negative effects if the result is to increase income through relief.

Growth Is Good

The gut reaction to AFDC's rampant growth was to condemn welfare for breaking up families and for supporting shirkers. Both contributed to welfare's expansion, but the crucial factors were much less complex and much less inimical. There are millions of families in this affluent nation who must live at the margin of subsistence unless they receive help. Prior to the 1960s aid was given grudgingly to only a small portion and benefits were niggardly. AFDC's growth was primarily the result of establishing a welfare system which provided adequately and universally for needy families headed by women.

In 1960 the average monthly AFDC benefit equaled roughly two fifths the poverty threshold for a family of four. Five years later it was one half and by the beginning of the 1970s, it had risen to 56 percent. The welfare package was further improved by the addition of in-kind benefits. By 1972 two thirds of AFDC recipients were receiving free or subsidized food and almost all were getting free health care. While both these in-kind benefits are available to families eligible for but not receiving cash, and to many with incomes above AFDC cutoffs, there is no doubt that this supplementation increased the adequacy and attractiveness of welfare by raising the well-being of the average recipient to a level near the poverty line. A GAO survey of 100 areas found that the combined value of food stamps, commodities, school lunches, public housing, and AFDC potentially available for a mother with three children and no other source of income was $4,100, or just $100 less than the poverty threshold in 1972.[31] While actual benefits would be lower since not all recipients can get into public housing or may participate in other programs, the welfare system now provides for most basic needs.

Improved benefits increased the reliance on welfare among those eligible. In 1960 a third of the two million women with children under 18 years heading families or subfamilies were on the AFDC rolls. The number of potential female recipients grew to 3.2 million by 1970, but the proportion on relief rose to three fourths. The average AFDC caseload equaled only two fifths of the poor or near poor in female headed families with children under 18 years in 1960, but had reached three fifths a decade later; in the latter year the AFDC caseload exceeded the number of poor families headed by females.[32] AFDC became widespread, if not universal, among low-income families with a female head, and a source of support whenever a woman headed a family.

Having reached this point, a leveling off of growth was inevitable. The number of near poor female-headed families with children under 18 years rose 5 percent annually in the first half of the 1970s. This rate would essentially have been the cap on growth unless benefits continued to be raised and eligibility extended to the nonpoor. In fact, however, welfare benefits were lowered and eligibility was restricted. Where the annualized benefit per family was 56 percent of the four-person poverty threshold in 1969, it was only 52 percent in 1973 (meeting a roughly constant proportion of needs when the decline in AFDC family size over this period is considered). By the same token, the average monthly benefit fell from 43 percent of average spendable earnings of a family head with three dependents in December 1970 to 36 percent in August 1974. The relative attractiveness of AFDC was thus eroded for those with a work option.

A Colossal Failure?

Ninety-four percent of AFDC benefits in 1975 went to those who would otherwise have been poor. For the roughly 3.5 million families and 11.4 million persons on AFDC rolls in 1975, the assistance spelled the difference between deprivation and at least a modest subsistence. If benefits had been less generous or eligibility more restricted, some, no doubt, could have found work and could have eked out an existence. But the difficulty of placing even those who have received training and other assistance should indicate that employment is not a realistic alternative for the bulk of the AFDC population beset by a multitude of handicaps. This is especially true in a slack labor market.

By the same token, less adequate or no benefits might make marriage more attractive for some by eliminating an option which improves income and well-being. However, to the extent that illegitimacy and family break-up occur for other reasons, the effect would also be to cut off aid to those most in need.

Policy options to encourage work or discourage family break-up are also limited. Reducing marginal tax rates can only be accomplished by raising break-even points, reducing target efficiency and increasing costs, or else lowering assistance for those who do not find jobs. The payoff in increased self-support does not appear to justify any of these steps. The extension of welfare to male-headed families is not likely to greatly change marital and family patterns.

As long as women are protected, the "reluctant papa" always has an excuse not to marry, and as long as per capita benefits are inversely related to family size, with high marginal tax rates, there will be an incentive to split a family or not to marry. Aid to poor families headed by males may be justified on humanitarian grounds, but is not likely to offset any effects AFDC may have on marital and family patterns.

In retrospect AFDC's massive and seemingly uncontrollable growth was necessary if the nation were to provide adequately for needy female-headed families with children. Combined with in-kind benefits, a poverty level minimum was guaranteed. More inclusive income eligibility criteria expanded the universe, and more lucrative benefits increased usage, so that AFDC came close to covering the bulk of low income female-headed families and subfamilies. While there has been extensive criticism of the inequities of widely varying state benefit levels, there has been little praise of the much more significant expansion of coverage. Universality is a necessary condition to achieve equity, and AFDC is close to meeting that test for poor female-headed families.

Having raised the benefits of most recipients to the poverty level, halting the further expansion of AFDC was justified, especially when economic conditions reversed and a growth dividend was no longer available for improving welfare standards. There is less reason for increasing payments once they begin to edge above levels which provide a subsistence income. If real benefits are stabilized, the impacts of welfare on work and family patterns will gradually decline to the extent they are related to the differences between welfare payments and wages.

The charges that AFDC has been a colossal failure must be recognized for what they are, simplistic political sloganeering. The developments during the Great Society and subsequent years were more positive than negative, moving toward a comprehensive system with adequate benefits. Though the development process was somewhat of an ordeal, it was positive in its directions and effects. The danger now is of going too far in the opposite direction, letting the system erode through inflation and unreasonably strict administration to a point where it no longer serves its primary purpose of providing for those with the greatest needs and most limited options.

The 1970s Growth Sectors

With the maturation of the social security system, the reform of public assistance for the aged, blind, disabled, and the "greening" of AFDC, the forces of growth and change that transformed income maintenance during the 1960s stabilized by the mid-1970s. But new growth sectors emerged, continuing to alter and expand the transfer system. The food stamp program grew rapidly when nationwide eligibility standards and benefit schedules were established in 1970 while severe recessions and rising supermarket prices added new claimants for assistance. Faced with the highest joblessness in more than three decades, Congress passed emergency legislation to bolster unemployment compensation in 1974. Food stamps and unemployment benefits rose to about $22 billion in fiscal 1975, triple the outlays three years earlier and double those for all public assistance programs.

Almost unobserved, but no less consequentially, the veterans' compensation and pension programs grew rapidly over the last decade, paying $7.1 billion in benefits by fiscal 1975. Looking ahead, the aging of World War II veterans is likely to swell the number of beneficiaries in the next decade, making these programs an even more important component of the social welfare system.

These changes follow closely the patterns of the 1960s. To meet severe and pressing problems, to lift benefits to rising societal adequacy standards, and to improve existing programs, legislative changes have been made without full recognition of their broader long-term implications. With potential claimants underestimated and spillovers unforseen, costs will accelerate unexpectedly and the public will perceive a crisis at hand. In all likelihood, legitimate problems will then be exaggerated and the negative emphasized in order to justify retrenchment. Following this familiar pattern, food stamps and unemployment compensation—perhaps even veterans' pensions—could become as controversial in the late 1970s as AFDC was in the late 1960s.

It is important, then, to recognize the overwhelmingly positive effects of the present system, so that when costs and problems become apparent, achievements will not be forgotten. The changes in unemployment compensation, food stamps, and veterans' programs promise to eliminate many inequities in the welfare system, to raise the level of benefits for many in need, to extend them to groups which have previously been shortchanged, and to diffuse opposition to "handouts." These new income support provisions have the potential to substantially improve our nation's social welfare system, even though they will also unquestionably create a number of problems.

Unemployment Compensation—Insurance or Welfare?

The welfare system's priority on aiding female-headed families is not unfounded. Males, at all education and skill levels, are more likely than females to find better paying jobs. In a tight labor market, almost all nonemployment of male family heads is transitional or volitional unless related to illness or disability. In March 1969 less than 2 percent of married males age 25 to 64 with a spouse present were outside the labor force, and the unemployment rate was a low 1.4 percent. There were 3.1 million poor families headed by a male (down from 6.4 million a decade before) and only 1.4 million of the heads were in their prime working years, age 25 to 64 years. The gap between income and poverty thresholds averaged two fifths more in poor families with a female head than in those with a male head, despite the more frequent income transfers to the former group. It makes sense, then, to concentrate scarce dollars on females with the most severe problems, presuming that males unable to work because of illness or disability will be covered by social insurance.

The same logic does not apply, however, when the unemployment rate is 5.8 percent among married men, as it was in May 1975. The basic assumption of the income support system—that able-bodied male heads can find jobs to support their families—does not necessarily hold during a prolonged slump.

The federal-state unemployment compensation program was designed to protect workers against short periods of forced idleness in a normally functioning economy. Financed by an employer tax, it allows states to set payment standards and eligibility rules. Most states pay a fixed proportion of previous earnings up to a stated percentage of average wages and salaries in covered employment.

There were several modifications in state benefit levels and eligibility rules, but no fundamental changes in unemployment compensation, over the 1960s and early 1970s. The average weekly benefit nearly doubled between 1960 and 1974 but increased only slightly as a proportion of spendable weekly earnings. The unemployed worker's chances of receiving aid also changed little. In 1971 beneficiaries represented 43 percent of the unemployed, the same proportion as in 1963, a year of similar overall unemployment.

Unemployment compensation was not a growth area because of the tight labor markets in the 1960s. When joblessness increased massively in 1974 and 1975, the number of unemployment compensation recipients skyrocketed. With 4.1 million unemployed in December 1973, there were 1.7 million recipients. A year later, when the number of jobless had risen to 6.1 million, there were 3.4 million recipients getting $1 billion a month. The system was effective in cushioning the plight of these unemployed recipients and offsetting some of their lost purchasing power.

However, as the unemployment rate rose to even higher levels in 1975, and the prospects of an early return to moderate levels of unemployment dimmed, the effectiveness of the system began to be questioned. Basic benefits lasted 26 weeks, with up to 13 weeks of extended aid in states with high and rising unemployment. As the recession deepened and lengthened, many recipients unable to find jobs faced exhaustion of benefits. Coverage was also inadequate. Most farm workers, domestics, and state and local government employees were uncovered. In a period of widespread joblessness, the logic of denying them protection was more questionable than ever. Finally, more and more states exhausted their reserves and had to borrow money from the federal account to finance benefits.

Congress reacted to these shortcomings by extending benefits to a maximum of 65 weeks, with a major part of funding coming from the federal government rather than payroll taxes. As part of the emergency program, aid was extended to an additional 12 million previously noncovered workers, making them eligible initially for up to 26 (and later 52) weeks of federally financed benefits. In March 1975 a weekly average of 5.9 million persons received $1.5 billion in unemployment insurance benefits of one form or another, more than five times the number during the last year of the Johnson administration, and the costs increased eightfold.

What are the implications of this rapid growth and change?

Clearly, the insurance aspects of the program have been eroded. In the past, payroll taxes covered benefits; but with the prolonged recession, many states had to borrow from the federal government and may never be able to repay. Federal contributions—not related to payroll taxes—cover half of regular extended benefits and all of benefits beyond that. That expansion of coverage is totally an income transfer to those in need, since no taxes have been levied against employers in previously uncovered sectors.

Whom does this new welfare system serve? Three fourths of the insured unemployed are males; almost all are adults; an overwhelming proportion are family heads with dependents. Persons who exhausted unemployment compensation in the past tended to be older and less educated. The liberalization of eligibility and the extension of benefits helps primarily those who may not be eligible for other welfare programs—low-income male family heads and the structurally unemployed. Unemployment compensation has thus filled the gap in the income maintenance system, while at the same time serving its originally designated goal of protecting covered workers. The changes were a reasonable response to the drastic economic slump that negated the assumption of the 1960s that nondisabled, prime-age males could find work if they looked and should not be provided relief except under the most stringent standards.

Food Stamps

The food of one in ten American families is purchased at a reduced cost under the food stamp program. A hybrid between cash and in-kind aid, food stamps are purchased for less than their value, with the price based on income and family size. Those with no income get stamps free and the amount of subsidy is reduced as income rises up to the eligibility maximum. The stamps can only be used to purchase food, but the consumer has more choice than under a direct commodity distribution program. In fact, where the allotment is less than a family would ordinarily spend on subsistence, it is little different from a cash subsidy.

Revived in 1961 after some experience during the New Deal, the food stamp program was state operated and directed. Paralleling the experience with other welfare programs, many states adopted restrictive eligibility and benefit standards, while others simply refused to implement the program. By mid-1969, 3.2 million persons were receiving food stamps, but subsidies were meager and federal outlays represented only a small proportion of welfare outlays.

Fiscal Year	Participants (in thousands)	Federal cost (millions)
1961	50	$ 1
1965	633	33
1969	3,227	229
1973	12,154	2,134
1976 (est.)	20,900	6,009

In the late 1960s, hunger in America became a national issue when severe malnutrition was "discovered" among millions of low-income households. The response of the Nixon administration and Congress was the federalization of the food stamp program and the liberalization of benefits in 1970. Nationwide income eligibility criteria were established based on the costs of providing a nutritionally adequate diet. The raised standards and their universal application greatly expanded the clientele. In December 1973, for instance, a family of four with $30 monthly net income could receive $116 in food stamps free; the cost increased up to the full price at a monthly income of $360 after deducting taxes, retirement contributions, union dues, medical costs in excess of $10 monthly, child care, and housing costs above 30 percent of income. An unknown but large proportion of the population, probably between a sixth and a fifth, could qualify for at least some aid under these standards.

Persons already in the welfare system qualified automatically and were the first to take advantage of the changes. At the end of 1973 seven out of ten AFDC recipients received subsidized food and they constituted three fifths of the 12 million food stamp recipients.

The combination of inflation and massive joblessness in the mid-1970s caused millions of unemployed and persons with fixed incomes to turn to food stamps. Between November 1973 and June 1975, the number of recipients rose by two thirds to roughly 20 million. The majority of these new participants were not welfare recipients (who were mostly receiving stamps already). By mid-1975, probably more than half of participating nonaged households were headed by a male.

Though sharing responsibility for growth, the Nixon administration was philosophically opposed to in-kind aid as inherently inefficient, distorting consumer patterns, and requiring expensive processing and distribution bureaucracies. There was carping at so-called food stamp cheaters—college students and strikers, considered by some to be undeserving. HEW estimated that $110 million could be saved by disqualifying students from non-needy families, but this represented less than 3 percent of the cost of the program at the time.[33]

A more basic charge was that the program was serving many who could well afford their own groceries. Detractors noted that families with more than $10,000 income could qualify for benefits and concluded that the food stamp program was not a welfare program but a "rip-off" by the middle class. These allegations were based on some serious misconceptions. In 1974 the absolute cutoff was $8,300 net income, which meant that a family with an annual gross income of more than $10,000 could qualify. But these high income limits applied to a family of eight, for whom the 1973 poverty threshold was $7,500. Further, the value of the subsidy declines with income and this "affluent" family would get only $40 a month worth of subsidies. The hassle of getting stamps may not be worth the few dollars for families with minimal needs and in November 1973, less than one fifth of all food stamp recipients were in households with after-tax incomes above poverty levels, and less than one in twenty had incomes exceeding 125 percent of poverty thresholds.[34]

While far from a perfect system, the food stamp subsidy formula does give more to those with less income and greater needs, and it phases out subsidies gradually. Lower-middle class families can get help if they suffer a loss of income; the near poor get less than the poor, but they nevertheless get something. Furthermore, because everyone who pays a grocery bill can sympathize with the plight of those with limited income, the food stamp program does not carry the same negative stigma as AFDC and the public is more willing to aid male-headed families. This support was demonstrated by the massive resistance to the Ford administration's proposal in early 1975 to cut back the subsidy level. The growth of food stamps has, thus, helped fill gaps in the income maintenance system in a publicly acceptable fashion.

Veterans' Pensions and Compensation

Income support programs for veterans have been characterized as a model welfare system, where aid is distributed generously and compassionately, with maximum concern for the dignity of recipients. Veterans' compensation helps those suffering service-connected disabilities. While nominally compensating for income loss, there is no means test. Survivors are also protected—widows until they remarry and children until age 18 (or age 22 if attending school). Benefits depend on the degree of disability, with completely disabled veterans getting nearly $500 a month in 1974 and the average recipient around $100.

Disabled or aged indigent veterans and their survivors are eligible to receive pensions. These are structured to augment social security and public assistance, providing a higher standard of living for the needy who have served their country. The 1975 minimum monthly benefit was $160 for a single veteran and $172 with one dependent. Up to $300 in other annual income is exempted with benefits gradually declining to zero for those with annual incomes of over $3,000.

The price tag of veterans' pensions and compensation has grown steadily as benefits have been raised. In 1960, $3.4 billion was paid out to 3.1 million veterans and their survivors; by 1975 cash benefits totaled $7.1 billion for 4.9 million cases. The caseload grew slowly as mortality among World War I veterans offset the rising number of World War II pensioners. Looking ahead, however, the prospect is for a much more rapid increase in beneficiaries. By 1985 there will be 5 million veterans 65 and over, more than double the number in the mid-1970s, and a further increase to 7.5 million can be expected by 1990.[35] If the proportion receiving benefits remains constant, there will be three times as many pensionsers within the next 15 years. Improvements in social security and private pensions may reduce the proportion of older veterans who are needy. But to date Congress has tended to raise qualifying income levels apace with welfare and social insurance increases. Undoubtedly, veterans' programs will play an expanding role in the social welfare system in the years ahead.

Veterans' pensions and compensation are, if not sacrosanct, rarely questioned. Pensions are quite clearly a welfare program, but they do not have the stigma of public assistance. Benefits are paid without red tape and with minimal checks on the income statements filed by claimants. The taxpayer has also been less parsimonious in providing for veterans. The expansion of the pension program will raise benefit levels for many of those who would otherwise have relied primarily on the other welfare system, while protecting dignity and self-respect. With their greater public support, the expansion of veterans' programs will increase the overall acceptability of income support efforts.

The "Welfare Mess" Revisited

These various income maintenance programs are part of a complex and interrelated web of cash and in-kind assistance. One fifth of aged social security recipients also receive welfare. Four fifths of SSI clients benefit from OASDI, as do three fourths of pensioned veterans. Most of these receive subsidized health care under either Medicare, Medicaid, or veterans' programs. Similarly, AFDC cash payments are almost universally supplemented by food stamps or distributed commodities as well as by free medical care. Food stamps are more and more frequently augmenting unemployment compensation. Subsidized housing, workman's compensation, government retirement, and school lunches add to the overlap and complexity. These separate programs provided over $125 billion in benefits during fiscal 1974 to separate caseloads totaling 130 million. Yet there were probably fewer than half this many individual beneficiaries, as the majority of recipients participated in two or more programs.

Given this extensive overlap, the combined impacts are critically important though difficult to pin down. While benefits under each program may be reasonable, the total package might be far above subsistence levels or publicly accepted needs standards. Equity demands that like people be treated equally, and if likeness is measured by per capita income, benefits are inequitably distributed as a result of the unplanned overlap of programs. Work disincentives are a primary issue. Not only can high combined benefits provide an option to employment, but the layering of programs, each reducing aid by some proportion of earnings, can increase the marginal tax rate, making it unprofitable for some low earners to seek work. With so many programs, administration is exceedingly complex. Changes in one part of the system can have perverse effects on other parts. Bureaucracies are needed for each categorical program, and the separate agencies may establish differing eligibility standards, certification procedures, and red tape. The probability of error, whether in favor of or against clients, is multiplied. All these issues have been part of the continuing 1970s debate over the adequacy of the welfare system, and to assess them the system must be viewed in its totality.

Is the System Too Generous?

Given the multiplicity of welfare and social insurance programs and the diversity of eligibility rules and certification procedures, there is room for exploitation of the system. It is a widely shared suspicion, sustained by occasional unrepresentative examples, that large numbers of welfare recipients are growing fat at the public trough.

In 1972 the General Accounting Office interviewed a number of households in low-income areas across the nation to determine the level and overlap of benefits under cash and in-kind social welfare programs. Household responses were cross-checked with administrative records to authenticate the data. The dollar amount of benefits was determined in each case under the cash programs, and in-kind aid was valued at average cost.

Not surprisingly, considering the low income group sampled, there was a significant degree of reliance on public programs, and

Benefits	Percent of recipients
Cash	*77%*
Social insurance only	40
Need based only	25
Both	12
In-kind	*78%*
Cash and in-kind	55
In-kind only	23

very extensive overlap. Three out of every five sampled households received at least one benefit. Of these recipients, two thirds participated in two or more programs, and almost a fifth benefited under five or more.[36]

The permutations and combinations were numerous, but the major nexus was public assistance. Four fifths of public assistance recipients participated in three or more programs compared with only two fifths of all beneficiaries (Table 3-2).

Table 3–2. Overlap of social welfare programs in low-income areas, 1972 (percent)

Program	Public assistance programs	Social security cash programs	Veterans' cash programs	Other cash programs	Food programs	Health care programs	Housing programs	Education and manpower programs	Other aid in kind
					Households also receiving benefits from—				
Cash benefits:									
Public assistance	100	28	4	4	64	82	26	18	14
Social security	25	100	10	7	23	53	14	4	6
Veterans' programs	22	22	100	11	19	44	15	3	42
Other programs	12	12	6	100	24	27	6	12	2
In-kind aid:									
Food programs	62	25	3	8	100	67	24	21	16
Health care	54	39	5	5	46	100	21	14	11
Housing	55	33	6	48	52	65	100	23	13
Education and manpower	100	13	1	11	63	58	30	100	14
Other	68	21	5	3	55	59	21	18	100

Source: James R. Storey, Alair A. Townsend, and Irene Cox, *How Public Welfare Benefits Are Distributed in Low-Income Areas,* Joint Economic Committee, 93rd Cong., 1st Sess. (Washington: Government Printing Office, March 1973), pp. 70–75.

Participation in more than one social welfare program is no guarantee of affluence. Multiple benefits are often the result of special needs and the combination of benefits rarely raises recipients far above poverty thresholds. Actual examples from the 1972 survey included an 85-year-old man and his wife living on $155 monthly old-age assistance and social security plus an estimated

$405 worth of aid under four different food and medical programs; a male-headed family of 11 with no cash assistance but $131 monthly from five noncash assistance programs; and a three generation family of five receiving checks from public assistance, social security, and the veterans' administration and participating in six noncash programs as well.[37] In the first case, even if medical and food needs were met, the $155 a month would hardly have covered rent in many large cities. In the second case, government aid was barely adequate to forestall starvation. And in the last case, income above a poverty level for the unit was maintained only because of participation in programs which were not needs-based, where benefits had presumably been earned through employment and service to the country.

Most families received multiple benefits because of their very limited incomes or heavy family responsibilities. Only 14 percent of all households in the GAO sample had six or more members, but 42 percent of the units receiving five benefits were this large. Nine out of ten households with five or more benefits were public assistance recipients. The cash transfers alone left 43 percent of the families receiving multiple benefits poor; a fourth remained below poverty thresholds even when the value of in-kind benefits received was added to cash income.[38]

Families in the same financial circumstances are not treated equally by the social welfare system. There are significant geographic differences. The 1974 maximum AFDC benefit for a family of four was six times higher in New York than in Mississippi, though the cost of living was less than twice as high. Similar disparities exist under other programs where needs standards are locally determined. There are also differences in eligibility standards, so that a family in one area may receive many benefits while one with similar characteristics and income in another might be ruled ineligible. Only one in eight poor families in Indiana, North and South Dakota, Nebraska, Virginia, Wyoming, and Nevada received public assistance in 1969. Twice as many were on relief, overall, in Massachusetts, New York, California, and, perhaps surprisingly, Georgia, Mississippi, Louisiana, and Oklahoma.[39]

More equal treatment is certainly a desirable goal, but it is important to recognize the last decade's progress as well as the practical constraints. Disparities have narrowed, by federal law in the case of SSI, but as a result of state actions under AFDC.[40] The benefits of recently expanded in-kind programs are inversely related to cash income, further reducing disparities in real well-being. In 1972 the annual AFDC payment to a female-headed family with two children and no earnings amounted to $576 in Bolivar, Mississippi, compared to $2,820 in Contra Costa, California. But because of the Mississippi family's lower cash income, the food stamps subsidy would be greater, $1,104 compared to $708 in California, bringing the ratio of benefits from a fifth to nearly a half, or roughly in line with living cost differences.[41]

Complete equalization is unlikely for political and practical reasons. There are very significant income disparities among areas. The 1969 median family income in the 12 states with lowest AFDC benefits averaged only three fourths of the median incomes in the 12 states with the highest benefits; the incidence of poverty averaged 18 percent for the first group, but only 8 percent for the second. Furthermore, both groups provided public assistance to 21 percent of their poor.[42] If standards were raised in the low-benefit states, costs would increase very substantially; unless these were borne completely by the federal government, there would be an onerous financial burden on these states. Alternatively, if the federal government intervened, the high cost of subsidizing low benefit states would have to come from the citizens of more affluent ones who would be reluctant to shoulder these additional burdens. By the same token, the fact that the maximum annual AFDC benefit for a three-person family in the low-payment states averaged only 20 percent of their median incomes compared to 33 percent in high benefit states, does not mean that equalization of these proportions is necessary or proper. The public may think in terms of absolute standards rather than ratios, and generosity may be a luxury that low-income states cannot afford.

Work and Welfare

Multiple needs-based programs can increase the marginal tax rate on earnings. If an AFDC family receiving food stamps and living in public housing earns an extra dollar, the cash payment is reduced by the $30 and one third rule, while food stamp costs and rents will also rise. Where Medicaid is available only to public assistance recipients, an extra dollar of earnings which raises a recipient above the welfare eligibility maximum may disqualify a family from free health care.

The overall work impact of the welfare system depends on the incidence of multiple benefits, the benefit offsets under the separate programs, the strictness with which these are enforced, as well as the work propensity and potential of multiple beneficiaries. Simulations have been used to estimate the prevalence of work disincentives. The Joint Economic Committee calculated potential benefits for a variety of recipient groups and program combinations in 100 areas in 1972. In Boston, for instances, a mother and two children with no earnings participating in AFDC, food, and public housing programs would receive benefits costing $5,371. If the mother worked half-time at $1.60 (the then minimum wage), her net income after reductions in benefits would have been only $5,079. A male with three dependents could receive food stamps, general assistance, school lunches, and public housing worth $5,701, whereas if he worked full-time at $1.60 he would have had a net income of $5,661.[43] Under one or more hypothetical combinations of after-tax earnings, unemployment compensation, AFDC, general assistance, food programs, and public housing, a mother with two children could actually lose income by earning more in nine out of 100 areas. The husband with a family of three could possibly lose income in 58 of the 100 areas under certain hypothetical eligibility conditions and benefit combinations.[44]

Gathered to document work disincentives, these simulations were stacked to emphasize the failures of the welfare system. For instance, the frequent finding that male family heads receiving unemployment compensation would lose by working rested on the assumption that potential earnings were only $1.60 per hour while potential unemployment benefits would be the average for the area. Needless to say, few males with dependents worked full-time at $1.60 per hour in 1972 and the disadvantaged male with such limited earnings prospects would be unlikely to have earned enough in the past to qualify for average unemployment insurance benefits.

A few extreme (and, in the above case, unrealistic) situations notwithstanding, the welfare system does reward work on the average. Considering cash, food, and housing programs in all areas, a mother with two children ends up with 30 percent more real income by doubling earnings from $1,600 to $3,200. A father with three dependents and no earnings has only three fourths the real income of the one who earns $1,600 (Figure 3-2).

Eligibility rules are rarely enforced with the rigor suggested by the simulations. The same welfare system which is blamed for overpaying and for slow reaction to income changes should not be assumed to respond automatically and with precision to penalize recipients who attempt to improve their economic situations. It is more reasonable to assume that the welfare machinery will favor them.

The work impact depends on the responsiveness of different groups to the various disincentives that they may encounter. A

Figure 3–2. Estimated average value of social welfare benefits available in 100 areas, 1972

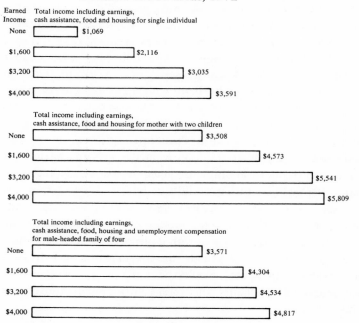

Source: James R. Storey, *Welfare in the 1970s: A National Study of Benefits Available in 100 Areas,* U.S. Congress, Joint Economic Committee, 93rd Cong., 2nd Sess. (Washington: Government Printing Office, 1974), p. 37.

disproportionate number of the households receiving multiple benefits are large and headed by either females, disabled, or elderly persons, that is, the groups least likely to or able to work. The unresponsiveness of welfare mothers to the 1967 work incentives should raise doubts about the leverage of tax rates changes. In the case of males, a number of studies have suggested that income guarantees do not noticeably discourage work, even with high tax rates. The New Jersey income maintenance experiment provided supplements ranging from 50 to 125 percent of the poverty level with a range of tax rates. Those aided reduced work only slightly and actually increased earnings. There was no correlation between tax rates and work reductions.[45] The welfare system provides much less generous aid than the income maintenance experiment, and its work impact on male heads is probably limited.

A final question is how much work is lost overall as a result of the welfare system's disincentives. Consider the case in which offsets make it unprofitable to move from part-time to full-time employment. Only one in twelve welfare mothers nationwide is working part time. Many of these may not be able to find full-time jobs or may not be able to take them. Thus, in the few areas where a disincentive exists, only a portion of the one twelfth of mothers potentially affected will actually curtail their hours of work by some marginal amount. When these reductions are averaged out over all recipients in all areas, they are minuscule.

Moreover, reduced employment is not all negative. Unemployment compensation, for instance, may allow the worker to discriminate in job selection rather than accepting the first available job in order to keep food on the table. In the long run, the loss is greater if the skilled worker is forced to take an unskilled job rather than seek a position better utilizing his or her skills. Another consideration in light of the high unemployment rate among welfare mothers is that, if more of them looked for jobs, they might displace economically self-sufficient persons who would have to turn to relief.

Whatever good may come from increasing work incentives must be balanced against the costs. The imposition of a 50 rather than a 67 percent offset rate under the proposed family assistance plan would have raised costs by three fourths, as eligibility would expand among low earners and recipients already working would keep more of their earnings. There are also costs in phasing out benefits gradually with rising income, rather than cutting them off completely at a given point. Ratchets increase target efficiency and reduce costs while creating work disincentives and vertical inequities. Whether or not they are retained depends on a judgment about the work impact, the ability to bear the costs, and the trade-off between helping those worse off as against having a smoother phase-out. In the case of the AFDC–Medicaid ratchet, the work impacts are probably inconsequential. Only a small share of AFDC recipients in states without a program for the medically indigent have earnings anywhere near the cutoff point. Since these few are already working near full-time, a small proportion of the potential earnings are lost if they try to keep below the eligibility threshold. The benefits of eliminating disincentives and increasing work marginally may not equal the costs of extending aid to persons with greater earnings.

It is also an unfortunate fact of life that the costs of increased work incentives are frequently levied on the needy who cannot find or seek jobs. As "workfare" was increasingly emphasized, the mean real cash income of four-person AFDC families with employed adults rose 8 percent between 1969 and 1973; but for those without a worker it fell by 6 percent.[46] It is important to remember that only one in eight AFDC mothers was employed in 1973. They gained while the other seven eighths who could not find jobs suffered.

Failings Do Not Mean Failure

The complex array of welfare, social insurance, and in-kind programs is difficult to understand, administer, or alter. The system is indisputably "messy," but this is unavoidable where there are so many needs, goals, and tradeoffs. There are problems, but these have been exaggerated by critics who have tended to ignore the many positive features and the progress.

The work and welfare issue provided grist for a corps of economists who could apply their marginal theories and quantitative methods to issues of tax rates and work disincentives. Their underlying assumption that ratchets and high benefit offsets could discourage work was correct, and their analysis was rigorous, yet their conclusions were frequently naive. When weighed in light of economic and institutional realities, the work losses do not appear to be massive nor largely dysfunctional. By the same token, there is very little proof that proposed measures to reduce tax rates or to eliminate ratchets would have increased work enough to justify raising break-even levels and expanding eligibility. Where welfare is concentrated on a group with limited employability, it is realistic and reasonable to accept work disincentives as a tradeoff for higher target efficiency and lower costs.

The welfare system may have contributed to family disruption by denying aid to male-headed units, but attempts to isolate the welfare system's impact on marital and family pattern changes do not substantiate a massive cause and effect relationship as postulated by critics. Moreover, the provision of aid to male-headed units does not promise to reverse or substantially alter current trends. Any feasible system would involve high marginal tax rates, with lower per capita benefits going to large families, so that two separate units with low or no earnings could almost always have a higher income than one combined unit. Aid to male-headed families should be judged on its own merits, in the knowledge that its effects on stabilizing marital and family patterns are questionable.

Much has been made of geographic inequities in the welfare system. Yet regional disparities in cash aid levels have been declining and the growth of in-kind programs has equalized total benefit packages even more. Experience with the reform of aid to the aged, blind, and disabled indicates that for political and practical reasons, differentials can be reduced but not immediately eliminated.

Similarly, criticisms of the sex bias of the welfare system fail to recognize that unemployment compensation and food stamps have reached large numbers of low-income male-headed families. The idea of treating all family units equally under the welfare system, while superficially appealing, ignores the fact that male heads are much more employable than female heads and that their work patterns differ. Comparable treatment is neither necessary nor necessarily preferable, and a comprehensive, single system of aid is a rather simplistic notion.

The administrative complexities of the welfare system have been subjected to a great deal of criticism, but it has not been very sophisticated. Claims that half or a third of welfare costs are eaten up by "swollen bureaucracies" are derived by including the expenses of personnel delivering a wide range of social, medical, and other services to recipients. The elimination of duplicative procedures could cut down on the paper work, but experience with consolidation suggests that the payoffs of reform are modest. Substantial economies could only be achieved if the casework approach, work registration, and income certification procedures were eliminated, but such steps would increase the risk of fraud and cheating.

A balanced appraisal requires recognition of the positive developments over the last decade and a half:

1. Cash benefit levels have been raised significantly, while food stamps, Medicaid and other in-kind programs have come to provide many of the necessities of life. Together, these meet the minimal needs of most of the poor.

2. The income support system has become more comprehensive. Social security is almost universal. The scope of unemployment compensation was increased by the mid-1970s amendments. Most low-income female-headed families receive AFDC and in-kind assistance. Food stamps and unemployment compensation have assisted increasing numbers of male-headed families. All eligible households are not served, and all those with real needs are not eligible, but the growth in coverage over the last fifteen years has been significant.

3. The constructive diversity of the income maintenance system has been retained. Social security has been made more redistributive, but the system remains a good insurance buy even for higher paid workers. Veterans' benefits are viewed as a reward for honorable service rather than a handout. Food stamps are popular in combatting a nationally recognized problem in a straightforward way and Medicaid is by now generally accepted as necessary and useful despite alleged shortcomings. Because aid to those in need is funneled through a number of diffuse channels and because insurance, service-based, and in-kind benefits do not have the same onus as cash "handouts," total assistance may be greater than if all aid came under a single income support system.

4. The welfare system has weathered the rapid transformation of the 1960s without major dislocations or untoward burdens. The maturing of the social security system will provide a larger proportion of benefits on the basis of prior contributions rather than mere

transfers. AFDC has passed its period of exponential growth. Medical care for the poor and aged has become a reality without ruining the nation's health care system. In brief, the nation developed over the last decade a relatively generous, complete, and comprehensive social welfare system.

5. There was an underlying logic in the pattern of developments. Redistribution was pushed under social security while still maintaining an insurance basis and thus broad popular support. The aged and low-income female-headed families with children were given a priority which was justified by their greater needs. With poverty declining among male-headed units in the tight labor markets of the 1960s, it made sense to target aid on the least employable group. Welfare reform proceeded slowly, but this helped to expose the hidden problems and constraints. Food stamps and unemployment compensation were expanded to provide aid to male-headed families in the 1970s, in lieu of initiating a guaranteed income program with uncertain results and costs. The evolution during the last decade followed rational and fairly equitable priorities, providing a basis for constructive progress.

4 Health Care

The Growing Federal Role

President Johnson's health message in 1965—his first priority in that eventful legislative year—staked out a major new area of federal social responsibility: "Our first concern must be to assure that the advance of medical knowledge leaves none behind. We can—and we must—strive now to assure the availability of and accessability to the best health care for all Americans regardless of age, geography, or economic status."

Most of the administration's proposals were approved that year. Medicare and Medicaid were the landmarks, but Congress also expanded maternal and child health care, provided scholarships for needy medical and dental students, overhauled the vocational rehabilitation program, established community mental health centers, and launched a nationwide attack on cancer and heart disease. In subsequent years Congress took steps to expand allied health manpower, to train more nurses, to modernize and build hospitals, and to rationalize the medical delivery system.

These measures had a massive impact on medical care in the United States. In 1960 public programs accounted for a fourth of per capita expenditures. The federal role was minor, concerned mostly with military personnel and veterans. By the end of the Johnson administration, per capita expenditures had more than doubled, but public outlays tripled and federal efforts quintupled. Nearly two fifths of health expenditures were publicly financed in fiscal 1969 compared with a fourth at the beginning of the decade.

The Great Society programs continued to grow during the 1970s. Federal health program expenditures, which had risen from $2.9 billion in 1963 to $13.1 billion in fiscal 1969, increased further to $25.3 billion in fiscal 1974. Medicare and Medicaid accounted for more than two thirds of the increase in the last five years (Figure 4-1).

Government intervention did not ruin the medical care system or result in socialized medicine, as the more vociferous enemies predicted. The "revolutionary" steps of the Great Society were quickly accepted by the public and the medical establishment. The debate of the 1970s was not whether Medicare and Medicaid should be continued but whether comprehensive national health insurance should be established. Still, this acceptance was grudging in some quarters, and the Great Society medical care programs have borne their share of criticism. Rapidly increasing price tags brought charges of inefficiency and inequity. The coincident inflation in hospital and other medical care costs was blamed on federal intervention. The failure of the government to exercise its market leverage was condemned by some, while its few efforts in this direction were criticized by others. Advocates of more comprehensive assistance as well as champions of reduced budgets and minimal government intervention joined forces in pronouncing a national health care crisis.

Caring for the Aged

Historical perspective is needed to understand the combined attacks from such diverse sources. Medicare was preceded by more than 20 years of debate and was passed over the active opposition of the American Medical Association. To gain support, major compromises had to be made. Taking a clue from King Solomon, Congress divided the program into two parts to satisfy advocates of alternative legislative proposals: Part A finances hospital and related costs for the elderly out of mandatory payroll contributions, and Part B pays doctor, drug, and other bills through voluntary insurance contributions supplemented by federal

Figure 4–1. Federal health expenditures, 1963–1974 (billions)

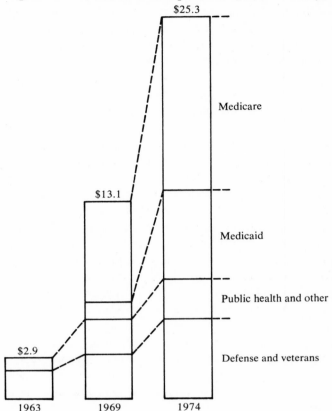

Source: Dorothy P. Rice and Barbara S. Cooper, "National Health Expenditures, 1950–1966," *Social Security Bulletin,* April 1968, pp. 10–11; and "National Health Expenditures, 1929–1970," *Social Security Bulletin,* June 1971, p. 11; and Nancy L. Worthington, "National Health Expenditures, 1929–1974," *Social Security Bulletin,* February 1975, pp. 8 and 10.

payments. The initial deductible and coinsurance levels were a compromise between supporters of medical care as a right, who felt that any charges would discourage usage by low-income families, and advocates of high deductibles and substantial recipient payments to discourage overutilization and to restrict coverage only to major hospital costs.

There were some innovations with uncertain consequences. Medicare provided for a continuum of aid from the hospital to extended care facilities to home treatment. The aim was to provide an option to lengthy and costly hospitalization for those who could be treated by other, presumably cheaper, means. The law also established quality standards and utilization review procedures though these were not a part of most private insurance contracts in existence at the time. Nondiscrimination was a prerequisite for hospital participation, requiring a major change in the dual systems of hospital care prevailing in many areas.

Thousands of detailed yet decisive issues were left to be resolved administratively. Billing procedures and cost reimbursement formulas had to be implemented, minimum quality standards determined, utilization procedures established, intermediaries selected, and payments allocated between hospitals and physicians. Besides the administrative complexities, these decisions involved substantial trade-offs and compromises. Improvements in the quality of care required changes in the delivery system but governmental meddling was to be avoided. Coverage of full costs encouraged overcharges, overutilization, and excessive costs but also insured that the most needy would not be discouraged.

With conflicting or competing aims, legislative and administrative compromises, and herculean implementation tasks, the wonder is not that there were problems but that there were so few. Getting the program designed and underway in a reasonable fashion was a major achievement itself.

Medicare's Immediate Impact

Medicare had immediate effects on health care for the elderly.[1] Hospital utilization increased for social security beneficiaries. The increases were greatest among those persons least likely to be able to pay for care—those age 75 years and over, blacks, unrelated individuals with low income, and residents of the South.

	Year before Medicare	Year after Medicare
Percent hospital inpatients	16.7	18.6
Number of stays per 100 persons	22.2	24.7
Average stay (days)	14.2	15.9

While the total days in nursing homes and extended care facilities per 100 persons declined, there was a shift from the former (not covered by Medicare) to the latter (which were). The percent of the elderly making visits to physicians' offices rose only slightly despite the provisions for home health care, in part because of the increased reliance on hospitalization.

Medicare also shifted the financial burdens of health care from the individual to the government. Between 1965 and 1967, the charges per institutionalized patient rose by a third, yet out-of-pocket costs declined by 15 percent as Medicare picked up almost half of the average tab (and almost 85 percent of the bill for short-term hospital stays.)[2]

Cost, Quality, and Utilization

Despite achieving the primary purposes of extending care to groups previously excluded because of low income or other factors, and reducing the costs for the elderly, Medicare experienced some serious problems.

Extended care facilities providing more care than nursing homes but at less cost than hospitals were meant to serve older persons recovering from hospitalization. That is not what happened. The average duration of short-term hospital stays for elderly patients increased rather than decreased after the introduction of Medicare. Extended care facilities were filled not by persons who would otherwise be hospitalized, but rather by persons who might have been cared for in nursing homes. Certification standards for extended care required 24-hour nursing service and the provision of treatments, medication, and diet according to the needs of the patient. Yet in July 1967, only 770 of the 4,160 certified extended care facilities were in full compliance with HEW guidelines, and by July 1969, only 1,374 of 4,776.

Utilization of Medicare raised a number of issues. Did the persons going into extended care facilities really need more attention than was available in nursing homes, or were patients simply referred because the cost was subsidized? Were extended hospital stays medically necessary or a matter of convenience for physicians? Were medical services vital or overused because of their low cost to the consumer?

Medicare required hospitals to establish utilization review committees (only half had them before 1965). Intermediaries were also supposed to assure that only reasonable physicians' costs were being charged for reasonable amounts of care. But there was only nominal compliance in most cases by hospitals and intermediaries, and investigations revealed some excesses. The staff report of the Senate Committee on Finance reported in early 1970:

> The detailed information which the staff has collected and developed indicates clearly that the utilization review requirements have, generally speaking, been of a token nature and ineffective as a curb to unnecessary use of institutional care and services. Utilization review in Medicare can be characterized as more form than substance.[3]

Cost was another concern. Initially, hospitals were paid full costs plus a 2 percent bonus to provide revenue to finance expansion. Cost-plus contracting provides little incentive to increase efficiency. In determining reasonable physician charges, the Department of Health, Education, and Welfare was to consider the doctor's customary charges for similar services as well as those prevailing in the locality. But in order to assure that the elderly would have access to the highest quality care without having to make extra payments out of their own pockets, the Department of Health, Education, and Welfare established reimbursement guidelines which paid on the basis of the customary charge of the physician or the prevailing full charges in the locality. The established rates were substantially higher than those under private insurance programs. Patients had little incentive to shop around, and perhaps in some cases the expected ceiling on fees turned into a floor.[4]

Medicare's often declared failure in these three areas is debatable. In light of the opposition which existed at the outset of the program, it must be questioned whether institutional change could have been achieved more rapidly. The doubling of fully certified extended care facilities between 1967 and 1969 was a significant accomplishment. The establishment of utilization review systems in hospitals was a necessary first step toward usage control. Many of the failings discovered in the 1970s were also the result of conscious policy decisions. Reimbursement formulas were designed to increase hospital revenue to provide the wherewithal for expansion; the subsequent growth in the supply of hospital beds may have reduced the need for subsidies. Likewise, the idea of buying the best available care was reassessed subsequently when the bill came due. Changes in policy are not an indication of failure but of response to changing circumstances.

In due course, Medicare treated its problems. Certification procedures for extended care facilities were tightened and referral procedures for hospital patients were made more restrictive. The "plus" in the hospital reimbursement formula was eliminated, and in 1970 HEW restricted payments for medical services to the 75th percentile of customary charges for the previous calendar year. The 1972 Social Security amendments further limited physician and hospital charges. Finally, excess utilization was more carefully policed with the establishment of professional standards review organizations to monitor charges and services.

These treatments were effective. The number of claims for extended and skilled nursing home care declined from one million in 1968 to 437,000 six years later with costs dropping from $342 to $194 million.[5] The number of annual claims for hospitalization continued to increase, but the total days of covered care was nearly stabilized as the average stay became shorter.[6] The proportion of hospital charges reimbursed dropped from 80 percent in 1968 to 76 percent in 1974.

	1968	1974
Medicare hospital claims (millions)	5.9	7.8
Total covered days (millions)	79.6	83.5
Average days per claim	13.4	10.8

These economies were not achieved by merely removing the fat from the system; it was also necessary to take some bone and gristle. The tightened reimbursement regulations for physicians charges resulted in a declining proportion of claims accepted by assignment or provided at Medicare established prices. The proportion of doctor's bills covered by Medicare fell from 61 percent in 1969 to 53 percent four years later.[7] The increases in the deductible and changes in coinsurance to discourage excessive usage had the greatest effects on those least able to pay. Elderly persons with income above $15,000 visited physicians 60 percent more often than those below $5,000 in 1972. Fifty-five percent of the upper-income group used medical services in excess of the deductible, compared with 43 percent of the lower-income group.[8]

There are those who feel that economies have gone too far, and that Medicare no longer provides easy access to quality care for low-income patients. But others believe that costs need still further cutting, and that more stringent controls over reimbursement and utilization are necessary. A trade-off between economic efficiency and welfare is involved. Policy makers initially chose to do as much as possible to insure the best care at the least cost to the elderly. More recently the government attempted to reduce outlays and to discourage utilization. This is a fundamental policy choice of providing more or less at the margin. Medicare is not to blame for whichever choice is made.

Ministering to the Poor

In contrast to the long debate over health care for the aged, Medicaid emerged rather suddenly and was accepted uncritically and perhaps unwittingly. It was initially viewed as a mere consolidation of medical vendor payments for public assistance recipients and the medically indigent aged not on relief. The exponential growth of Medicaid was, therefore, a surprise to many in Congress who voted for the legislation. The Department of Health, Education, and Welfare estimated during the legislative deliberations that Medicaid would add $240 million to medical vendor payments in its first full year of operation. This was exactly the cost in 1966, but only six states had the program in operation. While the 1968 budget projected a $2.3 billion state and federal price tag, once fully implemented, the outlay was $3.5 billion with a fourth of the states still not participating.[9]

Out of Control?

The scapegoats for this unexpected growth were "greedy" doctors and "hypochondriac" beneficiaries. In truth, however, the projections were wrong because they failed to recognize the dismal state of medical care for the poor as well as the growth factors built into the program. Between 1967 and 1972 the welfare explosion more than doubled the number of persons on AFDC and increased recipients of other public assistance programs. Medicaid payments to AFDC recipients rose by 8.1 percent quarterly over this period, but two thirds of this increase was the result of the 5.5 percent quarterly growth in welfare clients. A fifth of the rise was due to the increased propensity of persons on welfare to utilize Medicaid. Rising medical care prices accounted for another fifth of cost increases.[10] Meanwhile, the real cost per AFDC client actually declined, belying the notion that excessive usage was a major factor.

The initial design also contributed to Medicaid's growth. The system was structured to increase spending for the health care of the needy. The federal matching share was more liberal than under previous medical vendor programs and higher for low-income states, encouraging expanded eligibility and services. The law required that all persons eligible for cash aid be automatically eligible even if not on relief. Aid to the medically indigent (with income above welfare levels but unable to afford medical care) was encouraged by the availability of federal subsidies. Participating states were required to finance inpatient and outpatient hospital care, certain laboratory and x-ray expenses, skilled nursing home care and physicians' services; prior to Medicaid many had paid for much more limited services.

Given this impetus to expansion, it should not have been too surprising that costs quickly escalated. This may have been a case where advocates of increased assistance understated the price tag in order to achieve support. But clearly, the initial increase in outlays was because the federal foot was on the accelerator.

The brakes were used timidly at first but with increasing desperation. The 1967 Social Security Act amendments required states to implement cost, utilization, and quality review procedures, providing funds to support the administrative costs. A maximum income eligibility limit was established one third above public assistance maximums to stop affluent states from setting very liberal standards of medical indigency. The 1969 amendments reflected a similar concern with costs, postponing the target date for states to provide comprehensive care from 1975 to 1977.

Faced with continuing exponential growth, Congress took more dramatic steps in 1972. The goal of providing comprehensive services to all in need was eliminated. The law required the medically indigent to pay enrollment fees graduated by income as well as nominal deductibles and copayments. States were also allowed to establish higher payment requirements for optional services used by cash assistance recipients. States without effective utilization review programs were threatened with a reduction in federal subsidies. Professional standards review organizations were established to review local services to insure that they were needed and competent. Doctors' bills were limited to the 75th percentile of prevailing charges in the area.

These changes and saturation of the universe of need slowed the growth in Medicaid. From fiscal 1968 to 1970, federal, state, and local expenditures rose by two fifths, from fiscal 1970 to 1972 by 54 percent, but from fiscal 1972 to 1974 by only 11 percent.[11]

The Cost of Care

While overuse and abuse do not account for Medicaid's growth, they are important concerns in their own right. In 1970 the Senate Finance Committee issued a report concluding that Medicaid "has not nearly approached the congressional objectives of assuring good health care for the poor in an effective and economical fashion." First, few of the states were found to have reliable cost and utilization review systems. Second, the liberal reimbursement formulas were felt to contribute to inflated prices. Third, Medicaid shared in and sometimes intensified the problems of the welfare system: the eligibility determination system was inadequate; the cutoff of benefits when incomes rose above public assistance levels created a work disincentive; and there were serious inequities.[12]

These sweeping negative judgments were based on evidence which was, at best, circumstantial. For example, abuse by doctors was documented by compiling a list of those receiving more than $100,000 in Medicaid payments, implying that there was something innately wrong in earning so much money by serving the poor. Nationwide, doctors had a median income of $47,000 in 1974. In 1968 there were only 32 doctors who received more than $100,000 in Medicaid reimbursements, and they accounted for less than 1 percent of all payments for doctors' services. These reimbursements were gross rather than net income, and office and staff expenses had to be subtracted to get earnings. The doctors with high reimbursements were located mostly in California and

New York where earnings are above average; most were obstetri-
cian-gynecologists, a speciality characterized by very high income
and mass practice.

As an example, a Washington, D.C., doctor was examined by a
subcommittee of the District of Columbia Medical Society because
he received $532,000 in Medicaid payments from 1971 to 1973.
The only private obstetrician located in a low-income area of the
city, he saw an average of 60 patients per day, three fourths of
whom were Medicaid beneficiaries. The doctor's large staff
handled all medical and social histories and took blood samples.
The whole operation used the most sophisticated time-saving machinery. Despite the high patient load, the expert reviewers concluded that the obstetric care offered by this physician was better
than that available in the area's public clinics and at least equal to
that offered by private obstetricians elsewhere. His sins were those
ascribed with equal validity to his peers—assembly line practices
and too frequent hospitalization and testing. On the positive side
of the ledger, he was doing everything to economize on his own
time through the use of paraprofessionals, nurses, and equipment.
Since no other private physicians were working in this area where
most residents were poor, a large publicly subsidized clientele was
inevitable.

Medicaid and Welfare

From its inception, Medicaid was mired in the welfare mess.
The law specified that all recipients of public assistance had to be
eligible for a range of services but states determined public assistance needs standards, and had the option of paying for extra
services and of serving the medically indigent not on relief.

It was clear that state control would result in wide variations
just as it had under public assistance, but this was considered
reasonable at the time. Medicaid was viewed as little more than a
consolidation of existing medical vendor payments, so the existing
system was taken as a given. States differed markedly in medical
care costs and medical care utilization patterns, and to alter these
would have required significant outlays. The only feasible means
of achieving greater equality was to move toward it gradually, and
incentives were built into the Medicaid reimbursement formula,
with greater subsidies for low-income states.

The critical question is not whether inequities exist, but whether they are being corrected. In March 1969 California and New York received 45 percent of all Medicaid payments; their share declined to 35 percent five years later. Alabama, Arkansas, Louisiana, Mississippi, Florida, Delaware, Georgia, South Carolina, Tennessee, and West Virginia increased their share of payments from 4 to 9 percent.[13] This suggests that some equalization is being attained, but it is still far from satisfactory.

Viewed with some historical perspective, then, the shortcomings of Medicaid do not seem so telling. The program was designed as an open-ended effort to increase the availability of health care for persons of low income. The evidence indicates that services expanded rapidly for those in need, and waste was kept in bounds. Equity and efficiency were gradually increased as the program matured. It is, in fact, a testament to the program that the various national health insurance proposals introduced in the 1970s generally planned to continue Medicaid for cash assistance recipients, recognizing that it had attained a reasonable degree of effectiveness.

Achieving Broader Aims

The broader issue is whether Medicaid, Medicare, and the other Great Society health programs helped to realize the goals they set out to achieve: to alleviate the expense and anxieties of medical care for those with limited resources; to increase and reallocate the supply of medical care making it more available for those in need; to moderate the resulting price increases; and, ultimately, to improve the health of those whose ailments are related to the lack of care.

Health Care as a Right

There can be no doubt that as a result of government intervention adequate medical care has become a reality for the aged and many of the poor. Health expenditures for persons aged 65 years and over rose by 172 percent in the seven years following the passage of Medicare, and public programs accounted for 84 percent of the increase. On the other hand, cost-cutting efforts in the early 1970s increased the burdens. From fiscal 1966 to fiscal

1969 individual payments for health care for persons 65 years and over declined by almost a fourth, from $237 to $181. In fiscal 1970 they rose to $229 and continued upward to $311 in fiscal 1973.[14]

Those with limited income receive more complete health care as a result of Medicare and Medicaid. In fiscal 1964 persons in families with less than $2,000 income averaged 4.3 doctor visits, while those in families with $10,000 or more income averaged 5.1 (Figure 4-2). By 1971 the poorest families were more likely than the richest to have visited a doctor (as warranted by their more frequent health problems). Middle-income families were apparently sqeezed most by the rising doctor bills, but overall, the average number of visits for the entire population rose from 4.5 to 4.9 between 1964 and 1971.

The redistribution is also evident in hospital utilization patterns. In the 1963–65 period, persons in families with income under $3,000 averaged only 1.5 hospital days annually. By 1968–69, they averaged 2.1 days. For families in the $3,000 to $4,000 income classes, the increase was from 1.2 to 1.7 days. The increases were minimal in families with income over $7,000.[15]

Increasing Supply

These increased days of hospital care, more frequent physician visits, and other services required expanded medical resources. The Great Society sought to increase the supply of doctors, nurses,

Figure 4–2. Number of visits to physicians' office by income, 1963–64 and 1971

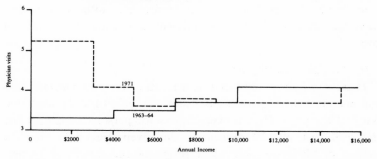

Source: National Center for Health Statistics, *Physican Visits,* Series 10, No. 18; and 1971 unpublished data.

and allied health personnel as well as to build and modernize institutional facilities. It is difficult to determine the net impact of these programs. If federal financial aid had not been made available to low-income medical students, others with higher income who were rejected from medical schools might have taken their place. The number of nurses and technicians would have expanded through normal market processes given rising wages and growing job opportunities. There is no doubt, however, that government assistance hastened the process. Between 1965 and 1971, the number of physicians per capita rose by a seventh; the number of nurses per capita by 11 percent; the number of short-term hospital beds per capita by 9 percent; and the number of hospital personnel per patient by 22 percent. The shortage of doctors was also met by changing the mix in the medical delivery system. In 1960 there were 1.8 nurses for every physician, and 5.6 other persons employed in health and related industries; by 1971 the ratios had risen to 2.0 and 9.0, respectively.

By the mid-1970s the increases in supply had been so extensive that many questioned whether there was a surplus of doctors and hospital beds or at least whether continued federal assistance was necessary. While geographic disparities persisted, progress had been made toward alleviating shortages in most areas. Hospital beds expanded most rapidly in low-income states and government financial aid was a significant factor.[16] Neighborhood health and maternal child care centers provided resources for a number of low-income areas in central cities and rural America. Public health services expanded in many depressed areas such as Indian reservations. This made care more accessible to the needy.

Inflationary Impact

The rapid increase in medical care prices over the last decade has been blamed on government intervention. Liberal reimbursement formulas and the lack of effective incentives or controls under Medicare and Medicaid have been charged with distorting the market. It has been alleged that doctors raised their rates for nonbeneficiaries in order to get more reimbursement from the government. Hospitals have billed for supervisory teaching physicians who may have little contact with a patient. More broadly, hospitalization is encouraged because it is relatively costless for the patient and convenient for the doctor; this artificially inflates demand.

As noted, however, the reimbursement procedures have been tightened, excess utilization has been curtailed, and average stays have dropped. Further, it has never been well documented whether or to what extent doctors raised their rates arbitrarily. Government subsidization of treatment for the poor, which was previously offered on a charity basis, should have contributed to a reduction rather than increase in average nonsubsidized fees.

Medicare and Medicaid raised prices largely as a result of drastic expansion and reallocations of demand over a very short time. Price is the mechanism for attracting resources and inflation is the unavoidable by-product of giving the medically indigent subsidies to bid away scarce health care resources from other potential users. The patterns of price change manifest basic laws of supply and demand. Total health expenditures, which had risen by an average of $2.6 billion annually between fiscal 1960 and 1965, increased by $3.2 billion between 1965 and 1966, $5.8 billion in the next year, and $6.4 billion the following one. In real terms, health expenditures increased 3.8 percent annually between 1960 and 1965, but 6.2 percent in the next year, 5.5 the following one, and 6.7 percent between 1968 and 1969.[17]

The demand for health care outstripped the demand for other goods and services. Between 1965 and 1973 U.S. real personal income rose 36 percent while real health expenditures (weighted by the medical deflator of the CPI) rose 57 percent. Society demanded more health care and this required a bidding away of resources from other areas.

While all other components of the consumer price index increased by 65 percent between 1960 and 1974, medical care costs went up by 90 percent. Most of the accelerated rise took place before 1970, and since then health care costs have risen at the same rate as other consumer purchases. Supply has caught up with demand over time, easing the inflationary pressures.

The incredible increase in hospital care costs is not as easy to explain. Between 1966 and mid-1975 the cost of semi-private rooms with board, routine nursing, and minor medical and surgical supplies rose an alarming 175 percent. There is no doubt that

Medicare and Medicaid were major contributing factors. The per capita increase in hospital days between 1965 and 1967 was greater than in the entire preceding decade. The rate of price rise accelerated from 5.6 percent between 1960 and 1965 to 10.0 percent the next year and 19.8 percent the year after. It decelerated slowly through 1971, then rose with overall inflation when prices were decontrolled.

Year	Percentage annual increase in hospital room costs
1964–65	5.6
1965–66	10.0
1966–67	19.8
1967–68	13.6
1968–69	13.4
1969–70	12.9
1970–71	12.2
1971–72	6.6
1972–73	4.7
1973–74	10.6

Supply and demand forces alone do not explain the upward secular trend. One factor is a change in the typical day of hospital care. The goods and services purchased for $44 in 1965 are not the same as those purchased for $119 in 1974. There were a fourth again as many employees per patient in the latter year. Since payroll expenses are roughly three fifths of total hospital expenses, this was a substantial factor in the rising costs. There was some cost push also resulting from unionization and minimum wage coverage of hospital workers. The physical plants of hospitals were improved significantly—the rooms were more spacious, the amenities greater, the facilities more accessible. Accreditation standards became more rigorous, improving health and safety features. Altogether, between 1966 and 1970, it is estimated that the increased inputs per patient day in short-term community hospitals accounted for 44 percent of the increase in costs.[18]

All this is not to imply that the rapid rise in hospital prices could not have been moderated. Cost reimbursement formulas were initially very generous, and utilization may have been excessive. But the basic cause of inflation was the rapidly increasing demand, which was only gradually balanced by an increasing supply plus rising standards of care.

Improvement in Health

While government programs have had a demonstrable impact in subsidizing, reallocating, and expanding care, the payoff in improved health is difficult to document. Medical care is only one of the factors affecting health, and government programs are only one of the means to deliver health care.

Nonetheless, friends and foes of government intervention have frequently blamed the nation's health problems on the medical delivery system. Introducing his 1970 Health Security Act, Senator Edward Kennedy charged:

> . . . America is an also-ran in the delivery of health care to our people. In the midst of the rising cost of health care, we have endured a decline in the overall quality of the care we give our citizens. The figures are shocking:
> In infant mortality . . . the United States today trails behind 12 other countries . . .
> We trail six other nations in the percentage of mothers who die in childbirth.
> The story told by other health indicators is equally dismal. The United States trails 17 other nations in life expectancy for males, 10 other nations in life expectancy for females, and 15 other nations in the death rate for middle-aged males.[19]

Such arguments are simplistic to the point of inaccuracy. Our nation's higher incidence of smoking contributes to lung cancer; pollution is a cause of heart disease, respiratory and other ailments; cardiovascular problems are related to the pace of living, diet, and lack of exercise. The quality of medical care has little to do with the increase in such ailments.

To discern the impact of expanded medical care, it is necessary to sort out all these factors. Life expectancy at birth rose by only a year in the 1960s compared with a year and a half in the 1950s, which some have interpreted as a failure of the health care system to lengthen life. Yet the causes of death such as accidents, suicides, and homicides, which have little relationship to medical care, plus those causes related to environmental factors and life patterns such as heart disease, cirrhosis of the liver, diabetes, and cancer were the major reasons for the slow improvements in life expectancy. Between 1960 and 1971, the crude death rate per 100,000 population fell from 954.7 to 929.0. The accident, suicide, and homicide rate rose by 9 percent, the environment related causes remained constant. Other causes which were medical in origin and medically treatable declined by 29 percent.[20]

High infant mortality rates are not proof of the medical system's failure. Infant mortality is related to education, socioeconomic status, race, age, pregnancy out of wedlock, marital and social problems, malnutrition, and a number of factors in addition to medical care. Studies of infant deaths in the United States in the mid-1960s suggested that only a fourth to a fifth could have been avoided by better pre- or post-natal care.[21] There have been some major improvements since the mid-1960s. The infant death rate fell from 24.7 per 1,000 live births in 1965 to 18.5 seven years later compared with a decline of 1.7 cases per thousand during the whole preceding decade. Likewise, maternal deaths per 100,000 live births dropped twice as fast over the last half of the 1960s compared with the first half.[22]

These data do not prove that expanded health care has improved health, but they do discount the assertion that national health problems are proof of the medical system's failure. The payoff of better care is presumably over the longer run, and the improvements of the 1960s will be felt in the future. Further, some portion of health assistance replaces personal outlays without affecting the level of care.

Most federal health outlays have gone to low-income individuals with documented needs for income subsidies and with established health problems that can be alleviated or eliminated with medical treatment. A very small proportion of all aid may be considered over-doctoring. However, it is clear that federal intervention through Medicare, Medicaid, and other programs has accomplished the primary goals of increasing "the availability of and the accessibility of the best health care for all Americans regardless of age, geography, or economic status."

5 Low-Income Housing

Great Society Housing Initiatives

Dilapidated homes, faulty plumbing and sanitation, and blighted neighborhoods are hardly consistent with a great society. Eight million households occupied substandard housing units in 1963, and one in seven could not afford minimally adequate shelter without spending more than a fifth of their income. Federal efforts to alleviate these conditions dated back to 1937 when the public housing program was initiated. The Housing Act of 1949 defined the nation's housing goal as "the realization as soon as feasible . . . of a decent home and suitable living environment for every American family." Congress authorized construction of 810,000 public housing units over the next six years, but less than a third of this number was built by the time President Johnson assumed office. New programs and new commitment were needed if the housing goal was to be realized, and the Johnson administration tried to provide both.

The Housing and Urban Development Act of 1965 established the Department of Housing and Urban Development. It lowered the interest rate on direct government loans to nonprofit sponsors of rental housing for the elderly and for low- and middle-income families, reducing financing costs in order to reduce rents. The law authorized local public housing agencies to lease private dwellings for use by their clients. Rent supplements were established for nonprofit sponsors of low-income housing which allowed them to make up the difference between one fourth of occupants' incomes and the market rental rates.

The Housing and Urban Development Act of 1968 expanded the tool kit by subsidizing interest costs on private loans for low-income housing. Two programs were initiated, one for rental units built for low-income tenants and the other to assist low- and moderate-income families to purchase homes. These two interest subsidy programs were envisioned as the primary elements in achieving the act's articulated goal of producing 6 million subsidized units in a decade.

Only 34,000 subsidized units were produced in 1963, mostly under the low-rent housing program. By Johnson's last full year in office, production had risen to 162,000 units; while half of this output was traditional public housing, the leasing and rent supplement programs initiated in 1965 accounted for 16 percent of those units. The two low-interest direct loan programs accounted for 36 percent. With the addition of the interest subsidy programs, and with the active support of the Nixon administration, output rose to 399,000 assisted units in fiscal 1970; 29 percent under the new homeownership program, 28 percent under the rental interest subsidy program and 10 percent under leasing and rent supplements (Figure 5-1).

These efforts made the federal government a major factor in the housing market. Subsidized production, which had averaged only 3 to 5 percent of total building in the first half of the 1960s, increased to a peak of 27 percent in 1971. By the end of fiscal 1974, there were about 2.7 million occupied units under the federal subsidy, representing 4 percent of the housing stock.

The subsidized units provided shelter to between 9 and 10 million persons at an annual cost of about $1,200 per unit, which represented a major supplement to the annual $4,000 income averaged by subsidized households. Housing efforts had a substantial $3.2 billion price tag in fiscal 1974.

Whatever the flaws in the housing assistance programs, they have clearly improved the quality and reduced the cost of housing for a substantial number of low-income households. They also affected the distribution of low-income and minority housing.

Figure 5–1. Production of housing units under federal subsidy programs, 1963–1972 (thousands)

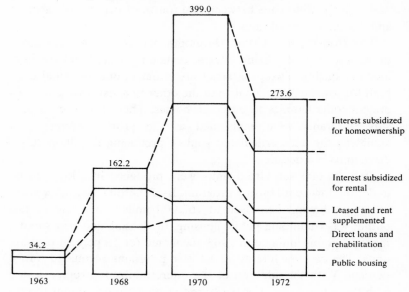

Source: Department of Housing and Urban Development.

Under the two interest subsidy programs, 18 percent of black residents had moved from the central city to suburban areas, compared with the national 7 percent black suburbanization rate.[1] Since blacks and other minorities are overrepresented in these programs relative to their proportion in the population, subsidized housing contributed to dispersion. More refined measures might reveal even greater dispersion within central cities from blighted, all-minority areas to more integrated neighborhoods.

The courts have used the subsidy program as a lever to encourage fair housing efforts. In some cases judges have banned con-

Total occupied units, fiscal 1974 (thousands)	2,696
Public housing including leased	1,109
Rent supplements	148
Interest subsidy for home ownership	419
Interest subsidy for rental	294
Housing for the elderly	42
Rehabilitation loans and grants	70
Farmers Home Administration programs	614

struction in segregated central city areas, and in others they have specified the distribution of units.

The Critical Litany

President Nixon endorsed subsidized housing efforts in his 1970 housing message. Based on "an extensive analysis of our housing goals and the prospects for meeting them," the administration concluded that "the construction and rehabilitation of 26 million housing units in a decade—including 6 million for families with low and moderate income—should meet the Nation's needs, and is consistent with other urgent claims on our productive resources." But criticism began to mount in the early 1970s questioning the costs, effectiveness, and equity of the programs. Predisposed to cash over in-kind aid and looking for ways to trim the federal budget, the President about-faced in January 1973, proclaiming the subsidy programs unworkable and putting an 18 month moratorium on project approvals. What caused such a major policy reversal in just three years and was it warranted?

Cost and Value

The major factor was cost. Not only was the housing assistance price tag high and rising; it was largely uncontrollable. Annual contributions were required to amortize the capital costs of each new unit of public housing, as well as those completed decades previously. Leasing and rent supplement agreements for new projects included long-term guarantees to the owners. The interest subsidy technique involved long-term commitments requiring annual payments to retire the mortgages. Thus, the high levels of production in the early 1970s soon transformed into healthy and continuing cash outflows. Further, under the public housing and rent supplement programs in which the government made up the difference between what tenants could reasonably pay and operating plus capital costs, the combination of rising maintenance expenses and declining tenant income dramatically increased federal outlays.

Total present and future subsidy commitments of units under contract through fiscal 1973 were estimated to be $86 billion; discounted at 7.5 percent, this would require a current federal

investment in low-income housing of over $30 billion. If construc-
tion had continued at the pace of the early 1970s, these costs
would have mounted rapidly. As the President stated in his 1971
message, "Present estimates (projecting current construction
rates) suggest that the federal government will (by 1978) be paying out at least $7.5 billion annually in subsidies. Over the life of
the mortgages, this could amount to the staggering total of more
than $200 billion."

Such Brobdingnagian figures, while of obvious discomfort to
federal budgeters, must be put in perspective. The $2.5 billion for
housing assistance was dwarfed by the estimated $6.2 billion in
homeowners' interest deductions from income taxes and the $3.0
to $4.0 billion other tax savings associated with home and apart-
ment ownership. The subsidies were about 1 percent of total public
and private housing expenditures.[2]

Lifetime cost estimates in the hundreds of billions of dollars are
somewhat frightening but must be considered in context. We rarely
stop to estimate the long-range commitments underlying current
outlays in other areas. Each year new weapons systems, highways,
dams, and other capital outlays are initiated which will ultimately
cost many billions. The same is also true for most social welfare
programs. Once benefits are legislated for a large number of
people, they are almost certain to continue at the same level, as a
minimum, for the coming years; if benefits are raised under social
security or veterans' pensions, they will continue as ineluctably
and uncontrollably as future mortgage payments. Alternatively,
providing cash allowances to subsidize housing costs would realistically have to be viewed as a long-range commitment with a very
significant present value. Because mortgages look into the future
and this is rarely done elsewhere, the costs of meeting housing
needs should not be considered out of line with meeting other
demands.

The pertinent issue is whether the government is getting its
money's worth. Critics have charged that when the government
enters the marketplace, it is hoodwinked by sellers and middlemen
who charge too much or deliver too little. A rash of scare stories
circulated in the early 1970s alleging shoddy rehabilitation, exorbi-
tant prices, and collusion between government officials and
builders to bilk the public. Such problems existed but in retrospect

were neither so frequent nor so severe as to condemn the housing programs. A 1972 General Accounting Office study documented some of the shortcomings of the homeownership interest subsidy program, finding that: "Houses with significant defects were sold to low- and moderate-income families under the programs. Because many of the defects concern the safety and health of the occupants, the program objective of providing low- and moderate-income families with decent, safe and sanitary housing has not been met in many cases."[3] This conclusion was based on an inspection of 1,281 properties, 433 of which had defects. Of these, 298 had what GAO considered "significant defects affecting safety or livability" and 35 units, all rehabilitated ones, were considered in such bad shape that they could not have been insured by FHA.

Some of these problems were indeed very serious. But others seem less so, such as familiar complaints involving cracked walls, loose tiles, poor drainage, and leaky roofs. Unsubsidized new and rehabilitated houses in the same price bracket would probably have far more numerous defects. FHA inspection procedures are rigorous, and though they may have been laxly applied in some cases, they are better than having no protection. Defects are more likely to occur in low-priced housing, and the more rigorous the standards the higher the price tag.

If higher standards are desired, the reasonable course is to try to improve inspection techniques. The FHA's field resources were strained by the massive increase in subsidized housing activity in just a few years, but it took steps to beef up and improve its inspection staff after problems became apparent. The GAO recommended reinspection of houses within one year, making the sellers or builders responsible for serious deficiencies. This might be considered a prudent step, though again such insurance would involve added costs.

A similar GAO investigation of the interest subsidy program for rental units did not reveal any significant problems of quality but raised questions about cost, alleging that since HUD's land appraisal procedures gave little or no consideration to the owner's cost, acquisition prices were inflated. The data did not support this charge. In almost a third of the projects examined the HUD appraisal was less than the previous property owner's purchase price and in another half, it was less than 25 percent higher—a reasonable difference allowing for inflation, turnover, and carrying costs. Only one in six projects had valuations exceeding the previous owner's cost by more than 25 percent.[4] It does not seem that the government was cheated any more than private purchasers from developers who put together large tracts of city real estate.

According to other internal estimates by the Department of Housing and Urban Development, construction costs were estimated to be roughly a fifth more, and operating costs a tenth higher, under the rental interest subsidy program than for comparable conventional units.[5] Some differential is due to building and operating in areas and for populations which would not otherwise be served. Vandalism and theft at central city sites may raise construction costs substantially. Conforming to HUD standards involves extra costs, such as paying union rates.

Financing techniques were a major cost factor under both interest subsidy programs. Direct loans are less expensive, since the government borrowing rate is less than the market rate. Many advocated the direct loan approach for this reason, but interest subsidies were adopted to involve private sector lending institutions, to initiate a large-scale effort without requiring multibillion dollar federal borrowing and, most important, to postpone and disguise the cost. Direct loans could have been used if the government had been willing to make the commitment and wanted to economize over the long run. The housing program should not be blamed for higher costs resulting from the conscious decisions of Congress to use more costly approaches rather than cheaper alternatives.

Maintenance and Management

Mismanagement was another charge against the assisted housing programs. Under the public housing subsidy formula which existed until 1970, rents had to cover operating expenses, which were rising faster than tenants' income and ability to pay. Contingency funds for maintenance and repair were drawn down to meet ongoing expenses, while improvements were postponed. The quality of housing deteriorated in many cities. The Brooke amendment in 1970 provided an extra subsidy covering the difference between rents adequate to cover operating costs and one fourth of each tenant's income, but the Nixon administration did not request the full authorized amount, held back appropriated funds, and engineered a crisis by allowing conditions to deteriorate when they could have been improved.

Much was said about the shortcomings of private nonprofit sponsors and of local public housing authorities. Yet the question must again be asked: compared to what? Owners and operators of low-income units generally have limited concern for the needs of clients and want to avoid tenants with undependable incomes or social problems. Profit motivated, their aim is to spend as little and collect as much as possible. In contrast, assisted housing sponsors are expected to serve the most disadvantaged, providing not only shelter but also social services, community organization, and protection. The use of private firms to run public housing units—called turnkey management programs—has produced little evidence of any savings or improved performance. Essentially, the effectiveness of management depends on how much money is available for maintenance and security, how carefully the clients are screened, and how rigorously standards are maintained. Public managers usually do not have control over these variables. Vandalism could be reduced by evicting all drug addicts and screening out all families with teenagers, or rents could be assured if a higher income group were housed. But would this serve the needs of more disadvantaged groups?

The viability of assisted housing projects has also been questioned. A critical review by the Department of Housing and Urban Development suggested that a fifth of all interest subsidized rental projects would fail within a decade, and a third or more over the period of their mortgages. One sixth of subsidized owner-occupied units were projected for default.[6]

Again, some perspective is needed to determine whether the projections are accurate and a cause for alarm. As of the end of 1973, HUD had acquired through foreclosure or conveyance only 0.6 percent of all units built under the interest subsidy rental program. Another 3 percent had been assigned to HUD, but, as under other housing, many of the problems were worked out without foreclosure.[7] There are start-up difficulties in all such efforts and defaults increase in a recession. Under the major HUD unsubsidized loan program for moderate-income rental housing, 17 percent of units were in default after the first five years, but the proportion then declined to 0.5 percent in 1968. It rose again to 3.6 percent in 1972. Under the unsubsidized FHA homeownership loan program, defaults also rose from 1.4 to 2.2 percent of all mortgages between 1968 and 1972. And while default terminations under the interest subsidy homeownership program represented 8.7 percent of insurance in force as of October 20, 1973, this was not higher than the actuarial projections which considered the high risk group being served but did not project the recession.[8]

In using nonprofit and limited dividend sponsors, building in what are frequently high risk areas, and providing shelter for households with low and uncertain income, the risks are clearly greater than under the more established programs for moderate and high income families. The problems noted in the early 1970s were the result of inherent start-up difficulties compounded by adverse economic circumstances.

Inherent Inequities

The housing programs have also been criticized on equity grounds. Some of those served were better off financially than others not being served, and with reduced housing payments, some were made better off than unsubsidized families. Generally, however, the programs focused on the neediest. The median income of two person families in public housing was $2,800 at the end of 1972, and families with four or more members had an average annual income of $4,500. Three fourths were on public assistance or receiving social insurance benefits. The tenants in rent supplemented and leased units had similarly low incomes. Under the interest subsidy programs, the restriction of subsidies to interest costs means that rents must cover operating expenses and amortization, placing a floor under the required rents and effectively setting a minimum income for prospective tenants. Yet rent supplements have been extensively piggybacked in interest subsidized rental units to serve a more disadvantaged clientele. In interest-subsidized, owner-occupied units, two fifths of the families had incomes below $6,000 in 1972, and only a fifth received more than $8,000 even though the average family size was 4.8 members. The very poorest cannot be served through the homeownership approach, but the beneficiaries are far from affluent.

As under other social welfare programs, the chances of participating vary from area to area. New York was ranked sixth in the allocation of interest subsidized rental units and thirtieth in home-ownership units from 1968 through 1971, yet according to estimates had the greatest need of any state in the country. The interest subsidy would not reduce the price of housing in such a high cost area to a level that low-income families could afford, while public housing could not be built within established price limits. On the other hand, in the South and West where building and land costs were lower, subsidized units could be built more easily.[9] Yet is the nation better off if a poor family in New York is sheltered rather than the two which could be housed in Mississippi for the same outlay? Refinement of the housing tools and use of different programs could shift the balance if desired.

On close examination, then, criticisms of the costs, inefficiencies, and inequities of the low-income housing programs are not persuasive. The housing programs are costly because they try to provide a decent home and suitable living environment to a large number of very low-income families. Inefficiency and mismanagement are not the products of bureaucratic bungling, but rather of the effort to maintain high standards, to build for people and in areas that the market will not, and to achieve other aims such as utilizing private financing or supporting union wages. Inequity is inherent where a program can serve only a small portion of the universe of need. Improvements are needed and can be made, but the shortcomings hardly outweigh the benefits to millions of persons who are better housed and more adequately provided for as a result of federal intervention.

In-Kind versus Cash Assistance

The Nixon administration's strident reaction to these alleged shortcomings was based on ideology and fueled by the promise of a better alternative. The ideology was that in-kind aid was inherently inferior to cash assistance and the alternative was a housing allowance or voucher program which would provide the needy with money to acquire their own housing without government intervention in the marketplace.

The housing assistance programs are the archetype of in-kind aid. Based on the evidence that millions of low-income individuals were unable to afford decent, safe, and sanitary housing, and that few, if any, homes or apartments were being built at prices near what they could afford, direct measures were taken to build or rehabilitate lower-cost units and to subsidize low-income tenants and buyers. The rationale was that the free market was not meeting their needs. It was felt that the upgrading process resulting from the rising income of the poor and the "trickle down" of construction for the more affluent was too slow, and that government intervention was required to combat neighborhood decay. The presumption was that interceding for those with the greatest problems would be the most direct and cost-effective way of helping them.

The arguments against the housing assistance programs typified the critiques of in-kind aid: consumers overuse the subsidized goods; government action distorts market operations and leads to inefficiencies; there is no housing problem but rather an income problem which could be better dealt with less cost by cash transfers. This philosophy, more than the scattered criticism, led the Nixon administration to halt new commitments and appoint a review committee to design alternatives. The underlying assumption, articulated explicitly by the Secretary of Housing and Urban Development, was that the programs were not only working poorly, but that they were unworkable because of the failings inherent in government intervention.

The report of HUD's National Housing Policy Review, *Housing in the Seventies,* was essentially an attempt to substantiate this ideology. Besides documenting the specific problems of the housing assistance programs, it sought to prove that the value of aid to recipients was substantially less than the cost to the government and that positive spillovers to nonrecipients were minimal.

> Government subsidized housing programs contain structural problems that result in considerable program inequities and inefficiencies. Certain problems could be remedied through legislative changes. However, legislative correction of one would tend to aggravate or create others. More importantly, while administrative changes would marginally improve the efficiency and equity of production programs, serious problems of inefficiency and inequity *inherent in using production as the basic approach* would remain.[10]

The Efficiency of Government Intervention

The claim of inefficiency was documented by cost data. Full operating and construction costs were estimated to be 15 percent greater in public housing than in comparable unsubsidized units. The construction costs of rent supplemented and interest subsidized rental units were nearly a fifth higher. There was no difference in the costs of units built for home ownership with or without subsidies.[11]

The review committee attempted a more basic challenge to the in-kind approach by comparing the total cost of government aid to the value placed on this assistance by subsidized residents. Rental subsidized tenants perceived only about $1 in benefits from each $2 spent, while subsidized homeowners perceived benefits equal to four fifths of actual costs.[12]

If one is looking for proof that the assistance programs are failures and that it would be better to distribute cash directly, there are several important caveats:

First, the accuracy of the data was questionable. One might wonder whether the full costs, such as income tax savings, were counted for unsubsidized units. Sample sizes were frequently inadequate. For instance, only 329 families in ten cities were surveyed to determine the participants' rating of the homeownership program.

Second, what is a comparable unit? Assisted housing must meet special government requirements. As previously suggested, affirmative action regulations and union wage provisions raise construction costs; but presumably these requirements have a payoff which justifies the extra cost so that by all rights the added outlays should be excluded for purposes of comparison. Very few, if any, units of lower cost housing were being built in most large cities, and the meaningfulness of comparisons between a Manhattan high-rise, less its amenities, and a unit built for use by large, low-income families, is questionable. Fire and theft insurance may be higher in low-income areas where subsidized units were built, with vandalism raising both construction and operating costs. Builders and lenders may have required incentives to compensate for the risks of providing housing for low-income groups in low-income areas. Finally, the clients of subsidized housing projects undoubtedly put more wear and tear on their apartments than more affluent residents of unsubsidized units.

Third, the residents' assessments of value may not be reliable. Consumers commonly perceive that goods are overpriced, and subsidized residents would in all likelihood increase their valuations of housing assistance if they were given that amount of cash and sent out to find shelter. Costs will never equal perceived benefits even under a housing allowance system, since there are always administrative expenses.

Fourth, the consumer might prefer cash to housing subsidies in order to spend a smaller proportion of real income on rent. Yet, one of the aims of providing in-kind aid is to assure that what the public believes to be basic housing standards are met. Some family heads with small children are willing to live in slums and spend the extra money on cars or other luxury goods, but the welfare of their children might be improved by providing the incentive to acquire better shelter. The implicit assumption underlying in-kind approaches is that societal values should receive somewhat greater emphasis under public programs.

Fifth, renters may normally value housing at less than the costs of construction and operation because someone else owns the property. Long after the public housing or rent-supplement tenants move out, the property will remain and either the public or the private sector owner will have the title. A tangible good has been created with an extended use-life, and renters will not benefit over its lifetime. It is not surprising, then, that subsidized homeowners gave a much higher valuation to benefits than renters.

The Impact of Subsidized Production

Even if participants perceive benefits to be less than cost, nonrecipients also benefit to the extent the increased supply of housing softens the market and thereby reduces price. Having asserted that in-kind benefits were worth less to recipients than their cost to the government, *Housing in the Seventies* went on to claim that the benefits had little impact on the housing stock and thus on housing prices.

In summary, the provision of housing subsidies undoubtedly increased the quantity and quality of housing for those relatively few who were subsidized while it reduced the con-

struction of new housing units for everyone else . . . Various
analyses suggest for every 100,000 units subsidized during the
1960s and early 1970s perhaps as few as 14,000 represent
net additions to the housing stock.[13]

The documentation for such a high offset was a regression analysis of quarterly data on housing starts from 1960 through 1972.
It was based on rather questionable grounds because it had to derive
quarterly subsidized starts by dividing annual figures by four. Supply and demand equations were simulated utilizing multiple regres-
sions, but these equations had no cost variable, a serious omission,
since the average unsubsidized start was two fifths more expensive
than the average assisted unit. The study used a linear estimation
technique despite the clear evidence that supply and demand factors changed markedly in the period under consideration as subsidized starts averaged only 55,000 annually from 1960 through
1967, but 313,000 from 1968 through 1972. The interest subsidy
programs, which competed for funds directly in the mortgage
market, as opposed to the earlier direct loan programs, were not
introduced until 1968. Demand factors such as the dramatic increase in mobile home purchases by low-income families and the
changes in income and family status were ignored as was increased
intermediation by quasi-government agencies such as the Federal
National Mortgage Association on the supply side. To cap it off,
the model did very poorly in predicting even past starts, with a
standard error larger than the production in any quarter. Without
belaboring the point, this study can be viewed as an exercise in
support of a basically ideological assertion.

Other studies suggest far less substitution. Indeed, *Housing in
the Seventies* cited an internal study estimating a 50 percent reduction in unsubsidized starts—a substantial and significant difference
which tended to be ignored in the above stated conclusions.[14]
Even more dependably, another study estimating housing starts for
1969 through 1971, using a national econometric model, concluded that "the expansion in subsidized housing production . . .
beginning in late 1968 constituted an actual net increase in total
production rather than a mere substitution of production within
housing markets—though substitution may also have taken
place."[15]

The raw data support this conclusion. When subsidized starts were at their highest point ever between 1970 and 1972, unsubsidized starts were also at their highest levels. Shortages of housing funds were overcome by the government's purchase of mortgages with money raised from general borrowing.

The purpose of assisted housing production is to increase the supply of decent homes for the low-income families whose needs are not being met by the free market. The percentage of all housing which will be built at the price level and for the income cohort in assisted units is close to zero, so that even if there is a decrease of 86,000 unsubsidized starts for every 100,000 which are subsidized, the number available for low-income families still increases by nearly 100,000.

Despite this fact, the critics on the HUD review committee concluded that: "Subsidized housing has not provided significant indirect benefits by opening up better unsubsidized housing at the same or less cost than tenants were previously charged."[16] This judgment was based on surveys of persons moving into units vacated by new tenants of subsidized housing. These unsubsidized persons were asked what they previously and presently paid and about certain characteristics of their previous homes. It was found that they had upgraded the quality of their homes but also paid more. The presumption would normally be that if they moved voluntarily, they were improving the quality of housing per dollar outlay. The HUD committee apparently did not agree.

The filtration process cannot be proved or disproved by looking at one step in what is a dynamic process. If, for instance, a family moves from a $40,000 house or a $200 a month rental unit into a $60,000 house or $300 rental, it is likely that due to inflation the prospective residents of the vacated unit will pay more than $40,000 or $200. Housing prices and rentals are constantly rising and because a particular unit is being vacated does not mean that its price will fall or even that it will rise less rapidly than other comparable properties. The impacts of increased construction are felt over time and in the total market, usually through a reduced rate of increase in total prices. The only alternative to the subsidized production approach is to maintain a healthy housing market and to rely on the filtering down of units. There is no reason to believe that, if the construction of upper-income units eventually opens up more adequate housing for lower income units, cutting in at a lower level will not result in an even more rapid and significant filtration.

Overall, then, *Housing in the Seventies* is more a polemic for the administration's predetermined ideological position that in-kind aid does not work rather than a reasoned assessment of the assisted housing programs. As the chairman of the Senate Committee on Banking, Housing, and Urban Affairs put it, "The mounting evidence of program failure, alleged by HUD officials, turns out to be more theory than fact. Its conclusions rest, like a house of cards, on an unsteady foundation."[17]

Realistically Appraising the Alternatives

To poke holes in these arguments does not prove the converse, that the assisted housing programs are effective. Neither does it deny some losses in consumer satisfaction when aid is given in the form of goods and services rather than dollars. Moreover, government entry into the marketplace may be associated with some inefficiencies, and unsubsidized production may decline somewhat when resources are bid away for subsidized construction.

Yet alternative strategies such as the housing allowance also have drawbacks:

First, it is doubtful that an administration bent on cutting welfare programs would be willing to initiate a new, categorical, large-scale program of cash aid. Neither the Nixon nor Ford administrations rushed forward with proposals to implement their favored approach.

Second, the housing allowance means settling for a lower quality product. The fundamental tenet is that existing units are good enough for low-income families. In welfare programs, benefit levels in most states are below minimum standards, which are far below the levels needed to afford shelter of the assisted housing quality. It would not be surprising to find the same thing prevailing under housing allowances, if enacted.

Third, inequities would not be easily swept away. Medicare, which is also a voucher program, has had problems, and similar issues are involved in housing allowances.

Finally, such allowances do not directly stimulate the building of new housing. There has to be a trickle-up of demand that may be constrained by high interest rates and the limited availability of money. Low-income populations are excluded from many areas by discrimination. Some proportion of housing allowances will be eaten up by inflated housing prices.

Recognizing the Good

The positive contributions of the housing assistance programs should also be clearly recognized:

First and foremost, they have placed families in better homes and have reduced housing costs. The massive waiting lists and low turnover in subsidized units suggest that the housing assistance programs are the most attractive or only options for a vast number of ill-housed, low-income families. Consumer preference curves, simulations, and other sophisticated theoretical estimates do not address the fundamental question of whether the same families would be better off without the program and whether the low-income housing market would have "loosened" as much as it did.

Housing assistance programs have spillover benefits. One is the community renewal impact. While some projects have been criticized as eyesores and health and safety hazards, the majority of projects in central cities are an improvement over the surroundings and provide some nexus for community development. The standard should not be whether public housing and rent subsidy programs generate complete neighborhood restructuring, but whether they improve substantially on what was previously there and would have otherwise remained. Also, the failure of some projects is really no different than the failure of some shopping centers or the rise or decline of whole communities. Housing production is an important tool in community renewal; in fact, the only way to make noticeable improvements without bulldozing slums.

Another spillover is that the programs provide some leverage to break down income and color segregation patterns in housing. While there are complaints about the concentration of assisted units in deteriorated central cities, court and administrative pressure has led to some dispersal into better central city neighborhoods and in some cases into the suburbs. The leverage is lost when enforcement pressure can only be exerted on behalf of individual complainants. Housing programs can hardly make a dent in segregational patterns but are a lever for some changes which might provide an impetus for integration.

A third argument for the housing programs is that they can be improved. Any effort doubling in two years, as the housing programs did between 1969 and 1971 is bound to experience inefficiencies. This does not mean that a continued production level of 300,000 or 400,000 units would encounter the same problems. The inequities in the distribution of units can be overcome by more realistically setting cost and subsidy limits. The high cost could be reduced by better appraisals, less rigorous standards, direct government financing, and elimination of the requirements that union wages be paid in construction. Qualitative deficiencies could be ameliorated by more frequent inspections, more expensive construction, or greater maintenance outlays. Dispersal could be augmented by tying water, sewer, and other grants to fair housing plans. To condemn the programs for concentrating in the central city while denying the leverage to disperse units, or to criticize high costs while agreeing to pay union wages, misplaces the blame; the programs should not be faulted because goals are sometimes in conflict.

Finally, the oldest argument for housing assistance is perhaps the most telling one at the present time—these programs can stimulate housing production. Economists have predicted the rebound of the housing industry from the low points in the mid-1970s, but a healthy pace of construction has yet to materialize. The housing goals of 1968 are certainly not being met.

The case for housing assistance programs is perhaps best summarized by Anthony Downs, one of the nation's foremost experts on housing problems and programs:

> *The most dramatic and most often repeated myth is that federal housing subsidy programs as a whole have failed, are disastrously ineffective, or are not working.* I believe this is false. Most of the more than 2.3 million housing units produced in the last 35 years through direct housing subsidies are highly satisfactory to their occupants, and have never experienced financial difficulty. Moreover, four of the primary objectives of housing subsidies adopted by Congress have been effectively served by existing programs since 1968. These objectives are: meeting the physical housing needs of urban

low- and moderate-income households, encouraging home ownership, stimulating the economy through greater housing production, and increasing the national supply of decent housing. If directly subsidized housing starts remain at close to 400,000 units annually for several more years, the four objectives listed above will continue to be met effectively.

Even if adequate non-housing programs related to poverty were adopted, large-scale direct housing subsidies for new construction would still be needed to expand the supply of decent housing units available to low- and moderate-income households.[18]

6 Compensatory Education

Faith in Education

In signing the Elementary and Secondary Education Act of 1965, Lyndon Johnson declared that "As President of the United States, I believe deeply that no law I have signed or will ever sign means more to the future of America." This faith in education was not just the testament of a former teacher but a view shared by most Americans. It was generally believed at the time that education was a primary determinant of each individual's and the nation's future well-being and that providing equal educational opportunity was a key to equalized economic opportunity.

This optimism may now seem naive. Education is no longer recognized as the prime determinant of an individual's future earnings or employment prospects. The 1966 Report on Equal Educational Opportunity (the Coleman report) cast doubt on the relationship between schools and learning, claiming that race and family background explained almost half of all achievement variation among students in 1965, and that the characteristics of the student body were far more important than differences in school facilities, curriculum, personnel, or spending.[1] Further doubts were raised when expenditures per pupil more than doubled over the 1960s and the teacher/student ratio rose by a fifth with little discernible improvement in the quality of education.

Another sobering realization was the immensity of the task of improving the quality of education. In 1972 there were more than 17,000 separate public school systems with varying degrees of autonomy from state and local government. There were 66,000 public and 14,000 private elementary schools, 25,000 public and 4,000 private secondary schools, plus 2,600 colleges and universities, together employing three million teachers. These thousands of units encompassed a staggering diversity of spending levels, curriculum content, personnel, and vested interests. In 1974 public agencies spent $79 billion on education while private sources added another $17 billion.[2] This complex system which had evolved over centuries and which affected almost every person in some way could not be easily changed by the injection of a few billion extra dollars in federal aid.

Finally, the economic payoff of increased education has been questioned. For certain groups, such as blacks, the relationship between schooling and future earnings is less pronounced than for the whites. There is some evidence that the return from added doses of education is declining for everyone, suggesting to some that the nation is overeducating its youth.

In hindsight, then, the Great Society's expectations for its education initiatives were inflated. The notion that federal dollars could be a lever for transforming the educational system did not materialize. The real issue is whether federal funds can be used to encourage gradual improvements. Schools alone cannot equalize opportunity and the policy question is whether better schools make enough of a difference to warrant the cost of improvement. Recognizing that the lack of credentials and schooling is only one factor contributing to socioeconomic inequality, the concern should not be whether increased education pays off as much for the disadvantaged as the nondisadvantaged, but whether relative improvements in attainment and achievement lead to meaningful improvements in the job market. Instead of assessing federal aid by the overoptimistic Great Society measuring rods, the compensatory education programs must be judged by reasonable standards recognizing what they can and cannot do.

Federal Aid to Education

Federal aid to education expanded dramatically in the 1960s and at the same time it was redirected to the task of equalizing educational opportunity for disadvantaged students. The Elementary and Secondary Education Act of 1965 was a landmark. Its Title I allocated funds to local school districts based on the number of schoolchildren from low-income families and the average school expenditure per child. These resources were for locally determined programs designed to meet the special educational needs of deprived youths.

Another major initiative was Head Start. On the assumption that the early childhood years were critically important for future development, and in light of the substantial evidence that poor children entering school were already behind their peers, the Economic Opportunity Act provided funds to community action and other agencies for the education and care of three- to six-year-old children from poor families.

At the other end of the educational spectrum, a work study program was also established as part of the war on poverty to assist college students from low-income families. The Higher Education Act of 1965 transferred this program to the Office of Education, provided aid to developing (mostly black) institutions, authorized economic opportunity grants to low-income students, established the Upward Bound program to help talented students from poor homes make the transition into college, and offered low-interest loans to needy students.

These programs expanded, and by fiscal 1970 total federal funds for preschool, elementary and secondary, vocational, and higher education were $9.6 billion or 2.4 times those in 1965 (Figure 6-1). They then expanded another 73 percent by fiscal 1975 to $16.5 billion. The proportion of aid specifically for the disadvantaged rose from next to nothing before the Great Society to $3.1 billion in fiscal 1972, a fourth of all federal educational expenditures in that year (Table 6-1).

Most of the criticism of federal educational efforts has been leveled at these compensatory programs for the disadvantaged. Powerful lobbies and the widespread appeal of programs which will help a broader range of students have shielded other education

Figure 6–1. Federal education outlays, fiscal 1965–1975 (billions)

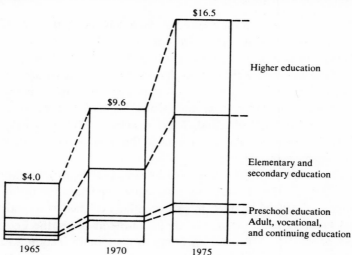

Source: Statistical Abstract of the United States, 1974 (Washington: Government Printing Office, 1974), p. 143; and *Special Analyses, Budget of the United States Government, Fiscal Year 1976* (Washington: Government Printing Office, 1975), p. 149.

efforts from equally searching criticism. A case can be made for compensatory education by comparing it with regular educational activities. This, however, begs the question whether Head Start, Title I, and the various scholarship, loan, and work programs for the disadvantaged are worthwhile and performing according to reasonable standards.

Early Education

It is well documented that children from low-income and minority families enter school with learning handicaps which subsequently become more severe. Preschool programs are needed to equalize chances at the educational starting gate.

Head Start, one of the most popular initiatives of the war on poverty, provides funds, mostly to community action agencies, for child development programs ranging from complete child care services to part-day summer sessions for children about to enter the first grade. By fiscal 1973 there were 179,000 children in part-day,

Table 6-1. Federal education programs for the disadvantaged, 1972

Program	Obligations (millions)	Participants (thousands)
Total	*$3,140*	*9,619*
Early childhood	376	356
Head Start		
Full year	} 376	270
Summer		86
Elementary and secondary education	1,633	6,290
Follow-Through	63	90
ESEA, Title I	1,570	6,200
College	1,131	2,973
Direct student loans	317	614
Guaranteed student loans	231	1,256
College work-study	272	600
Educational opportunity grants	210	304
Upward Bound	30	25
Talent Search	5	125
Special services for disadvantaged	14	49
Support to developing institutions	52	–

Source: U.S. Department of Health, Education, and Welfare.

and 91,000 in full-day, full-year programs, plus 86,000 in summer activities.

These participants received intensive assistance costing an average of $1,300 for full-day and $1,100 for part-day care per pupil. Education accounted for roughly two fifths of costs; health and nutrition an eighth; administration, parental involvement, and family services a fourth; transportation and facilities the remainder. There was intensive supervision and aid, with a professional staff/child ratio of 1 to 12, and counting volunteers, an adult/child ratio of 1 to 2. Individual projects varied markedly in their emphasis on play, social development, and basic training in language and quantitative skills. Following traditional nursery school practices, the development of self-esteem and social competence was emphasized as much as learning specific academic skills. The idea was not to advance achievement so much as to improve the readiness to learn. Almost all of the full-year centers served lunch and at least one other meal, and a majority of full-day centers served three or more meals a day. Almost all children received physical or dental exams and about two fifths had medical or dental problems which were treated. Parental involvement was achieved on several levels. Parent advisory committees provided inputs into decision making and served as an information channel to parents. Most centers also employed parents—with one sixth of paid staff members having children in the program and an additional 15 percent the parents of previous participants. Many more parents worked as volunteers.[3]

Did this combination of services, on the average, significantly improve the educational future of participating children? The evidence is limited, but not overly sanguine. A 1969 follow-up study of former Head Start participants found that those previously in full-year programs entered first grade with somewhat greater learning readiness than a matched sample of nonparticipants, but children enrolled in summer programs gained little. Self-concepts were no more positive, classroom behavior no better, and even more critical, there was little difference in achievement between participants and controls at the second grade level.[4] Apparently, then, summer programs had meager impacts while the modest benefits of full-year programs washed out quickly.

Though criticized for using culturally biased tests, for control selection deficiencies, and for an unrepresentative sample, this study probably provided a fair assessment of Head Start's impact at the time. But full-year programs were not initiated on a large scale until fiscal 1967, and full-day programs until fiscal 1969. The second graders sampled in 1968 and 1969 were in most cases the first graduates of the early projects, providing a poor basis for assessing the potential effectiveness of preschool compensatory education.

In order to preserve the small but important gains from preschool education, Congress established the Follow-Through program in 1967 to help disadvantaged students in grades 1 through 3 who had previously participated in Head Start or an equivalent preschool program. A wide range of strategies were tested augmenting normal school offerings, some focusing primarily on basic education, some emphasizing structured learning and the use of special equipment, and others self-realization through progressive education formats.

Follow-Through demonstrated some success. According to most tests of affective and cognitive development, participants improved relative to controls with the impact more noticeable the longer they stayed in the program. Moreover, successive cohorts realized greater gains, reflecting program improvements. Recent Follow-Through gain rates, in fact, approach national norms. There were also significant improvements in parent and teacher attitudes.[5]

These positive conclusions depended in part on the statistical techniques used in the evaluation of Follow-Through. Comparison of participants and controls was made on the basis of the frequency of positive impact, rather than the size of the improvements. Nevertheless, the finding that the measurable benefits not only continue but increase over the years was not biased by this methodology and can be tentatively accepted. More recent data which show Follow-Through students learning at average rates are based on tested gain scores and are not biased or inflated by statistical manipulations. There are grounds, then, for believing that intensive programs beginning before regular enrollment in school and continuing several years thereafter can improve learning.

Improving Elementary and Secondary Education

Title I of the Elementary and Secondary Education Act has been plagued since its inception by administrative problems. The act allocated funds directly to school districts on a needs formula and subjected them to only a few general federal guidelines. From this standpoint it was a precursor to revenue sharing, a fact which was ignored by the Nixon administration critics who in other cases favored this approach. Many difficulties of compensatory aid stemmed from the lack of needed federal regulations.

In the early years, some local educational agencies used federal funds for swimming pools, football uniforms, and administrative offices. Pressed to spend money or lose it, school districts initially took the opportunity to reduce construction backlogs while developing new instruction programs. In fiscal 1966, a third of all outlays were for construction and equipment, and only half for instruction. But by 1969, as federal guidelines became more restrictive and as locally initiated programs got underway, less than 4 percent of outlays were for construction and equipment while instructional outlays accounted for three fourths of the total.[6]

A more fundamental problem was the inclination to try to feed the multitudes with sparse loaves. Title I funds were allocated on the basis of poverty and welfare caseloads, and most school districts qualified for some money. School systems, in turn divided the allocation among schools, usually by a similar formula, rather than concentrating resources in areas of greatest need. In fiscal 1967 the less than $1 billion in aid was spread among 9 million participants, with an average outlay of $108 per student. The national average per pupil expenditure in that year was $475, so that spending for participants increased resources by more than a fifth. While there is no proof that achievement is related to spending levels, or that there is minimum concentration which will result in substantial gains, many claim that this is the case.[7] Some changes in the funding formula were made to encourage greater concentration, but local school districts were reluctant to choose among students with equal needs.

Another problem was the use of Title I funds to aid nontargeted schools and nondisadvantaged students in targeted schools, or to support activities with questionable impact on the education of the disadvantaged. HEW audit reports showed that funds were used for general aid in 33 of 37 states, frequently to upgrade the quality of minority schools. While this served the disadvantaged, some of the federal aid might have displaced local funds. Changes were subsequently made requiring equal local spending per pupil in Title I and non-Title I schools within districts, but the actual redistribution of local funds has been slow.[8]

Despite these problems, the charges of total noncompliance with federal guidelines are based on early experiences and frequently lack a reasonable sense of perspective. According to a recent comprehensive analysis of ESEA's administration:

> When the evidence of illegality is compared to the more numerous instances of compliance, or when it is analyzed to determine the magnitude of its impact (in terms of students or dollars), it does not lead to the conclusion that lawlessness characterizes the administration of Title I. To the contrary, the evidence indicates that in the majority of [school districts] the administration of the program is in compliance with the regulations.[9]

Whatever the administrative shortcomings, ESEA reached areas and students with serious needs. Fifty-three percent of all students in schools receiving Title I funds in 1969 came from families with an income below $6,000 (median family income that year was $9,433) and nearly a third were minority group members. Four fifths of second grade participants, and nine tenths of those in the sixth grade, were below national reading norms.[10] States able to afford a high level of expenditures per pupil received less federal aid than less affluent states.[11]

The crucial question is whether the disadvantaged students receiving compensatory aid are helped. The evidence is mixed. On the negative side, an evaluation of compensatory education programs in eleven school districts in fiscal 1966 and 1967 found no overall achievement gain and in some cases even slippage by participants.[12] In fiscal 1968 the Office of Education conducted a national survey of grades two, four, and six. Participants started off with much lower achievement and fell farther behind nonparticipants and national norms. There was no relation between the remedial reading courses and the amount of reading gain. The same survey was repeated in fiscal 1969. The number of participants below school norms increased despite compensatory aid, while nonparticipants held their own.[13]

These studies were seriously flawed. The 1966–67 survey was premature, reflecting administrative problems encountered in the early years of the program. The 1968 and 1969 national surveys had extremely low response rates and the usable data applied to only a few large central city school systems facing the most difficult problems. In all these cases the controls were much better off to begin with, and since past achievement is related to future gains, they could have been expected to gain faster, negatively biasing comparisons.

The studies indicating positive impact are more numerous, and more dependable, as well as more current. A 1969 nationwide survey of teachers in Title I elementary schools found that most believed compensatory programs had improved reading proficiency and the understanding of written and oral instructions. While this might have been a self-serving judgment, an analysis of 24 state reports for 1969 and 1970 found participants attaining school norms in the fourth grade and surpassing them in the sixth grade, though at each grade level they started off farther behind.[14]

A review of state and school district reports by the Department of Health, Education, and Welfare in 1971 and 1972 found that most programs achieved gains greater than the .7 grade equivalent per year usually averaged by disadvantaged students. A significant percentage surpassed national norms. A massive sampling of Title I students in California found that 7 percent gained at a rate of 1.5 grade equivalents or more, 19 percent at 1.0 to 1.4, and 36 percent at .7 to .9. In Colorado four of every five participants gained at a rate of .8 grade equivalents or better, and a fourth advanced at a rate of 1.5 grades. In Connecticut 109 of 142 compensatory district programs averaged gains in excess of school norms during the 1970–71 school year. The assessment concluded that "the drift of evidence seems to be unmistakable, that compensatory education often enhances the achievement for poor children."[15]

Finally, an analysis of 14 fiscal 1972 state Title I reports again indicated that the gain rate of disadvantaged students was significantly above the .7 norm; in fact, at almost all grade levels, the average disadvantaged student exceeded national norms. There may have been some positive bias because California and Alabama, which had the most successful programs, also had the largest samples. But separate data for different states and grade levels revealed that out of 113 reported discrete cases only 11 were below the .7 standard, while 55 were above the national norm.[16]

The early national surveys which cast doubt on the impact of compensatory education were premature and far less comprehensive than later state reports. On the other hand, the later evaluations demonstrating significant gains, although more broadly focused and based on larger samples, rarely had any controls, using rather a crude gain of .7 grade achievement as the standard for assessment. These reports also have been biased to the extent that effective programs were the ones most likely to provide usable data. There is no doubt, however, that compensatory education programs have the potential to significantly raise the learning rates of the disadvantaged as they have done in some areas. The positive evidence is also more recent, probably reflecting real improvements in design and administration. Whether the results justify the costs remains a matter of individual judgment, but compensatory efforts can make a difference.

Higher Education

Even in states with publicly supported college systems, higher education puts substantial financial burdens on those of limited means. Not surprisingly, less than a fifth of poor families with a college-age dependent have a member attending school full-time compared with more than half of families with incomes above $15,000.[17] While the exceptionally able poor youth may get private scholarships and help from other sources, the lower achieving high school graduate with a deprived background has only half the chance of college attendance as a youth of equal ability from an affluent family.[18]

To overcome the financial obstacles, federal aid for needy students was dramatically expanded over the last decade. Under the Higher Education Act of 1965 low interest loans were provided to 634,000 students in 1974, half of whom came from families with less than $6,000 annual income. The government also guarantees loans made by private institutions and subsidizes the interest due until after graduation. A third of the 700,000 guaranteed loans in fiscal 1974 went to persons from low-income families.[19] The college work-study program, initiated as part of the war on poverty, paid poor students wages for part-time jobs. Some 560,000 students were employed in 1974, roughly half of whom came from families with less than $6,000 income. The earnings averaged around $600 and covered half the expenses in public colleges and a fourth in private schools. A fifth of the students participating in the program reported that they would have been unable to attend college without this money.[20]

Loans have to be repaid and work may detract from study, so direct subsidies are also needed. The Economic Opportunity Act authorized annual grants ranging from $200 to $1,000. The program helped 304,000 students in 1974, including two thirds from families with annual incomes below $6,000.[21] Despite their handicaps, the re-enrollment rates of grantees equaled those of other freshmen and, for those dropping out, finances were rarely a factor.[22]

In 1972 Congress initiated the Basic Education Opportunity Grant, designed to provide $1,400 to all college students, less the amount the family could reasonably afford to pay. While falling short of such comprehensive assistance, 689,000 students were helped in 1974, half from low-income families.

Social and personal as well as financial obstacles may dissuade low-income students from pursuing a college education. Under the Upward Bound program colleges are funded to use their campus facilities during summer recess to provide remedial programs and counseling to selected tenth and eleventh grade students from low-income backgrounds. Almost all Upward Bound students finish high school, and two thirds go on to college.[23] Of those who entered in the fall of 1970, 60 percent were still there in 1972—a dropout rate not far above that for all students.[24]

These and other programs aiding colleges and college students contributed to the massive expansion of higher education. Between 1960 and 1974 college enrollment rose from 3.6 to 8.8 million, and the proportion of 20 to 24 year olds enrolled in school grew from 13 to 21 percent. The 4.6 million grants, loans, and work-supported arrangements in fiscal 1974, representing a 27-fold increase in federal outlays within a decade, were no doubt a factor in the rising enrollment.[25] There was a tripling in the number of aided students from families with income below $6,000 between 1965 and 1973. The number of nonwhites attending college rose from 227,000 to 814,000 between 1960 and 1974, with more than two fifths of these in the latter year receiving some form of federal aid.[26]

Does Education Pay Off?

These federal education programs were based on the supposition that increased achievement and attainment would improve future socioeconomic status. This notion was subsequently challenged on several fronts. Evidence that many workers were overqualified for their jobs raised questions whether workers who were better schooled or who had better credentials were more productive.[27] The unemployment problems of scientists and engineers and declining job opportunities for teachers suggested an oversupply of college graduates, at least in selected fields. Other evidence suggested that blacks did not get the same returns from education as whites because of inequities and discrimination in the labor market. The career education concept challenged the notion that the purpose of schooling was the preparation for more schooling and advanced the idea of preparing students for immediate entry into the labor market. Finally, there was a widely publicized decline in college attendance in the mid-1970s as youths sought other means of realizing career goals.

Increased achievement and attainment still leads to improved income and earnings. Education programs can affect future well-being. Based on the age, education, and income distribution of the population, the projected income of a high school graduate in 1963 was 38 percent more than that of an elementary school graduate. College students could look forward to 57 percent higher life-time income than persons with only a high school diploma. Over the next decade, incomes improved at all levels, but projected income differentials remained essentially unchanged.[28] The increased numbers at higher attainment levels did not lower the relative return to greater education. It is reasonable to assume, therefore, that the investment paid off for those groups who increased their average attainment over the decade.

If increased schooling of the disadvantaged debased the value of a diploma, as some have alleged, then this should have been especially evident for blacks, since the proportion with a high school diploma doubled between 1960 and 1973. However, nonwhite males age 25 to 34 years with a high school diploma earned 15 percent more than dropouts in 1960, and the differential increased to 20 percent a decade later. Nonwhite college graduates earned 28 percent more than high school graduates in 1960 compared with a 65 percent differential 10 years later. As a result, the nonwhite high school graduate 25 to 34 years of age increased his relative earnings from 43 percent to 76 percent of earnings by whites over the 1960s, while the one third differential among college graduates was almost wiped out. The substantial return from increased education was a primary factor in the rising income and earnings of blacks.

Federal aid for higher education increased the chances of low-income students getting a college diploma. The sheepskin has a demonstrable value, and the evidence is persuasive that the federal investment has had and will continue to have a substantial payoff in improving the well-being of the disadvantaged. Whether this applies to preschool and elementary and secondary education is less certain. There is also some evidence that increased educational inputs affecting both achievement and attainment bear some relationship to future earnings. A study utilizing data from a massive longitudinal sample of American families concluded that a 100 percent increase in school expenditures per year was correlated with roughly a 10 percent increase in educational attainment (even higher for the poor) and a 14 percent increase in future hourly wage rates.[29]

Keeping the Faith

Whether this holds true for compensatory expenditures is unknown, but doubts about the payoff for such efforts should be no greater than doubts about all privately and publicly financed education. We do not know conclusively whether more teachers per student, new text books, better-equipped laboratories and libraries, specialized courses for those with problems or unique interests, or innovative teaching techniques really make a difference in student achievement. There is no guarantee that the nation or specific individuals will be better off with more educational attainment, or even with improved scholastic achievement in the future. Academics are still debating whether IQ differentials are hereditary, whether the progressive or fundamental 3-R approach is best, whether new forms of career education need to be substituted for scholastic training. It is, therefore, not surprising that experts have not reached a verdict on compensatory education. In the absence of any conclusive proof of failure (and with some indications of a positive impact), compensatory efforts must be judged by the same set of societal hypotheses which underlie the entire education system.

First, the prevailing belief that schools can help determine the quality of learning should also be applied to compensatory education efforts. Despite the Coleman report findings of a limited correlation between classroom characteristics and achievement, it is a rare parent who is indifferent to crumbling buildings, old textbooks, or archaic teaching methods.

Second, there is a fundamental belief that the quality of inputs is associated with the quality of outputs. Extra dollars do not always buy more or better services, but it is difficult to attract scarce resources without money. And while there may be diminishing returns to educational resources, improvements can be made on most educational systems.

Third, the pervasive conviction, resting on past experience, that improved education has a long-run payoff remains unshaken. It is doubtful that families would spend thousands of dollars to send their sons and daughters to Montessori schools, private elementary and secondary facilities, and most of all, to colleges, unless they were convinced that the investment would provide their offspring long-term advantages.

Fourth, there is a deep and abiding belief that education is a mechanism for equalizing opportunity. The rationale for a public school system is that wealth and income are unequally distributed while ability is equally (or at least less unequally) spread. Whether education can compensate for shortcomings in the home, negative peer group influences, and other factors is unclear, but it does provide an opportunity for upward mobility which has proved effective in the past for many with ability and motivation.

All these hypotheses may be wrong or at least overemphasized in our society. Yet as long as most people believe these notions, and act on them, compensatory education efforts are warranted. It has been demonstrated that even the most disadvantaged students can learn, and their learning rates can be improved. Extra resources may not always be the key but more money is one of the best ways to reorient institutions, to introduce and experiment with new curricula, and to reallocate attention to those with greatest needs. Added education has resulted in increased earnings for disadvantaged groups. The possibility that the payoff may be reduced in the future is no reason to cut back on aid to those with the most severe problems while more advantaged youths continue to hedge their bets with a diploma. It is a matter of faith that compensatory or any education investments are worthwhile—but unless there is much more convincing evidence to the contrary, there is good reason to "keep the faith."

7 Manpower Programs

A Decade of Manpower Policy

There are millions of Americans with bad jobs or no jobs who
are unable to support themselves and their families adequately.
Until the 1960s the federal government provided little assistance
other than to cushion periods of unemployment. The Employment
Act of 1946 established the goal of maximum employment, but the
unemployment rate rose above 5 percent in 10 of the next 18
years. The Great Society's goal was full employment, and between
1964 and 1969, unemployment averaged only 4.1 percent. In
addition to stimulative monetary and fiscal action (and of course
the stimulus of wartime spending) a wide range of structural measures was implemented to improve the workings of the economic
system. These included aid to depressed areas, increased minimum
wages, and most innovatively, a variety of manpower programs to
provide vocational training, remedial education, work experience,
counseling, placement, and other services for those failing in or
being failed by the labor market.

Proliferation and Expansion

The Manpower Development and Training Act was the first
major effort to train and retrain unemployed workers. Initiated in
1962 to serve those displaced by technological change, it was re-

oriented over the 1960s to help the unskilled and deficiently educated. The Economic Opportunity Act of 1964 spawned a number of programs for the poor—the Neighborhood Youth Corps, providing work and some training to in-school and out-of-school youth; the Job Corps, focusing on intensive remedial efforts in a residential setting geared to helping the most handicapped teenagers; the Work Experience and Training program, offering work relief for the needy, and adult education for all those without the verbal and quantitative skills needed for employment. In 1965 Operation Mainstream was added to provide jobs for older workers, mostly in rural areas. The New Careers program was begun in 1966 to restructure jobs in the public and nonprofit sector in order to create new paraprofessional openings for less skilled workers. By 1967 the proliferation of programs was recognized as a problem, and an attempt was made to consolidate and focus efforts under the Concentrated Employment Program. This legislation provided block grants, usually to community action agencies, to design, operate, and coordinate programs in low-income target areas, but it evolved as another categorical program and did little to reform the overall system. The Work Incentive or WIN program, created by the 1967 amendment to the Social Security Act, sought to increase the employment and earnings of welfare recipients to make them self-supporting. To involve private employers in the war on poverty, President Johnson established the Job Opportunities in the Business Sector (JOBS) program, offering subsidies to private firms hiring and training the disadvantaged. A National Alliance of Businessmen was established to administer the JOBS effort and to encourage volunteer job pledges. The vocational rehabilitation program was expanded in 1968 and extended to the socioeconomically as well as mentally and physically handicapped.[1]

In fiscal 1964 outlays for manpower totaled $450 million, mostly supporting employment services, vocational rehabilitation, and MDTA. Under the impetus of the Great Society, outlays increased to $2.6 billion by fiscal 1970 (Table 7-1).

Retrenchment and Reform

The Nixon administration was philosophically inclined to the notion of human resource investments that would increase the

Table 7-1. Outlays for manpower programs (millions)[a]

Program	1964	1967	1970	1973	1974
Total	*$450*	*$1,775*	*$2,596*	*$4,952*	*$4,666*
Department of Labor					
U.S. Employment Service	181	276	331	431	390
MDTA-Institutional	93	221	260	358 ⎫	
Job Corps	–	321	144	188 ⎪	
JOBS	–	–	86	104 ⎪	
Jobs Optional	5	53	50	73 ⎪	
NYC In-School	–	57	58	73 ⎬ 1,419[b]
NYC Summer	–	69	136	220 ⎪	
NYC Out-of-School	–	127	98	118 ⎪	
Operation Mainstream	–	9	42	82 ⎪	
Public Service Careers	–	–	18	42 ⎪	
Concentrated Employment Program	–	1	164	129 ⎭	
Work Incentive Program	–	–	67	177	218
Public Employment Program	–	–	–	1,005	598
Program Administration, Research, and Support	23	118	143	209	162
Department of Health, Education, and Welfare					
Vocational Rehabilitation	84	215	441	636	755
Work Experience and Training	–	120	1	–	–
Other programs					
Veterans' programs	12	19	141	292	351
Other training and placement programs	15	116	277	382	377
Employment-related child care	37	53	141	433	398

Source: U.S. Office of Management and Budget.

[a] Details may not add to totals because of rounding.

[b] Programs now authorized by Comprehensive Employment and Training Act.

employability of the disadvantaged. It accordingly supported the thrust of manpower programs and outlays had increased to $5 billion by fiscal 1973. From the outset, however, there was opposition to the methods and approaches of the Great Society. Over the 1960s manpower programs had increasingly emphasized aid to the hardest core and to reach them worked largely through community-based organizations. Ad hoc responses to a variety of different problems resulted in a complex maze of programs nominally directed by the federal government. These aspects of the manpower effort were opposed by the Nixon administration.

During the 1968 campaign, candidate Nixon singled out the Job Corps for criticism, charging that it cost too much and accomplished little in its effort to salvage the most disadvantaged youths. During the first year of his administration, the program was transferred from the antipoverty agency to the Labor Department, numerous centers were closed, and enrollment was halved. Other Economic Opportunity Act programs were also transferred, ostensibly to improve operational performance but with the effect of substantially reducing the role of community-based groups. These were only temporary measures until more complete reform could be achieved. The Nixon administration proposed that the separate categorical programs could be replaced with a single revenue sharing grant to governors, mayors, and county officials with which they could then design and implement efforts better suited to local needs, more accountable to the will of the people, and without the red tape of federal direction.

Decentralization and decategorization of manpower programs was the aim of the Comprehensive Manpower Act of 1970, but the President vetoed it because the bill also authorized a public employment program which he considered wasteful. When unemployment rose to the 6.0 percent level, the administration grudgingly accepted the Emergency Employment Act, which provided $2.25 billion for hiring the jobless. With this issue resolved, revenue sharing was implemented under the Comprehensive Employment and Training Act of 1973. The act consolidated the many programs initiated under the Manpower Development and Training, Economic Opportunity, and Emergency Employment Acts, substituting a single federal grant to local governments with populations over 100,000 and to states which were to distribute funds to less populated areas. The aim was to replace the previous panoply of separately funded, federally designed and administered manpower programs with a flexible locally run system.

Yet as the scale of manpower outlays continued to rise in the 1970s, retrenchment as much as reform became the administration's aim. In fiscal 1974 budgets were cut and inflation reduced resources even further. Criticism began to be leveled at manpower services, questioning the effectiveness of training and education in improving the employability of the disadvantaged.

The Effectiveness of Training

To a greater extent than in any other area of social welfare policy, there was a basis for making informed assessments of performance. Where the outputs of other endeavors such as education, health care, or community action were difficult to quantify, the primary purposes of manpower services were to raise wages, improve occupational status, and increase the stability of employment; all these could be measured in dollars and cents. By comparing the labor market experience of participants before and after enrollment, the changes could be determined. Even better, the success of participants could be compared to that of a matched control group of nonparticipants in order to eliminate factors such as aging or changes in economic conditions which might affect before and after comparisons.

The assumption underlying manpower efforts is that training, education, and other services will increase the productivity of the worker, his attractiveness to the employer, the quality of his job, and his personal attitudes toward work. As the proverb put it: "Give a man a fish, and you feed him for a day. Teach a man to fish, and you feed him for the rest of his life." Investments in humans, as in machinery, have a long-term payoff in increased productivity and wages. Supporters of manpower services have claimed that discounted future earning gains of participants in training programs exceed program costs by a significant margin, making the return on investments not only positive but comparable to other possible expenditures.

Positive Evidence

A number of studies, mostly in the 1960s, used this methodological framework to assess the effectiveness of institutional and on-the-job training, the basic building blocks of all manpower programs. There was a wide variation in the scope, timing, assumptions, and detailed findings of these studies, but their underlying message was essentially the same: training increased later earnings and the present value of projected gains exceeded costs. Put another way, the rate of return on the investment in human capital was positive and substantial.

Vocational training in schools, skill centers, and other institutions helped participants move into better jobs where they earned more and had greater stability of employment. There were nine major studies of institutional training under the Manpower Development and Training Act. When these were standardized by the use of the same projecting and discounting assumptions, the benefits to participants were found to exceed costs, with benefit/cost ratios ranging from 2 to 12 and all but three in the range between 2 and 3.[2] (A ratio less than 1 meant that the benefits were not equal to costs, while anything above this indicated a positive rate of return. For example, a ratio of 2 implied that the current value of future benefits was double the outlays.) When the estimated earnings foregone during training were added into costs, the rate of return was somewhat lower but still positive, ranging between 6 and 138 percent, according to the estimates of the individual studies.[3]

Training on the job is apparently even more effective than the classroom approach, since trainees can earn while learning and since they have greater incentive to stay where a job is assured at the end of training. Subsidies to private employers under the Manpower Development and Training Act cost half as much per enrollee and a third as much per completer as institutional training.[4] Completers of on-the-job training substantially increased earnings, yielding a high rate of return on the government's investment. Under standardized assumptions, the benefit/cost ratios for the five major studies of the Job Opportunities in the Business Sector program ranged from 1.5 to 4.3. The two for the MDTA–OJT program were 5.9 and 9.2.[5]

The Rebuttal

The consistently positive findings and the apparent rigorousness of the methodology were enough to convince policy makers in the heady days when manpower efforts were expanding exponentially that the investment paid off. However, as the price tag reached into the multibillion dollar level, and as the nation's resources became strained, more careful and critical reexaminations suggested that the proof of success was neither methodologically unimpeachable nor factually unequivocal.

While there had been a number of different studies of manpower programs, none was definitive in its approach or findings. Samples were limited in size and earnings data were frequently sketchy. Follow-up of enrollees was normally limited to a half a year or less, leaving the longer run uncertain. Benefit/cost estimates had to rest on long-range projections of short-term experiences. If participants encounter early transitional problems, the gains relative to controls might be expected to widen as trainees make better use of their newly acquired skills. But the benefits might also be lost if training is forgotten or the first jobs quickly left. If gains lasted only five years instead of the ten which was assumed in most benefit/cost studies, the human resource investment would not be profitable in many cases.[6]

Control groups were a common problem in the manpower studies. In the absence of control groups, studies simulated participant gains by assuming what would have happened in the absence of training. Where controls were used, match-ups were based on a few general variables. Since disadvantaged persons were being selected for training, controls usually tended to be better off. No-shows who were accepted but did not enroll matched up better, but they may have had different personal traits which deterred them from enrolling or perhaps more attractive options.

A basic question in all studies was how to calculate the benefits. The gains of participants might result from displacing other less skilled workers, reducing the net benefit to the disadvantaged. Those who enter training leave the labor force, and those who advance leave openings behind them; these vacuum effects help nonparticipants. Self-support is assumed to have a number of positive consequences and is certainly preferable to transfers, all else being equal. The indirect benefits from work might justifiably be added to the earnings gains.

Costs are also not as straightforward as they appear. Transfers and supportive services, such as health care, are major components of manpower programs. Allowances represented more than half the outlays under institutional training. Income transfer and health programs are presumed to justify their cost on the basis of the benefits they provide. It might make sense, therefore, to exclude allowances and supportive services when calculating the value of training. Foregone earnings are another uncertainty, since they are completely hypothesized.

All these issues have significant impact on the outcome of benefit/cost analysis. Ignoring displacement effects or projecting short-term gains over decades exaggerates the effectiveness of manpower services. Comparison with less disadvantaged controls or inclusion of income transfers as costs leads to an understatement. The net of all these considerations—whether studies as a rule understate or overstate effectiveness—is uncertain. While benefit/cost analyses usually operated on the most conservative assumptions and while almost all analyses demonstrated training to be worthwhile, the assumptions were crucially important and the proof was not as rigorous as it appeared.

More evidence of failure was needed to justify retrenchment. This was provided by a massive Manpower Administration evaluation, which examined the ten-year social security earning histories of 57,000 persons enrolled in manpower programs in 1964. This study was the most extensive and longest-term evaluation ever undertaken, and its intent was to provide a more definitive assessment of effectiveness.

The results were generally negative. Under the MDTA-institutional program, enrollees had average annual earnings $68 less than controls in the five years before training but $152 less in the succeeding five years. Black completers of both sexes and white female completers benefited relatively more than controls, but white male completers did not and all noncompleters lost ground. MDTA–OJT participants improved earnings $212 more than controls, but this did little to change their disadvantaged status, since they still averaged less than $2,400 annual earnings in the years after training. Under other manpower programs such as the Job Corps, participants also lost ground relative to controls over the long run.[7]

This study and its sobering conclusions were never officially released by the Manpower Administration, but the message quickly got through to decision makers. The negative findings were leaked to academic critics of the manpower programs and were quoted in the press by top economic officials proclaiming the failure of manpower efforts.

Further analysis, however, revealed major flaws in this study, which unknowingly preordained its negative findings. The control group was selected on the basis of age, race, sex, and patterns of earnings in the five years prior to training. Education attainment, a major determinant of labor market success, was not used because data were not available in the social security records. Without information on education, the control variables could not distinguish between a young black male college student and a high school dropout; both would have extremely low unsteady earnings in the base period, which would include the teen years. Subsequently, when the college student graduated and got a job his earnings would be higher than that of the trainee. The control sample containing the better educated would, over time, be expected to advance faster than the participants, who were selected for training on the basis of their educational handicaps. Further biasing the results, the average earnings of controls were higher in the base period, which would lead to a widening absolute differential even if both groups improved at the same rate and would explain why participants could lose ground in absolute terms even while gaining at a somewhat faster rate. Finally, the study did not include the year prior to training in the base period on the supposition that trainees were experiencing unusual transitional problems; because this was a year of low earnings for trainees, its exclusion tended to match them with a higher income cohort. In fact, when the Manpower Administration subsequently reanalyzed the MDTA-institutional data using 1959 to 1963 as the base rather than 1958 to 1962, it found that participants gained in both absolute and relative terms.[8]

The magnitude of the control group bias is suggested by another longitudinal study of MDTA using social security data (though admittedly of smaller scale and shorter duration) which compared 1968 enrollees with no-shows. Average earnings of male participants rose by $1,500, or two thirds more than that of no-shows. For females, the absolute and percentage relative gains were even greater for participants (Figure 7-1).

Weighing the Evidence

Extensive measurement and evaluation of the effectiveness of manpower training has not yielded any conclusive answers, but this is more reflection on the state of the art of measurement and evaluation than on the performance of manpower training. The evidence of success is extensive even if subject to reservations. A number of detailed and highly technical studies have used different methodologies to reach the same conclusion that training pays off for participants and society. Benefit/cost analysis has serious limi-

Figure 7–1. Annual average earnings of 1968 MDTA—institutional trainees and controls

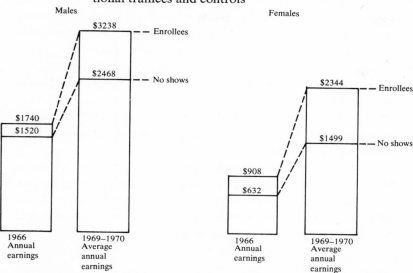

Source: Edward Prescott and T. F. Cooley, "Evaluating the Impact of MDTA Programs on Earnings under Varying Labor Market Conditions," Manpower Administration, U.S. Department of Labor, Mimeo, Table 1, 1971.

tations, and many of the issues raised by critics are telling; yet together they do not suggest and certainly do not prove that the separate studies were positively biased. Some considerations would lower benefits or raise costs, but others would have the opposite effect. The consistently positive findings of independent analyses remain a hopeful sign even though there are equivocations.

The proof of failure, on the other hand, was quite clearly biased. Disadvantaged participants were compared with nondisadvantaged controls and a widening gap between such groups would be expected with or without training. Parallel studies with better controls and reanalysis of the same data using realistic assumptions provided positive rather than negative evidence.

The failure of manpower training is supported by little more than the claim that we cannot be absolutely sure it is successful. The admissible evidence is positive and is more substantial than for most other governmental endeavors. A verdict of failure is, therefore, untenable.

Can the Future Be Changed?

The Job Corps, even more than other manpower programs, bears the stamp of the Great Society. Spawned by the Economic Opportunity Act of 1964, its aim was "total remediation"—removing hard-core youths from debilitating home environments and reshaping their behavior through concentrated education and vocational training combined with counseling, health care, and other services. As President Johnson put it, "One thousand dollars invested in salvaging an unemployed youth today can return forty thousand in his lifetime."

From the first publicity selling the Job Corps to the public, it became a symbol of the war on poverty and the punching bag for the Great Society's critics. Congressional investigations filled volumes and every untoward incident in Job Corps centers or neighboring communities was front page news.

Significant Benefits But Higher Costs

The central issue was the high cost of residential treatment. The annual cost per man-year during the first decade averaged about $9,000 or $4,600 per enrollee. Comparisons with the lesser cost of sending a youth to Harvard University did not apply, since few of the corpsmen—who averaged fifth grade level of educational achievement—were ready for the Ivy League. Nevertheless, there was little convincing evidence that the Job Corps worked according to the standards applied to other manpower programs—that the current dollar value of participant gains exceeded program costs by a significant margin.

A six-month follow-up of August 1966 terminees and a group of no-shows found corpsmen realizing an hourly wage gain of 14 cents. Projecting these gains over future work life, discounting them to the present, and comparing them to costs yielded benefit/cost ratios between 1.04 and 1.45 depending on the assumptions. Benefits could also be estimated by measuring the educational gains of the corpsmen and relating these to projected income by known education/earnings ratios. In 1967 the Job Corps claimed .9 years of achievement gain per enrollee, which yielded benefit/cost ratios between .79 and 1.22.[9]

In fact, the education gains of enrollees proved to be substantially less than the .9 grades claimed, while the earnings gains may have washed out over time. Six months after leaving the Job Corps, former trainees experienced a 27 percent reduction in unemployment but after eighteen months, their chances of joblessness were the same as for other disadvantaged youths.[10] Using the eighteen month data and comparing enrollees to dropouts rather than no-shows resulted in a dismal benefit/cost ratio between .2 and .4 for males and .3 and.6 for females.[11] While corpsmen did gain relative to controls, the estimated current value of these gains did not come close to equaling the costs.

These studies were prepared in the formative years of the Job Corps, and there is evidence of some improvements since. In the first half of fiscal 1969, 53 percent of terminees available for placement were employed upon termination; 5 percent went into the armed forces, and 6 percent returned to school. In fiscal 1973, when the national unemployment rate for 16- to 19-year olds was a third higher, placements were up to 58 percent, enlistments to 7 percent, and school returns to 20 percent. The educational achievement of corpsmen has also apparently increased. The .18 grade per month average in 1967 (which may have been exaggerated) was substantially less than the .26 average gain from April 1973 through March 1974.[12]

Recent data evidence further improvements. In fiscal 1974, two thirds of terminees were employed upon leaving the Job Corps, and more than a fifth returned to school or enlisted in the armed forces. Only one in twenty was available for and seeking placement but unable to find a job. This is an enviable record in dealing with such a disadvantaged group during a severe recession. Job Corps costs have also declined. Between 1967 and 1974, the total operating cost in men's urban centers dropped despite a 48 percent rise in the Consumer Price Index.[13] If the benefits remained constant in real terms, these economies would have doubled the benefit/cost ratio.

The fact remains, however, that the payoff of the Job Corps is still uncertain. The earlier studies suggested that the benefit/cost ratio was not significantly above unity and perhaps even less. Some rather heroic assumptions were required to demonstrate a positive rate of return on the Job Corps investment. In particular, transfer costs were subtracted. Most of the analyses of institutional training under the Manpower Development and Training Act did not use this method yet calculated rates of return which were substantially higher than those estimated for the Job Corps. While there are some indications of improved performance over the 1970s, there is no dependable proof that benefits significantly exceed costs.

Money Isn't Everything

Should the Job Corps be eliminated, or the resources transferred to other programs? If there are alternative, more successful or less costly methods of assisting the same clientele, the answer should clearly be positive. But it must be recognized that the Job Corps has focused on the most disadvantaged youths, who are less often served under other programs. It has not been demonstrated that any other approach can deal more effectively or economically with such clients as those in the Job Corps. Average performance comparisons are misleading.

An even more basic issue is whether social investments have to be profitable. Many of the benefits are noneconomic, or at least not quantifiable in dollars and cents. The Job Corps may have elements of a "consumption good." Like college, it may give the disadvantaged a chance to get away from home, to broaden horizons, and to mature. Seven of ten terminees rated the Job Corps facilities good or excellent. An equal proportion gave positive assessments of counseling. Two fifths found the vocational training very helpful and half gave high marks to basic education. Two thirds felt better prepared for marriage and child raising. A majority felt they learned more about the importance of school, of keeping oneself in shape, of staying out of trouble, and of getting along with the family. An overwhelming majority of relatives, friends, and employers perceived that corpsmen had changed for the better, becoming less trouble-prone, better able to get along with people, and more likely to make plans for the future.[14] What is the value of these attitudinal and behavioral changes?

Is an effort unwarranted if it only helps one or two in ten participants and if their future stream of extra earnings does not amortize the costs for all ten? Some may consider success of a small number worth the expense. Society will spend millions of dollars to rescue a trapped miner or to merely exhume his body, but demands cost efficiency in salvaging individuals trapped by their social and economic handicaps. In considering alternative capital investments, the only criterion is profit, but the effects on individuals are not so simple. An expenditure on college bound youths from upper income families might yield a higher return than an equal amount for Job Corps clients, but the needs of the latter group are certainly greater. Alternatively, some critics assert that if a benefit/cost ratio is less than one, an income transfer is preferable to training and other assistance. Yet it is doubtful that a cash payment of $4,600 would be of any long or even short-term benefit to the average 16 or 17 year old participant with a fifth or sixth grade education. The problem of the disadvantaged youth is not just current but future welfare, and it is more one of earnings than income.

Benefit/cost analysis is only one tool for assessing the worth of the Job Corps. While the human resource investment notion offered a justification for expanding manpower programs in the 1960s, it was a two-edged sword which tended to bias judgments against efforts for the hardest-core. The Job Corps may or may not be more profitable than other investments, but this is largely an irrelevant issue if the aim is to reach out to and improve opportunities for the most disadvantaged youths.

The Revenue Sharing Alternative

While the overall impact of manpower services was debatable, there was general agreement that effectiveness could be increased to yield more value for the money. The revenue sharing approach favored by the Nixon administration received bipartisan support. It promised to reduce the overlap, duplication, waste, and red tape resulting from so many federally funded programs. Consolidation of authority in the hands of local elected officials would permit better adaptation to local conditions, better integration with other governmental activities, and increased political accountability. Change itself could be constructive, sweeping away the cobwebs and providing an injection of local expertise.

The diehard supporters of the Great Society's centralized and categorized approach stressed the drawbacks of the revenue sharing alternative. Minorities, disproportionately served under federally run programs, would have less leverage at the local level;

manpower programs, which had been their "piece of the action," would be snatched away by local officials. The disadvantaged had received increasing priority in the 1960s, but given the propensity of program operators to cream among clients and given the limited political clout of the disadvantaged, decentralization could result in a shift in emphasis to those less in need. Local control could increase the leverage of vested interest groups and might reduce the emphasis on innovation and experimentation which blossomed under federal support. Finally, change could upset ongoing improvements in manpower programs, causing needless upheaval and dislocation.

Early experience with the Comprehensive Employment and Training Act of 1973 suggested that there was truth in the claims of both advocates and detractors of revenue sharing. CETA has resulted in some positive and some negative changes. Overall, the impact has been far less than revolutionary, demonstrating again the limits of reform and the difficulties of realizing ideal systems.

Under the old approach, with detailed federal guidelines and oversight, programs in different areas generally served similar clienteles in similar ways. CETA changed this pattern. Some capable local sponsors were able to take over programs, reorganizing ongoing programs to meet needs better, while reducing waste and duplication. There were others who did not establish their own efforts as previous delivery agents fought to maintain their control and administrative responsibilities. In some cases the politically stronger rather than the more effective delivery agents prevailed, adversely affecting the quality of services.

CETA required the appointment of broad-based local manpower planning councils to design programs, evaluate performance, and represent the community in decision making. While the councils usually did achieve balanced representation, those with the most to gain or lose—delivery agents and administrators—usually took charge, with community and client groups as well as business and labor representatives participating only nominally. In most areas elected officials had little to do with either planning or administration so the promised accountability was limited.

The focus of decision making shifted from delivery agents to beefed up local bureaucracies. Those hired by city and county governments tended to be college educated, many with specialized courses in manpower policy. This upgrading was useful. Yet the administrative staffs of delivery agents were pared, and since these positions had frequently been upward mobility routes for minorities and the less educated, the positive spillovers were reduced. Local community action agencies lost out as school systems, vocational educators, and other establishment institutions expanded their roles.

Perhaps most significant, there was reduced priority on the disadvantaged and members of minority groups. Previously stable workers forced into idleness by the recession fit within the definition of disadvantaged even though their handicaps were less severe than those of the traditional hard core. While minority group members continued to participate on a large scale, their proportion among all participants declined.

CETA did not radically alter the manpower system. With attention being focused on reorganization and on the implementation of emergency public employment programs to cope with massive joblessness, complete revamping of activities rarely occurred, and most sponsors continued the same manpower operations with the same deliverers as under direct federal funding.

Assessing success or failure is premature, as well as largely judgmental and dependent on the relative weight given to the varied developments. For instance, some may consider the shift away from the disadvantaged completely justified considering the severity of economic conditions, while others might view it as an abnegation of previous commitments. One lesson is clear, however. The potentials of revenue sharing were oversold, and the drawbacks of categorized programs were exaggerated in seeking reform. This left the lingering impression that manpower services are ineffective even though most available evidence supports the opposite conclusion.

8 Civil Rights Action

The Law of the Land

Economic, political, and social relations are built on legal foundations. The longstanding problems of minorities, the poor, and other disadvantaged groups are perpetuated and, in some cases, caused by the legal system. Property laws more often than not protect the haves against the have nots, and frequently become a tool for sustaining inequality. Legal action usually requires a great deal of resources, putting a price on justice. One of the major aims of the Great Society was to guarantee and secure the basic civil rights of all citizens. Through federal laws and administrative actions sustained and encouraged by Supreme Court decisions, efforts were intensified to achieve equality before the law for minorities, the poor, and other disenfranchised groups. The Great Society's civil rights record is probably its major achievement.

Legislative Landmarks

The record of successful civil rights legislation before the Great Society was almost nonexistent. In contrast, more was accomplished legislatively under Johnson's leadership than by any other President in the twentieth century. Until 1964 the only significant civil rights measures were the Civil Rights Acts of 1957 and 1960. The 1957 act proscribed attempts to inhibit persons from voting and authorized the attorney general to seek an injunction when an individual was deprived of, or about to be deprived of, his voting rights. The Civil Rights Act of 1960 strengthened the earlier law by authorizing the appointment of referees to supervise voting in cases where patterns of discrimination were revealed. Unfortunately these laws did not have much force because they relied on individual complaints and a drawn-out process of resolution. They were significant, however, in that they were only civil rights laws passed since Reconstruction.

When Johnson became President in November 1963 he moved vigorously to overcome discrimination in voter registration as well as voting, public accommodations, housing, employment, and education. The Civil Rights Act of 1964, initiated under John Kennedy, was the cornerstone. Title I barred unequal application of voter registration requirements and established a sixth grade education as a presumption of literacy. Titles II and III outlawed discrimination in public accommodations on the grounds of race, color, religion, or national origin. Titles IV and VI authorized the attorney general to file suits for desegregation of public schools and colleges and barred discrimination under any federally aided program. Finally, Title VII outlawed discrimination in employment and established a five-member Equal Employment Opportunity Commission (EEOC) to investigate complaints, seek voluntary compliance, and support plaintiffs in court. The attorney general was also authorized to file suit against patterns or practices of discrimination.

The next year the focus was voting rights. The Voting Rights Act of 1965 departed from the pattern of the 1957 and 1960 legislation by providing for direct federal action to enable blacks to register and vote, rather than relying on protracted individual legal suits. It gave the attorney general authority to supervise voter registration in areas where less than half of voting age minority residents were registered. Literacy tests were also barred in state and local elections (the twenty-fourth amendment to the constitution approved the previous year had already accomplished this in federal elections).

In President Johnson's last year in office, the administration achieved its final major goal in proscribing housing discrimination. Title VIII of the Civil Rights Act of 1968 prohibited discrimination on the basis of race, color, religion, or national origin in the sale, rental, advertising, or financing of housing. The Department of Housing and Urban Development was designated to establish investigative and conciliatory machinery to handle complaints. If no agreement could be reached, complainants were authorized to sue in federal court.

Subsequent civil rights legislation has been modest in comparison to the Great Society's record. The major landmark under Richard Nixon was the equal rights amendment of 1971 guaranteeing equality of the sexes, but this constitutional amendment had yet to be ratified by mid-1975. The Equal Employment Opportunity law was strengthened in 1972 but the administration could claim little credit. When the Johnson administration's 1968 proposal to give cease-and-desist powers to the EEOC was reintroduced the next year, President Nixon countered with a bill authorizing the commission to initiate suits in federal court. The Senate supported the first approach and the House the latter, so that a compromise was not reached until 1972. The Equal Employment Opportunity Act of that year authorized the EEOC to file suits on behalf of individuals or against patterns and practices of job discrimination. Back pay awards were also authorized, upping the potential cost of discrimination. Yet cease-and-desist powers, which might have had more widespread and immediate impact, were not granted.

The Courts

The legislatively defined civil rights had to be interpreted by the courts. The leadership of the Johnson administration in the area of civil rights was matched by the activism of the Supreme Court in its interpretations of the law. Because two branches of the government moved in the same direction, the rights of minorities and the poor were greatly expanded, the right of each citizen to an equal vote was obtained, and the rights of suspected criminals were protected.

These decisions drew strong opposition. Echoing attacks upon the Warren court, presidential candidate Richard Nixon declared in 1968, "We need a court which looks upon its function as being that of interpretation, rather than of breaking through into new areas." Upon election, he followed upon this declaration by seek-

ing the appointment of political and legal conservatives. To replace
the retiring Earl Warren, President Nixon selected Warren Burger,
a circuit court of appeals judge known for his strict construction
of the law. The liberal ranks were further weakened by the death
of two justices and resignation of another whose places were filled,
after much debate, by justices who the President claimed would
"interpret . . . not twist or bend the Constitution in order to
perpetuate personal political or social views."

The changing composition of the court was followed by new
rulings affecting civil rights. The famous Miranda decision of the
Warren Court, which protected the rights of criminal suspects, was
hedged. The court ruled that public accommodations could be
closed if they could not be feasibly integrated and the construction
of low-income housing could be made subject to approval by local
referendum. While the court did not retreat on school desegregation or equal employment opportunity, it avoided new initiatives.

Administration

In the exercise of executive authority, there were contrasts between the civil rights stance of the Johnson and subsequent administrations. This is perhaps best illustrated in education. The
initial HEW guidelines issued in April 1965 suggested that school
districts could desegregate either by the assignment of pupils on
the basis of geographic attendance zones or by allowing pupils and
their parents choice among a district's schools. A year later the
guidelines were revised setting targets to measure the effectiveness
of the desegregation plans, and to assure that the choices were in
fact free. Senator Richard B. Russell of Georgia led the southern
opposition claiming that "the administrators have abandoned any
pretense of the stated objective of the law at the time it passed, and
have undertaken to establish entirely new objectives in their administration of the act." Congress also challenged HEW's authority to cut off funds during the school year. But the 1968 revised
guidelines proscribed the freedom of choice approach and were for
the first time directed at northern as well as southern districts.

The Nixon administration aligned itself with the opponents of
these measures. In 1969 it announced that it would no longer
terminate federal funding to school districts violating the law but
would rely on the Department of Justice to initiate court action.

This change in policy was defended on the grounds that the disadvantaged were the ones hurt most by the loss of federal funds. But the NAACP Legal Defense Fund sued HEW in 1970 to force termination for noncompliance, and in 1973 this suit was upheld by the Supreme Court. The President also joined the opposition to busing and sought a moratorium. The Justice Department intervened on the side of antibusing forces in Detroit, Richmond, Nashville, Dallas, Oklahoma City, and Fort Worth.

The Nixon administration's fair housing record was modest. At the beginning of the 1970s the Secretary of the Housing and Urban Development spoke boldly of using full federal leverage to secure the adoption and implementation of fair housing plans, threatening the loss of housing subsidies and other grants. But the President backed away from this aggressive policy, declaring in 1971, "We will not seek to impose economic integration upon an existing local jurisdiction . . . This administration will not attempt to impose federally-assisted housing upon the community."[1]

There was also a marked contrast between the interventionism of the Great Society and the laissez-faire of the Nixon administration on voting rights. Eighty thousand blacks were registered by federal examiners within six months after the Voting Rights Act of 1965. President Johnson's Department of Justice kept a close watch on developments and moved aggressively. After 1971 no federal examiners were assigned to conduct registration though blacks were still under-registered in areas of the South.

There was less difference between the Great Society and the succeeding administration in their efforts to equalize employment opportunity. Presidents Nixon and Johnson both pushed to increase minority representation in federal employment. The Office of Federal Contract Compliance (OFCC), created in 1965 by executive order to police government contracts, remained relatively inactive under the Great Society. The Philadelphia plan requiring federal construction contractors to meet specific goals and timetables for the hiring of minorities was a Nixon administration innovation. When employment quotas became an issue, the President backed off and shifted emphasis to "hometown" plans. Still the administration must be credited for its initiative. While it resisted efforts to give the EEOC cease-and-desist powers, it bolstered enforcement activities, nearly quadrupling federal civil rights expenditures between fiscal 1970 and 1975.[2]

These legislative, judicial, and administrative developments are open to widely differing interpretations. Normative and philosophical judgments underlie all civil rights issues. Every advance has been bitterly opposed by some Americans, viewed with apprehension by many more, but considered inadequate by others. Court and administrative decisions translating general principles into specific prescriptions have been condemned both for moving too fast and for going too slow.

Overall the Great Society took a more active stance on civil rights than preceding and subsequent administrations. The paucity of civil rights initiatives in the following seven years was explained in part by the need to "flesh out" and apply the laws rather than to pass new ones. Despite the contrast, there was a continuity in civil rights developments. The 1960s were filled with drama: dogs attacking civil rights marchers, a proprietor blocking access to his chicken carry-out with an axe handle, a governor standing in the door of a southern university to keep out the first black student. The 1970s did not involve such overt discrimination. Efforts focused rather on overcoming systematic or institutional discrimination. The issue was not whether action should be taken to protect the rights of minorities but what tools should be used and how vigorously they should be applied.

The Civil Rights Record

The primary focus of the civil rights efforts of the last decade was to ameliorate the longstanding problems of minorities. These actions were important in improving the status of blacks.

Voting Rights

In 1960 only 29 percent of the nonwhite voting age population in Alabama, Arkansas, Georgia, Louisiana, Mississippi, North and South Carolina, Tennessee, Texas, and Virginia were registered, or less than half the percentage among whites. Largely as a result of the 1965 Voting Rights Act the number of registered blacks increased by half a million between 1964 and 1966 and more than doubled over the 1960s. By the beginning of the current decade, the 59 percent of nonwhites registered in the South approached the 65 percent registration among whites and the difference could largely be explained by demographic factors.

More black votes were the result. Where 44 percent of all southern blacks age 21 and over voted in the 1964 presidential election, 52 percent cast ballots in 1968.[3] In 1962 there were only 6 blacks in state legislatures in the South; by 1968 there were 53, and by 1974, 85.[4] While there may still be a few areas of the South where blacks are denied voting rights by government actions, this is no longer a pervasive phenomenon.

Equal Employment Opportunity

The efforts to equalize employment opportunity have steadily gained momentum. The Equal Employment Opportunity Commission was initially limited to information gathering, mediation, and friend-of-the-court legal support. The 1972 amendments extended the coverage and increased the leverage of the agency by granting it authority to file suits on behalf of individuals or groups. The courts also broadened the definition of discrimination and the employer's liability for such acts. In 1971 the Supreme Court ruled that practices which were fair in form, but discriminatory in operation, were illegal. Specifically, it outlawed pre-employment tests that were not job-related on the grounds that they were more likely to exclude blacks and other minorities. The court expanded this reasoning in proscribing the use of arrest records to screen employees. In another important 1971 decision the court established the principle of monetary relief in class action cases, raising the ante in civil rights litigation.

While the Nixon administration opposed granting the EEOC cease-and-desist powers, it did substantially beef up its staff. In fiscal 1971 the commission completed 7,320 investigations at a cost of $16 million. By fiscal 1975, 33,000 cases were handled at a cost of $55 million. The EEOC's staff of lawyers was increased more than fivefold in 1973 in order to utilize its newly legislated authority. In a landmark case, the American Telephone and Telegraph Company signed a consent decree in 1973 involving $15 million in restitution and back pay for several classes of female employees and a $23 million promotion package for women and minorities. This agreement was the first shot in a stepped-up campaign that resulted in a number of large settlements.

Another approach was to use the substantial market leverage of the government. The Office of Federal Contract Compliance (OFCC) since 1970 has required all federal contractors to establish affirmative action goals and timetables. The major action was in the area of construction. In 1969 the Department of Labor issued the Philadelphia plan requiring construction contractors in that city to increase the proportion of minority craftsmen from 2 percent up to 4 to 9 percent in the first year and 19 to 26 percent by the fourth year. The Supreme Court approved this approach and similar plans were implemented in a number of cities. Rarely did these achieve targeted employment goals but they apparently increased minority hiring at union wage levels.

Despite reluctance to use its full powers, OFCC pressure had an effect on employment. Between 1966 and 1970 firms with government contracts increased their employment of black males by 3.3 percent more than those not doing business with the federal government. Government contractors with no black employees in 1966 were 10 percent more likely by 1970 to have hired at least one black male. Overall the wage share of black workers in the average firm with government contracts increased by 28 percent between 1966 and 1970, compared with 25 percent in the other firms.[5] Additional studies have suggested even greater gains, especially for black females.[6]

Integrating the Schools

The government, spearheaded by the Supreme Court, has played an increasingly active role in pursuing equality of education. Building on the 1954 decision against separate but equal school systems, the court declared in 1964 that there had been "entirely too much deliberation and not enough speed" and forbade school closings and other measures states used to avoid integration. In 1967 the court ordered Alabama to desegregate its schools and the next year ruled against freedom of choice plans. A highly controversial 1971 decision upheld the use of busing, numerical ratios, and gerrymandering of districts as temporary measures to achieve integration where school systems had failed to end segregation by other methods. The court proved more reluctant when school financing was concerned, refusing to strike down property taxes even though they frequently resulted in the underfunding of schools in poverty areas.

At first, the task of enforcing the Supreme Court's decisions fell entirely to plaintiffs in lower courts. The federal government intervened occasionally during the Kennedy administration as a friend of the court or (using the authority of the Civil Rights Acts of 1957 and 1960) by threatening to deny funds to school districts entitled to receive federal aid because enrollment in their schools was affected by federal installations. But these efforts achieved very slow progress. In 1964, 89 percent of all black children in southern and border states still attended all black schools.

The responsibility for enforcement shifted more directly to federal shoulders with the passage of the 1964 Civil Rights Act. Title IV provided for assistance to help school districts desegregate and authorized the attorney general to sue to obtain compliance, while Title VI authorized a cutoff of federal funds to any program guilty of racial discrimination. Through fiscal 1969 the funds of 129 school districts had been cut off at least temporarily. The new administration elected to shift its enforcement efforts entirely to court action until the Supreme Court forced a return to the practice of terminating funds for noncomplying schools.

Despite the changes in policy, progress in achieving desegregation continued during the late 1960s and early 1970s. The percentage of blacks in majority black schools dropped from 77 percent in 1968 to 63 percent in 1972. The proportion in all black schools declined from 40 to 11 percent nationwide and from 61 to 12 percent in the South.

With white flight from central cities, *de facto* rather than *de jure* segregation became the problem. In thirteen of the fourteen cities with the largest number of black people, 90 percent or more of black children were in schools where black students constituted a majority in 1971. The only available tool to overcome such isolation was busing; and though more than two fifths of all elementary and secondary students were already traveling to school on a bus, the idea of busing to equalize racial imbalances set off strong, sometimes violent, opposition. A Gallup Poll in 1971 found 77 percent of respondents opposed to this kind of busing. Although congressional busing foes were not able to command majorities in

1968, the balance shifted during 1970 and 1971 until an anti-busing law was passed as an amendment to the 1972 Higher Education Act. The compromise measure prohibited the implementation of court-ordered busing to achieve racial balance until all judicial appeals had been exhausted, but the Supreme Court quickly reaffirmed its support.

The benefits of integrated schools are still much debated, and the many opponents of busing would claim that the payoff to better racial balance is not worth the trouble of uprooting students. Others have argued that the integration of cental city school districts has hastened white flight and intensified *de facto* segregation. There is evidence from the Coleman report and studies in some desegregating school districts that minority educational achievement can be improved by better racial balance; but it is entirely judgmental whether these improvements warrant the expense and dislocations involved in busing. In a more recent study James S. Coleman concluded that in the 20 largest cities induced integration brought about by court action was self-defeating because whites moved from the affected areas or placed their children in private schools. In smaller cities, he estimated that school desegregation seemed to have less impact on white outmigration. On balance, Coleman concluded that courts are not suitable "instruments for carrying out a very sensitive activity like integrating schools."[7]

Suffice it to say that busing has had at least a significant temporary impact on many large cities, especially those in the South. A survey comparing school integration in 1967 and 1972 found that when cities are rated on a scale from 0 for total segregation to 100 for complete racial balance, that there have been marked improvements in some cities, such as Charlotte, Denver, Jacksonville, Oklahoma City, and San Francisco, though in the largest urban centers, such as New York, Los Angeles, and Chicago, the school integration efforts have been offset by other factors[8] (Table 8-1). It is doubtful that progress would have been so substantial in some areas and possible that segregation in the largest cities might have increased even more in the absence of government pressure.

The Losing Battle

A national survey in June 1967 revealed that 63 percent of whites were opposed to any law forbidding discrimination in hous-

Table 8-1. Index of school integration[a]

City	1967	1972	City	1967	1972
Atlanta	5	19	Jacksonville	8	78
Boston	26	30	Los Angeles	11	13
Charlotte	23	87	New York	48	46
Chicago	8	7	Oklahoma City	3	75
Dallas	8	11	Philadelphia	24	19
Denver	18	42	San Francisco	33	80
Detroit	21	22	Tampa	12	85
Indianapolis	15	19			

Source: Newsweek, September 8, 1975.
[a] 0 = total segregation; 100 = total integration.

ing.[9] Most Americans believe that they should have the right to congregate in areas with compatible neighbors and that an owner should be able to sell or rent his home to whomever he pleases. Yet a 1968 national survey also found almost two of every three persons agreed that blacks should have equal housing opportunities. This public support of fair housing in principle but not in practice has been reflected in congressional and administrative action.

While court interpretations have been supportive of the 1968 fair housing law, ordering the dispersion of low-income housing and an end to discriminatory zoning restrictions, the Department of Housing and Urban Development has taken only marginal steps to implement these decisions. It established machinery to handle individual fair housing complaints. It has publicized that "unfair housing is not only unfair—it's illegal," and required fair housing posters in all real estate and rental offices and in model homes. Properties financed with government loans or guarantees were also required to meet affirmative marketing regulations insuring that sales and rentals would be advertised in the minority community. However, the government has refused to use the leverage of grants to eliminate exclusionary practices in many areas, or to move aggressively against discriminatory private practices.

Housing discrimination is harder to combat than either employment or educational discrimination because the decision makers are the millions of sellers and renters of individual units. A real estate broker may work aggressively for a white customer but may move more slowly for a black buyer in a white neighborhood. The seller may have two or three contract offers and choose a white client even when there is no economic justification for his choice. Bank lenders may be more demanding in assessing the financial dependability of black buyers and such discrimination is difficult to prove.

Yet given firm commitment, much more could be accomplished. Subsidized housing programs could be used as a tool for economic and racial integration, especially if combined with affirmative action requirements under community aid programs. Apartment complexes and large housing projects could be sued on the basis of patterns of discrimination just as employers are. Minority quotas could be established for lending institutions. Such actions might not reverse the trend toward residential segregation, but they could improve conditons.

Poverty and the Law

The poor are crucially affected by governmental policies and dependent on the government's protection. Concentrated in ghettos, barrios, reservations, or isolated rural areas outside the economic mainstream, they are preyed upon by usurious merchants, they are sold shoddy products, and they are frequently the victims of consumer frauds. Living on credit and with uncertain income, they are constantly harassed by bill collectors and the threat of garnishment. Dependent on government support, they have little leverage to challenge the decisions of faceless bureaucracies.

The Government Giveth and the Government Taketh Away

The idea that participants in government social welfare programs should have legal claims on benefits, much less any voice in decision making, did not emerge until the middle 1960s. As late as 1966 the prevailing legal view was, according to one court decision, "Payments of relief funds are grants and gratuities. Their disbursement does not constitute payment of legal obligations that the government owes. Being absolutely discretionary, there is no judicial review of the manner in which that is exercised."[10]

One aim of the war on poverty was to assure due process and equal protection under government social welfare programs by requiring that eligibility and benefit level criteria be related to need and by restricting procedures making the recipient subject to the whim of administrative agents. Due process litigation focused on decision-making procedures, that is, whether clients were given proper consideration, notification, and opportunity to respond. Equal protection litigation was more concerned with the results of these decisions, that is, whether clients were being treated fairly.

The principle of due process became firmly established. The Supreme Court affirmed that tenants of federally assisted housing projects were entitled to reasonable voice and a fair hearing before they could be evicted. It ruled that welfare payments could not be garnisheed without a hearing and that unemployment benefits could not be withheld during employer appeals. Most important as a precedent was a 1970 Supreme Court decision that explicitly disclaimed the notion that welfare is a gratuity and therefore outside the jurisdiction of the courts:

> Public assistance is not mere charity, but a means "to promote the general welfare, and secure the Blessings of Liberty to ourselves and our Posterity." The same governmental interests that counsel the provision of welfare, counsel as well its uninterrupted provision to those eligible to receive it; pretermination evidentiary hearings are indispensable to that end.[11]

Advances were also made in the area of equal protection. Supreme Court decisions in 1968 and 1970 overturned the man-in-the-house rules in effect in many states, declaring that a male resident could not be held responsible for support of an AFDC family unless he was the father of the children. Residency requirements were overturned in 1969 on the grounds that they restricted the rights of interstate mobility and denied aid to families with exactly the same needs as resident recipients.

However, the court resisted attempts to use the equal protection clause as a lever to raise benefits for particular groups or to demand an adequate level of support as a right. In an important 1970 decision which has served as a precedent for several subsequent rulings, it affirmed the states' fundamental right to set and change welfare standards:

> In the area of economics and social welfare, a state does not violate the Equal Protection Clause merely because the classifications made by its laws are imperfect. If the classification has some "reasonable basis," it does not offend the Constitution simply because the classification "is not made with mathematical nicety or because in practice it results in some inequality. . . ."[12]

The effects of these legal interpretations are difficult to isolate. The decisions overturning the man-in-the-house and residency requirements contributed to the growth of welfare rolls in the late 1960s and early 1970s, but the expansion of due process had a more indirect effect. There is no way to know how many social welfare beneficiaries would have had their benefits cut off or reduced capriciously or would have lost out in the absence of pretermination evidentiary hearings. The tide of legal interpretations may have contributed to the rapidly rising acceptance rates of welfare applications in the late 1960s.

Legal Representation for the Poor

These court decisions were based on suits filed by or on behalf of the poor; they involved millions of dollars of legal work and the commitment of many lawyers. Without legal resources, little progress would have been possible.

The Neighborhood Legal Services program was a major factor in the poverty law movement. The Economic Opportunity Act provided funds to community action agencies and to legal aid societies, which hired 2,000 lawyers in 800 neighborhood law offices. The antipoverty lawyers provided traditional legal assistance in establishing or asserting clearly defined rights, but also offered legal analysis and representation directed toward reform of the law through class action suits. Traditional assistance offered by legal aid societies helped alleviate the immediate problems of the poor but tended to swamp poverty lawyers with insurmountable caseloads. Test case litigation and class action suits were more glamorous and had broader implications, though they also generated political problems.

The initial priority of the Neighborhood Legal Services program was law reform. The first national director argued, "We cannot be content with the creation of systems rendering free assistance . . . Lawyers must uncover the legal causes of poverty and design new social, legal and political tools and vehicles to move poor people from deprivation, depression and despair to opportunity, hope and ambition."[13]

These reform efforts generated a furor. California Rural Legal Assistance (CRLA) brought a number of suits, preventing the state from implementing certain restrictions under Medicaid, petitioning the Food and Drug Administration to ban the use of DDT, and pressing the workmen's compensation claims of persons injured by pesticides. Such activities drew opposition from powerful interests and led to attempts to give governors veto power over legal services activities. Vice President Spiro Agnew voiced the administration's position:

> What we have is the federal government funding a program designed to effectuate major political changes. What we may be on the way to creating is a federally-funded system manned by ideological vigilantes who owe their allegiance not to a client, not to the citizens of a particular state or locality, and not to elected representatives of the people, but only to a concept of social reform.[14]

The Nixon administration wanted to replace the Neighborhood Legal Services program with a national corporation which would make grants and enter into contracts to support noncriminal legal services for the poor. The implicit aim was to move the effort out of the community action framework and into more reputable and responsible hands. This change was effectuated in 1973 when a federal legal services corporation was authorized to make grants to law firms, individuals, and community action agencies and also state and local governments. Lawyers could not engage in demonstrations, picketing, boycotts, strikes, lobbying, or political activities. Class action suits could only be undertaken with the express approval of the project directors, and no grantee could use more than half its resources on such cases. Antipoverty lawyers were thus restricted from organizing the poor to represent their own interests and from pursuing legal reform for its own sake.

Debate over contrasting philosophies and approaches should not detract from the successes of the Neighborhood Legal Services program. There is no question that it substantially increased legal representation for the poor. Nearly two fifths of the caseload dealt with marital and family matters, another fifth with juvenile and civil offenses, and an equal proportion with sales contracts, garnishment, and bankruptcy. Only one in eight cases dealt with state and local welfare, income support, or housing—cases likely to challenge actions of government agencies. The normally critical General Accounting Office gave its stamp of approval in 1971 concluding that "the program grantees provided the poor with the same scope of civil representation that was available to persons able to afford private attorneys."[15]

Antipoverty lawyers also represented the poor in administrative rule setting. Procedures have been implemented in recent years to allow prior comment on regulations and to consider suggestions from interested parties before making final decisions. This practice has proved useful for well-heeled interest groups with legal representatives keeping an eye on regulatory developments, but the poor were generally left out because of their ignorance and lack of spokesmen. Permanent legal services projects magnified the voice of the poor in these processes.

Law reform was a secondary but very important activity. Most cases were not abstract legal actions but efforts to secure for the disadvantaged the basic rights available to the more affluent. The plaintiffs faced real problems with government agencies, landlords, bill collectors, and other institutions. And the batting average of legal service projects was high. For instance, the California Rural Legal Assistance was the focus of so much opposition because it succeeded in court and not because it failed. It only went to court in 5 percent of the cases in which it was involved, and through 1969 had won nine tenths of these suits.[16] Most other projects had equally high success rates, and the claim that legal service lawyers engaged in ill-considered legal actions or undertook them for purposes of harassment is not supported by the evidence. If the courts are accepted as the final arbitrator of the law, then legal services for the poor have been most successful.

A Continuing Quest

Civil rights laws, court interpretations, and governmental actions markedly altered the status of minorities and the poor. Blacks gained access to almost all public accommodations within the course of just fifteen years. Black voter registration in the South increased significantly, resulting in political gains. *De jure* school segregation was largely eliminated, and the number of blacks going to racially mixed schools increased significantly. There is statistical evidence of reduced labor market discrimination against minorities as well as some documentation of the gains resulting from the affirmative action efforts by EEOC and OFCC. Supreme Court decisions which overturned rules and procedures used to keep poor people off relief contributed to the growth of welfare.

The concept of civil rights has been expanded. Until the 1960s, a beneficiary of government aid had no legal basis to question how it was given or taken away; by the 1970s the fundamental guarantee of due process was an established principle. Free choice in the selection of schools was initially considered enough to assure equal opportunity; eventually, equality came to be defined in terms of results. Rights in the job market increased from the right to equal treatment at the hiring door to the right to compensatory treatment implicit in affirmative action plans.

New tools to achieve compliance paralleled this redefinition of rights. Class action suits with damage penalties replaced individual cases and ad hoc conciliation. The courts have supported busing to overcome educational segregation, affirmative action and quotas to fight labor market discrimination, and metropolitan-wide fair housing plans to correct residential segregation.

Limits of the Law

Despite these positive developments, the experience of the last fifteen years has also demonstrated the limits of the law. The nation was willing to pass a fair housing law, consistent with the majority belief that minorities should have equal access; however, policy makers have been realistically leery of pushing enforcement, consistent with the even firmer public belief that a man's home is his castle. When efforts toward equal education resulted in busing and attacks on *de facto* segregation, which affected large numbers of the population, opposition mounted. Laws are not likely to be actively or effectively enforced where they are opposed by a majority.

It is also inherently easier to correct some problems than others. Discrimination in voting rights and in the use of public accommodations could be eliminated because the problems could be easily identified and the offenders recognized. In employment and education, it was possible to exert pressure on large employers and school systems having responsibility for decision making within their domains. In the housing market, however, where millions of individual decision makers were involved, corrective action was difficult to achieve.

Finally, efforts to combat employment discrimination were effective as long as blacks were needed in a tight labor market. Similar attempts to end housing discrimination had to contend with the massive exodus of whites from central cities and the uncertainty and fear related to the polarizaton process.

Unfinished Business

While the dramatic and sweeping legislative actions of the 1960s accomplished much, important tasks remain to be completed, and in many cases the payoff of past legislation has yet to be realized.

It took a decade to establish the procedures for effectively attacking labor market discrimination. In the early 1970s these were applied in only a few cases, but in these instances they were markedly successful for minorities and women. Future commitment will determine whether such efforts are broadened. There also remain a number of issues which need to be resolved in the courts and in the law. For example, seniority, a foundation of our industrial relations system, has been challenged as perpetuating past discrimination. (A ruling upsetting seniority practices would have massive repercussions.)

Progress in integrating schools slowed in the middle 1970s and proponents struggled to hold the line. Busing, though implemented successfully in many areas, remains the center of controversy. In the face of accelerating white flight, the crucial issue is whether metropolitan-wide busing will be required. School financing is another critical issue. If busing is deemphasized or has no meaning in city school systems that are now virtually black, changes in financing will be necessary to assure that "separate" schools are "equal" schools.

In housing much could be done by more vigorous enforcement of existing laws. More leverage could be exercised under expanded housing assistance programs. Patterns and practices of housing discrimination might be more actively prosecuted as they are in cases involving employment.

The effort to establish welfare as a right under the equal protection clause has also stalled. Given the broad geographic diversity in the welfare system, the cost of correcting all the inequities would have been staggering and would have required major intervention by the courts. With aid becoming more comprehensive and with the federal role increasing, judicial reexamination may be required. If the equal protection doctrine were applied, the poor would have a much greater voice in welfare reform, since they could exert leverage through the courts.

The civil rights progress of the 1960s and 1970s has led to substantial improvements, but much remains to be done. There are forces in our society which tend to nurture inequality and erode the equal protection of the law. The quest for equality must be constant.

9 Community Organization

The Community Action Concept

A fundamental concept of the Great Society was community participation in decisions concerning the level, mix, and delivery of public services. The Economic Opportunity Act of 1964 provided that projects were to be "developed, conducted, and administered with the maximum feasible participation of the residents of the areas and the members of groups served." Unlike other federal grants-in-aid dealing primarily with state and local government, the Community Action Program (CAP) contracted directly with nongovernmental community-based groups with the authority to develop and implement local antipoverty efforts as well as to administer national poverty programs. Residents of poverty areas and poor persons were to be represented on the boards of these community action agencies (CAAs). The model cities program, begun in 1966, established community-based model demonstration agencies (MDAs) to concentrate and coordinate urban development efforts in poverty areas.

A variety of community-based service institutions evolved under the umbrella of model cities and community action. Antipoverty, welfare, housing, manpower, and other funds were used to establish neighborhood health centers, community development corporations, cooperatives, and manpower centers. These community-based groups shared the goals of developing new approaches and service mixes challenging the establishment, in order to improve services and concentrate resources on persons most in need.

Not surprisingly, these efforts to change institutions alarmed some interest groups. Advocacy of client needs was frequently perceived as disruptive and innovation was criticized as wasteful. One erstwhile supporter explained that the efforts of community-based organizations had resulted in "maximum feasible misunderstanding." It is possible, however, that misunderstanding was less a product of community action's failure than a reflection of the complexity of building new, multipurpose institutions.

Community-based organizations took many forms. Some were democratically elected, while others were dominated by activists. A few were run by city halls or other establishment institutions. They included profit and nonprofit corporations, bureaucratic agencies with advisory committees of community representatives, and ad hoc groups organized around specific issues. Some concentrated on planning, organization and confrontation, others on service delivery. Given this diversity, generalizations are difficult and can be misleading. Advocacy and institutional change conflicted with smooth service delivery; planners and innovators had to choose between activism and bureaucratization. Furthermore community participation was a process that could not be judged by tangible products alone. Individuals and groups tend to have greater security and satisfaction when they have the power to control their lives. Innovation, organization, and representation have long-run payoffs which are difficult to measure.

The Umbrellas: CAP and Model Cities

The Community Action Program encompassed a wide range of activities. The initial idea was to distribute federal monies to local organizations, letting them decide how to spend it. But early in the game the federal government got into the act, earmarking funds for national emphasis programs. In fiscal 1965 more than two fifths of CAP allocations were used for Head Start. By 1971 the federal government earmarked almost four fifths of outlays for Head Start, health and family planning, legal services, and other national emphasis activities.

Early education was the primary activity of community action agencies (Table 9-1). Social services accounted for another very significant segment, mostly relating to the establishment and support of some 2,500 neighborhood service centers in poverty areas.[1] Job training was of lesser importance, followed by health, housing, and legal services. Less than a tenth of funds were used for community organization and 14 percent for coordination and support of community groups and training of local leaders.

An equally broad range of activities was undertaken by model cities. Education was again a major component, but urban renewal and housing together accounted for about a third of the funds. Citizen participation efforts received less than 1 percent of model cities budgets (Figure 9-1).

Within these broad functional categories there is an even more diverse range of activities. Community based groups provided home care for the aged, funded community service workers to improve relationships between the police and the community, established experimental drug treatment programs, funded day

Table 9-1. Elements of community action programs in 51 cities, 1969

Program	Percent of funds available
Services	78.1
Educational	28.6
Social services	25.4
Job training	12.8
Health services	5.7
Housing	2.5
Legal services and delinquency	3.2
Community organization	8.4
Organization for program involvement	3.7
Organization in neighborhood centers	3.0
Settlement house organization	1.7
Other community action	13.5
Use of indigenous staff	5.7
Use of indigenous community groups	3.0
Training of local leaders	2.5
All other	2.5

Source: Kenneth Clark and Jeannette Hopkins, *A Relevant War Against Poverty* (New York: Harper & Row, 1969), pp. 64–65.

Figure 9–1. Share of model cities funds going to various activities, 1971

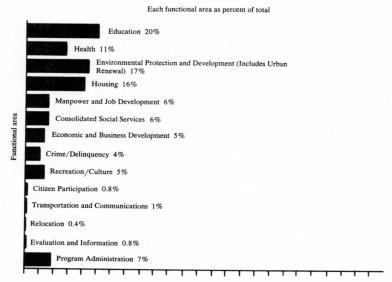

Each functional area as percent of total

Source: Model Cities: A Report on Progress, Model Cities Service Center (Washington: Government Printing Office, 1971), pp. 41–76.

care centers in poverty neighborhoods, developed business sites in urban and rural areas, restored houses, supported adult and continuing education and street academies, established neighborhood health centers, supported tenant organizations, worked to enforce housing codes, sponsored local arts programs and other recreation activities, and trained and placed the disadvantaged.

Aggregate Effect

There is no way to determine whether the mix of services was most appropriate for each area, or whether the services were delivered efficiently. The same is true of most governmental endeavors. Because established agencies minimize controversy, are run by a set of articulated rules, and keep their books in order, they are (often wrongly) assumed to be operating efficiently. Evaluations of community-based groups assumed that confrontation, sloppy bookkeeping and loose personnel policies were *prima facie* evidence of ineffectiveness.

There is no doubt, however, that most of the services provided by community organizations were sought by the clients. Many activities and approaches they introduced have since been provided by establishment agencies or received support from other sources. One survey of 591 CAAs found that between 1965 and 1973 they received $200 million from federal agencies other than OEO and $750 million from other sources, including $200 million from local governments and $285 million from states.[2] These outside resources increased over time suggesting a recognition by state and local governments that CAAs were filling useful purposes.

Community organizations were innovative. There was extensive experimentation with paraprofessionals in education, child care, health, and social services. The one-stop neighborhood service, manpower and health centers were all attempts to establish decentralized and comprehensive service institutions. There were scattered experiments with housing allowances, prepaid health care for low-income families, continuing education, supplemental transportation systems, and many other approaches.

Most important, the CAA and model cities activities had high "target efficiencies" and many valuable spillovers. Services were focused on the poor and near poor, or restricted to poverty neighborhoods and their residents. Minorities received a large share of the benefits, with blacks representing 56 percent of enrollees in the Concentrated Employment Program, 55 percent in the Neighborhood Youth Corps, and half under Head Start. If employment services, schools, or other established agencies had initiated similar operations, it is doubtful that minorities and the poor would have fared as well. Delivery of services with at least nominal participation of recipients had other payoffs. Community action and model cities agencies employed as many as a hundred thousand nonprofessionals (most of whom were disadvantaged) as social workers, counselors, day care aides, and outreach workers. Poverty area residents also filled many of the professional slots.

Representing the Poor

Community participation and control had intrinsic benefits in addition to their tangible impact on services and resource allocations. Community action started out on the defensive. A few CAAs were captured by militants and became involved in radical activities. With a background of riots and civil unrest, this radical stereotype became implanted in the public mind. Yet community action was hardly revolutionary. A study of 51 urban CAAs in 1968 found that "despite the designation of community action, programs seem to be functioning primarily in terms of services."[3] A Senate study of CAPs in 35 communities concluded that

> . . . except in a very small number of communities the Community Action Program does not involve a predominant commitment to the strategy of giving power to the poor, of deliberate confrontation with established powers, of purposefully created conflict. This is a stereotype placed on CAP in its early days by a few articulate advocates of this approach and echoed ever since by journalists who have not examined what is actually going on.[4]

Another study of 20 agencies, which broke down activities into 350 elements found that only 3 percent were exclusively related to the political strategy.[5] Any radical inclinations were further constrained by the 1967 amendments to the Economic Opportunity Act, which gave mayors and county officials authority to take control over community action agencies.

Community participation was limited under model cities in order to avoid the early confrontations experienced with CAP. The law called for "widespread citizen participation" rather than "maximum feasible participation" and placed local agencies under the authority of elected local officials. Rather than quick results for model cities, there was a lengthy planning period and it tempered precipitous action on the part of community-based organizations. The influence of poverty area representatives was also diluted in the 1970s when "planned variations" were initiated in many cities, expanding the target area to include the entire jurisdiction.

Given these constraints, the extent and impact of community participation under CAP and model cities was limited. OEO regulations required that one third of CAA board members be target area representatives, but frequently they were the elite from the poor neighborhoods. In March 1968 two thirds of board representatives were white, seven tenths managers and professionals, and almost two thirds college graduates.[6] Poverty area representatives were usually either appointed or elected on the basis of a very small plurality of all residents.

Yet activism and community participation must be distinguished from community representation. Even if the poor did not control decisions, the mission of community-based organizations was clearly to serve the needs of poverty areas and their residents. This was possible even though the boards were not dominated by low-income representatives. The crucial question is whether the agencies were responsive to the needs of the poor and effective in meeting their needs.

Not surprisingly, with over a thousand CAAs, there was widely varying success. An analysis of Seattle's CAA concluded that the "attempt to develop local neighborhood self-improvement associations through the efforts of an indigenous community organizer was a failure."[7] Conversely, a study of the Baltimore agency concluded that "federal programs and federal funds have been the main means, directly and indirectly, by which the black poor have gained a foothold in Baltimore's political system."[8] A study of public welfare systems found that the Great Society's community-based agencies were important in opening welfare programs to the poor.[9] An analysis of five California CAPs concluded that "they demonstrated some ability to bring about minor adjustments and modifications in environmental conditions, but very few groups made the transition from a concern with social services to a more political involvement."[10] A broader analysis of CAAs in 50 cities concluded that "changes directly credited to CAP have tended to be auxiliary in nature . . . These changes may be meaningful first steps toward a basic reordering of these institutions to provide more substantial satisfaction to the needs of the poor, but cannot be interpreted as a commitment to follow such an evolutionary course."[11] On the other hand, a parallel study of the same data stated, "Cities in which the CAA emphasizes organizational goals are much more likely to be undergoing institutional changes than are cities in which the CAA emphasizes service goals."[12] An internal analysis by the Office of Economic Opportunity documented the CAAs' success in increasing the involvement of the poor in decision making through participation in program planning, development, and operations. Changes were made in the employment practices of state and local governments and of private employers, while government services were made more accessible as a result of CAA activities.[13]

Finally, a study of model cities programs in eight areas concluded that despite underfunding, red tape, and a wide variation in the degree of citizen participation, "The model cities program has been the single most effective instrument to give the broadest range of services to disadvantaged areas and to improve local government operations."[14]

It appears, then, that while participation and control by the poor was limited, the leverage of a continuing interest group speaking for the otherwise deprived and disenfranchised did change the way state and local governments and other institutions treated these individuals in a number of areas. Some criticize model cities and CAAs for failing to mold the poor into a viable political force, while others insist that agencies should not engage in any activities other than service delivery and that the "maximum feasible participation" of program clients should be minimized. Controversy over the activities of community-based agencies continues, but the evidence is persuasive that they were relatively effective in serving the needs of the poor.

Service Delivery by Community-Based Organizations

A variety of community-based service institutions evolved under the umbrella of model cities and CAP. Neighborhood health centers were established to increase the access of the poor to comprehensive health care. Various forms of community development corporations and cooperatives were initiated to develop businesses, to support minority entrepreneurship, and to raise the incomes of poverty area residents. The Concentrated Employment Program (CEP) funded manpower training, placement, and other services for target area residents, usually through established CAAs. These more focused community-based efforts can be compared with other traditional approaches to the same ends, yielding a more detailed view of the effects of community participation.

Neighborhood Health Centers

In the middle 1960s the health crisis was not perceived as one of rising costs, but of inadequate or nonexistent care for large segments of the population. Because of the flight of middle- and upper-income families from core city areas, there was a dramatic decline in the number of physicians in poor neighborhoods across the country. Residents in these areas had to rely more on hospital emergency rooms, a costly and inefficient delivery system discouraging preventive care. Furthermore, inner city hospital systems declined in quality as their clientele and patrons changed.

New approaches were needed to increase health resources in low-income neighborhoods. The initial success of demonstration neighborhood health centers led to an amendment to the Economic Opportunity Act earmarking funds for the "development and implementation of comprehensive health service programs focused upon the needs of persons residing in urban or rural areas having high concentrations of poverty and a marked inadequacy of health services." About 100 were initiated by 1971. Health center advocates urged their extension to serve all eligible patients in a network of some 500 to 600 centers.[15]

As with other poverty efforts, mounting criticism accompanied growth. Some centers experienced internal conflicts pitting medical personnel against community representatives. Horror stories of high costs and inadequate service were circulated. Yet such criticism ignored a great deal of positive evidence that neighborhood health centers were providing more accessible care at no more cost and at no less quality than other suppliers.

1. *Cost.* A detailed study of costs in six centers with several years of operating experience found that a cost per visit for primary clinical medical care in 1970 was comparable to the average payment under Medicaid. The cost of a physician encounter was the same as under the two largest group health plans, while the medical service encounter cost was lower because of the more extensive use of paraprofessionals and technicians to treat neighborhood center patients.[16]

2. *Quality.* Neighborhood health centers provided more than adequate care. A 1971 study compared the treatment records of patients in OEO health centers, medical school-affiliated outpatient departments, and group practices. Medical and pediatric care in neighborhood health centers was more complete than that in both hospital outpatient departments and private group practices, while obstetric care was about the same. Health centers did much better in giving routine laboratory tests and physical exami-

nations, taking histories, and completing assessments quickly after initial contact.[17]

The consumers also preferred the care offered in neighborhood health centers. At the Columbia Point center in Boston 63 percent of registrants claimed they would still use the health centers if all sources of care were free, compared with only 20 percent preferring a private doctor and 13 percent a hospital. Three fifths of users of the Rochester neighborhood health center rated the quality of care better than previous sources, and only one in eight considered the center care inferior.[18]

3. *Availability.* Cost and quality comparisons are inappropriate where the alternatives to the health center are inaccessible to the clients which it serves. An isolated rural center may have to pay bonuses to attract medical personnel and may not realize all economies of scale. Yet, in its absence, the patients would have to rely on other distant or discriminatory suppliers. The evidence is that neighborhood health centers provide care which is not otherwise accessible and minister to health needs which frequently would go otherwise untended. At Columbia Point, only 28 percent of neighborhood residents reported ever having had a general health examination for preventive purposes before the opening of the center, 17 percent had done so in the previous year. Two years later, three fifths reported having had a check-up within the previous year. Initially, a fourth responded that they or someone else had put off seeking needed medical care in the last six months because they were unable to pay or could not arrange care; after two years of operation, the proportion postponing care dropped to about one in ten. The percentage of children without polio immunization declined from 22 to 8 percent. Moreover, hospitalization fell 30 percent in the first year of the center because of better preventive care and the alternative to emergency room treatment.[19]

These scattered pieces of evidence do not prove that the neighborhood health center is the best of all possible methods of delivering medical care to persons with low income. But existing institutions are not doing the job fully and promised new institutions, such as health maintenance organizations, have not proved themselves. Neighborhood health centers must, therefore, be counted as one of the substantial successes of the Great Society's community-based service approach.

Economic Development Endeavors

Another battlefront in the war on poverty was the economic development of poverty areas. Community-based organizations were established to initiate and support businesses and to perform a number of welfare and service functions with the hope that they would eventually be self-supporting. Legislation proposed in 1968 which would have provided federal borrowing power plus various tax incentives failed passage. However, antipoverty funds were used to support a large community development corporation (CDC) in Bedford-Stuyvesant in New York, and Congress expanded these efforts in fiscal 1969 by funding 15 CDCs.

While no one CDC is typical, the Bedford-Stuyvesant Restoration Corporation and its auxiliary, the Development Services Corporation, is the largest and probably best-known community development effort. Created with the active support of Senators Robert Kennedy and Jacob Javits, and a galaxy of business leaders, the Restoration Corporation had received commitments of $31 million from the Office of Economic Opportunity through fiscal 1972, roughly a fifth of all funds going to support community development groups. In addition the Restoration Corporation received $11 million in loans, grants, and technical assistance from foundations and corporations, plus $3 million in Small Business Administration loans and guarantees and $65 million in Housing and Urban Development funds.[20] These resources exceeded manyfold those received by other CDCs. The Restoration Corporation experience, then, suggests what can be accomplished with the most generous support.

The primary goal was business development. Using its own loan funds and SBA guarantees, Restoration had funded 13 manufacturing firms, 15 service ventures, 17 retail establishments, and four construction firms through 1972. Restoration owned two of the companies, and held a minority interest in two more. The rest were owned by private entrepreneurs. Through 1972 most of these were unprofitable and total losses exceeded total profits. But the 458 employees in funded ventures and the 232 on the CDC payroll in 1972 earned half a million dollars more annually than in their previous year.

Property acquisition and development were another major focus. One of the first projects was a face-lifting for neighborhood housing and the rehabilitation of a community center. The Restoration Corporation arranged for the construction of a 53-unit apartment building and rehabilitated 151 family units through 1972.

The intangible products, such as community pride and a sense of control, are difficult to assess. But the latter was a slogan more than a reality because of the Restoration Corporation's continued dependence upon outside help. There was little turnover of funds to reinvest or profits to plow into social and welfare activities and the corporation could not operate without continued outside help.

Most other community development corporations have accomplished much less. A study of the business ventures of 30 CDCs, which received the bulk of OEO money, found that only a fifth were in the black at the end of fiscal 1972, with an aggregate loss of over $4 million. Optimistic projections suggested that half of the firms would be out of the red after another year, but the worsening economic conditions unquestionably undermined this target.

Before passing sentence on the idea of community-based development efforts, it is necessary to assess alternative ways of encouraging ghetto and minority enterprises. A brief review of other economic development programs suggests that CDCs were not alone in their business failings. In the late 1960s a number of large corporations established branch plants or subsidiaries in ghetto areas to employ low-skilled minority workers. The intent was to sell some or all of the stock to employees and area residents. Most of these operations foundered, demonstrating that the problems of operating in the ghetto were more intractable than expected. Most corporations found that sophisticated technology could not easily be applied to unskilled labor-intensive ventures and that a longer term commitment was needed to make the operations viable. Many firms gave up on these plants preferring charity to losses in their balance sheets.

One way to overcome such problems would be to provide tax and other incentives making it profitable to operate in the ghetto. A large-scale OEO experiment with this approach proved only that if the formidable obstacles were to be overcome, very sizable incentives and subsidies would be needed.

The Nixon administration favored minority entrepreneurship

but not by funding CDCs. Instead, it supported the Minority
Enterprise Small Business Investment Company (MESBIC), a
vehicle for packaging private sector expertise and leveraging private and public resources. The MESBICs were given $2 of Small
Business Administration loans for each dollar raised from private
sources; this sum, in turn, could be used to secure private financing, $5 for each $1, it was hoped, for a total leverage of ten to one.
With these funds, risk capital or long-term subordinated loans
could be made available to minority businesses. In practice, however, most of the 51 MESBICs formed during the first three years
of the program proved to be unprofitable and continued so despite
increased interest subsidies and the addition of tax bonuses in
1972.[21]

Another minority entrepreneurship approach was that of the
Small Business Administration (SBA). Economic opportunity
loans established in 1964 and other small loan programs were
increasingly concentrated on minorities. In 1973 the SBA made
loans and guarantees totaling $334 million to minority business-
men, a tenfold increase in four years.[22] But in expanding efforts
so rapidly, lending standards were relaxed and supportive services
were not adequate for the increased activity. By 1972 a fourth of
minority loans were in liquidation, delinquent 60 days or more, or
charged off, a loss rate four times higher than under the regular
business loan program.

In light of the difficulties encountered by MESBICs, the SBA,
and related efforts, the problems experienced by the CDCs should
not be surprising. Business development in low-income neighborhoods and support of minority entrepreneurship are very risky
ventures. The hidden subsidy going to MESBICs in the form of
low interest loans and tax incentives is just as necessary to sustain
them as the direct annual appropriations to CDCs.

Clearly, however, the benefits are greater for minorities and
residents of low-income areas when the groups handling the activities are community based. The overhead of business development
means jobs and income for residents. Any profits made by a
MESBIC are cycled out of the hands of small businessmen or the
low-income community. The jobs created in SBA offices are not as
likely to go to ghetto residents as those in CDCs.

More crucially, CDCs consider not just the viability of a business, but its likely employment and other impacts on the community. A radio station may be a marginal investment but a potential source of community identification and pride. The CDC would be more likely to fund it than a firm motivated by profit considerations. Much of the money going to CDCs is used for purposes other than business development. CDCs sponsor training programs, run housing projects, fund recreation centers and activities, and serve as a community advocate. Even though the achievements in these varied areas are mixed, it is misleading to assess the value of CDCs solely on their record of business development. Viewed as delivery mechanisms for a variety of services and assistance, including business development aid, the CDCs might be considered worthwhile investments.

Cooperatives

The case for cooperatives is more convincing. Under the Economic Opportunity Act, the Farmers Home Administration and the Office of Economic Opportunity were authorized to support purchasing and marketing cooperatives which would help poor farmers realize economies of scale. The Farmers Home Administration concentrated on small loans for product-related investment. During the first six years of operation, its loans averaged only $16,000, but their impact was positive. Members of machinery cooperatives reportedly increased their net farm income 11 percent annually, while those in marketing cooperatives increased income 15 percent.[23]

The Office of Economic Opportunity cooperatives were aimed at a lower income clientele and were used to organize the rural poor, especially minorities. Between 100 and 150 cooperatives received support from local community action agencies and 10 cooperatives were funded with OEO's research and development funds. The membership of these cooperatives was predominantly black and several coops challenged or were challenged by local white interests.[24]

OEO cooperatives raised the income of members by more than 10 percent. At least a third of the cooperatives would never be profitable, but the subsidies necessary for their continuance were substantially less than income support, which would have been needed to equal the extra earnings of members. The cooperatives also had other payoffs, giving blacks and other rural low-income individuals not only the leverage to compete on somewhat better terms with agri-business institutions but a base for pursuing community interests.[25]

The Concentrated Employment Program

The central concept of the Concentrated Employment Program (CEP) was to provide resources to poverty neighborhoods for a comprehensive attack on their employment problems. CEPs had the authority to subcontract or provide directly for outreach, counseling, training, basic education, placement, follow-up, and any other services needed to make disadvantaged participants employable.

Initiated in 1967, the Concentrated Employment Program has never had a glowing reputation among manpower efforts. At the outset, many CEPs were plagued by slipshod management, antagonism from agencies like the employment service, whose cooperation was vital, high turnover of staff, and in a few isolated cases, apparent misappropriation of funds. These initial problems generated a reputation which was difficult to live down. Yet the evidence was not as negative as many believed. Competition from CEPs had a major impact on state employment services. Rules were changed in many states to hire and assign individuals from the minority neighborhoods to work with the CEP target population. CEPs dramatized the employment problems of inner city residents. A number of job opportunities were provided, with more than half of CEP staffs residing in target areas. Most important, the disadvantaged, frequently ignored by other manpower programs, were served and were helped. CEP had a substantially larger share of minorities and persons with less than a high school education than did other adult manpower programs.[26] These participants almost doubled their median earnings between the six months prior to training and the six succeeding months, according to the most comprehensive survey of the program. Two thirds of participants felt they obtained jobs as a result of services received. The proportion employed as laborers and domestic and food service workers declined from 53 to 36 percent, with parallel increases in clerical and skilled jobs.[27] These findings were supported by the few benefit-cost analyses of CEP which suggested that the program was as effective as other manpower efforts.

The issue here is whether community participation and control, which diminished after 1969, were positive or negative factors. Undoubtedly, prime sponsorship by CAAs compounded start-up difficulties. If the employment service had been assigned the same mission from the outset, there would probably have been better management and administration. But in all likelihood this would have been balanced by a greater reluctance to experiment with new approaches such as manpower service centers in ghetto areas. There is fairly clear evidence that community control resulted in service to a more disadvantaged clientele. In fiscal 1968, 85 percent of CEP participants were from minority groups and had less than a high school education. With the transfer of power to the employment services in 1969, the minority share fell to 64 percent and the high school dropout percentage to 53 by fiscal 1973.[28]

Finally, community participation resulted in institutional changes. The idea of reaching out to those in need and serving them in a convenient and humane manner was demonstrated by CEPs and then gradually adopted by employment services. The one-stop comprehensive service concept adopted by many prime sponsors under the Comprehensive Employment and Training Act of 1973 was largely a CEP legacy.

The Case for Community Action

When Richard Nixon took office in 1969, the Great Society's community-based programs were already passing the initial stage of confrontation and were becoming integral parts of the social welfare delivery system. Yet policy makers in the new administration either did not recognize or did not care about these changes, having reached the judgment that community participation should only be exercised through political channels with control remaining in the hands of duly elected state and local officials. A number of antipoverty programs were transferred from OEO to other agencies. Plans were announced for the consolidation of model cities into a block grant program for community betterment, and this was achieved in the 1974 Housing and Community Development Act.

The decentralization and decategorization of manpower programs under the Comprehensive Employment and Training Act of 1973 eliminated direct federal support of CEPs in favor of block grants to state and local government. Resources were squeezed for neighborhood health centers through administrative action, and some were closed down. But most visibly, a frontal assault was launched on the Office of Economic Opportunity—which by Nixon's second term consisted basically of the Community Action Program and some demonstration projects. In 1973 the administration instructed the newly appointed director to close shop and the proposed 1974 budget contained no funding request for the antipoverty agency.

The demise of CAP was at this point assumed to be inevitable. But over the next year, pressure mounted from governors, mayors, local businessmen, and other establishment types. Governor George Wallace claimed, "There is strong support in Alabama, from all segments of the local communities," and the governor of Texas said, "The nation—and Texas—can ill afford to lose the capability which community action has developed to provide programs tailored to meet the needs of the poor."[29] Reflecting this sentiment, Congress gave an overwhelming bipartisan vote of confidence to the community action program in 1974. The Office of Economic Opportunity was ended, but a Community Services Administration was established in the Department of Health, Education, and Welfare and assigned the same missions as CAP at a somewhat higher funding level.

Whether this was a vindication of the community-based approach or simply the result of effective lobbying and the reluctance to cut off federal spigots, the fact remains that a majority of Congress felt the program was worthwhile. One suspects that the mayors, county officials, and other state and local politicians supported the continuance of OEO's programs when the chips were down because they realized that the demise of the CAAs would mean the end of these valued services or else increased state and local responsibility.

The products of the Great Society's community-based programs are significant. A variety of clearly useful services were provided: child care, pre-school education, vocational training, health care, narcotics treatment, and on and on. The innovations and institutional changes resulting from community participation and control were of lasting significance. CAP and Model Cities were the precursors of the contemporary movement for greater governmental responsiveness, more direct forms of citizen involvement in local public affairs, and the decentralization of municipal government.[30] The neighborhood-located multiservice center was firmly established as an effective way to deliver services to clients.

New types of jobs, first established in community-based programs, have gained wide acceptance. Many state and local civil service systems have since opened new entry and upgrading routes, eliminated artificial credential barriers, and established new classifications for caseworkers, aides, and trainees. Community-based organizations have generated leadership in the minority and poor community. A large majority of current black political leaders and spokesmen gained their initial political exposure and administrative experience in community-based organizations. The community-based groups contributed to the extension of social welfare benefits to increasing proportions of the eligible population. Neighborhood service centers helped secure all available benefits for clients, and the welfare rights organizations were clearly a by-product of the antipoverty agencies. Finally, community action must be credited with increasing the responsiveness of delivery agents to client needs. While there may be less than "maximum feasible participation" in decision making, recipients have a much greater voice than in the past.

The process of community participation and control proved reasonably effective, once the external and internal power struggles had died down. While frequently less efficient than established delivery agencies, community organizations made up for inefficiencies by their other payoffs. The unit cost of service might have been lower under a centralized delivery system in a single location, but many in need would not have had access. It would have been easier to serve individuals who had the most marginal problems, but these were the ones who could most likely have helped themselves without government assistance. It might have been more efficient to hire professionals and skilled workers to perform jobs, yet the overall impact was greater when upgrading opportunities were provided for the disadvantaged and outdated employment systems were changed.

Community participation was not substantial in terms of election turnouts or influence on the boards of community-based organizations. Yet these organizations generally did represent their constituencies. The large numbers of paraprofessionals and minority employees in the community-based organizations were one influence. Another was persons with an interest in the needs of the local community, who generally gravitated to these organizations, giving support of indigenous representatives. Most local politicians are carried into office by a minority of all registered voters. Community-based organizations did not fit the image of a town hall meeting, but rarely does any other organization in our society.

Looking back, then, the ideas and activities which once seemed so revolutionary are now accepted. The Great Society's community participation programs generated needed changes. Once priorities had been altered, and services redirected and modified, the need for such an approach diminished. But the time may come when circumstances require another dose of innovation and change. The experience of the Great Society's community-based organizations should be reviewed as proof that even a relatively minor redistribution of power and control can have long-run benefits for the social system.

Part Three

The Goals of a
Compassionate
Society

10 Aid to the Poor, "The True Test of Civilization"

Poverty Policies

In his first state of the union message, President Johnson made the commitment that is perhaps most frequently identified with the Great Society: "The Administration today, here and now, declares unconditional war on poverty in America." This was hardly a novel theme. In accepting the 1928 presidential nomination, Herbert Hoover had declared: "We shall soon, with the help of God, be in sight of a day when poverty will be banished in the nation." The difference was that the Johnson administration did not intend to wait for the workings of the Almighty. "Having the power," the President exhorted Congress and the nation, "we have the duty." The power was that of the federal government and the duty was to banish poverty.

The war on poverty was envisioned as an escalation of the efforts to alleviate poverty which had been expanding since the New Deal. By bolstering the redistributive features and raising payment levels of social insurance, and by expanding the scope and benefit levels under public assistance programs, the income of the poor could be augmented. Food, housing, and health programs would provide the most vital needs, which could not be purchased with low incomes. Even more basic, however, was the notion of eliminating the causes of poverty as well as treating its symptoms.

The Economic Opportunity Act of 1964, the cornerstone of the war on poverty, emphasized service and human resource investment programs to aid the poor in helping themselves. President Johnson said, "the measure . . . offers the answer that its title implies—the answer of opportunity. For the purpose of the Economic Opportunity Act of 1964 is to offer opportunity, not an opiate." Further, "The days of the dole in our country are numbered. Our American answer to poverty is not to make the poor more secure in their poverty, but to reach down and help them lift themselves out of the rut of poverty."

To realize these goals, the Economic Opportunity Act established the Community Action Program, Head Start, Upward Bound, VISTA, Legal Services, Adult Basic Education, the Neighborhood Youth Corps, the Job Corps, and the Work Experience and Training program. Over the Johnson years human resources investment and service programs for the poor were dramatically expanded. In fiscal 1964 these self-help programs accounted for only $0.4 billion in outlays, or less than a twentieth of the federal money spent on the poor; five years later their price tag rose to $3.2 billion and a fifth of antipoverty expenditures.

While these increases were significant and were most commonly identified with the war on poverty, expenditures by the Office of Economic Opportunity never amounted to more than one in eight dollars spent by the government to help the poor. The growth of income support and in-kind programs was much more significant in helping the poor. Needs-based programs accounted for most of this growth. At the beginning of the Johnson administration three fifths of the aid to the poor was under programs with entitlement based on work experience, veteran status, and mental or physical handicaps. In the next five years aid to the poor under such programs rose 60 percent, but expenditures under needs-based programs increased 160 percent. By the end of the Great Society period, needs-based poverty programs accounted for over half the resources going to the poor.

Seeking a Truce

Many of the fundamental components, if not the goals, of the war on poverty were renounced by the Nixon administration. President Nixon denounced the welfare system as a failure and advocated an alternative family assistance plan. Medicaid was condemned for inflating medical costs, treating the poor inequitably, and overpaying for the services provided. Compensatory education was downgraded for providing little demonstrable change in the learning rates of disadvantaged students. Most of the Economic Opportunity Act programs were attacked at one time or another, some were eliminated and the antipoverty agency was gradually dispersed.

However, federal outlays benefiting the poor almost doubled between fiscal 1969 and fiscal 1974 as they had during the preceding half decade (Figure 10-1). The real rate of growth (adjusted for inflation) declined from 77 percent during the Great Society years to 45 percent during the Nixon period, but the real absolute increase was greater in the latter period. Outlays for the poor increased from 6.7 percent of the federal budget in fiscal 1964 and 8.6 percent in 1969 to 10.6 percent in 1974. The momentum generated by the Great Society did not abate until the end of the Nixon years. In fiscal 1974 antipoverty spending (adjusted for inflation) was the same as in 1972.

Fiscal year	Percent of real growth over previous year	Percent of federal budget
1965	4.0	6.7
1966	21.0	7.1
1967	18.3	7.6
1968	13.5	7.9
1969	4.9	8.2
1970	7.8	8.6
1971	19.3	9.2
1972	12.3	10.6
1973	−2.1	11.2
1974	2.4	10.6

The continuance of the war on poverty during the Nixon years was not, however, a reflection of a deep commitment to the antipoverty effort. The recession which began in 1969 increased the number of poor and left those in poverty even further behind the rising cost of living. More persons became automatically eligible for welfare, food stamps, unemployment compensation, and other services. The needs-based antipoverty measures inherited by the Nixon administration were open-ended, and the expansion in out-

Figure 10–1. Federal aid to the poor,
             fiscal 1964–1974 (billions)

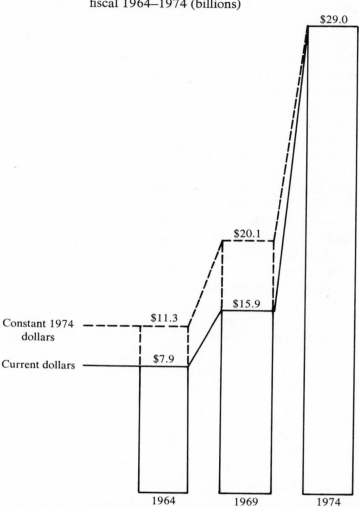

Source: Office of Management and Budget.

lays was not susceptible to control except by restricting aid or
lowering benefits—Spartan measures which Congress rejected in
most cases. Despite the rhetoric favoring workfare over welfare,
expenditures for human resource investment programs declined
from 20.2 to 17.8 percent of antipoverty outlays between 1969
and 1974. Needs-based human resource investment expenditures

rose by a third over the Johnson years but by less than a tenth during the Nixon administration.

It is important to keep in mind also that between 1964 and 1969 the number of poor decreased by 11.9 million or a third, while over the next half decade the poverty population stabilized. As income transfers became more effective in moving people out of poverty during the 1960s, aid to those lifted above the poverty thresholds was not counted in the poverty expenditures.

The Antipoverty Decade

The last decade's antipoverty efforts cannot be neatly dichotomized into the Johnson and Nixon years for comparison. The issue is the longer-run effect of mounting outlays and the possible impact if the leveling off of the last few years continues.

There were substantial changes in priority among different antipoverty approaches during the decade prior to 1975. Income support programs declined in relative importance with expenditures rising from $6.4 billion in 1964 to $11.9 billion in fiscal 1974, but falling to 41 percent of all federal antipoverty outlays (Table 10-1). The decline was partially a reflection of program effectiveness in lifting households above poverty thresholds. In 1963, for instance, the average social security retirement benefit was two fifths the poverty threshold for a two-person family, compared with two thirds a decade later. Under AFDC the percentage of funds going to the poor fell from 41 to 35 percent between 1964 and 1972, again because of the greater effectiveness of moving recipients out of poverty.

The most dramatic change in antipoverty strategy was the growth of in-kind and service programs. Policy makers chose to fight poverty not by the direct means of providing cash but by the indirect means of offering goods and services that would offset the need for cash and help to increase self-sufficiency. Such efforts carried a price tag of $17.2 billion in fiscal 1974, a twelvefold increase in a decade. While social security and public assistance remained the two most important programs for the poor, representing a third of all aid, Medicaid, food stamps, Medicare, and social services were close behind and growing rapidly.

While it may be difficult to clearly categorize the antipoverty efforts of the Great Society and the Nixon years, there were differ-

Table 10–1. Federal outlays for the poor, fiscal 1964–74 (millions)

Category	1964	1969	1974	Percentage of total		Percent of 1964–74 increase
				1964	1974	
Total	*$7,915*	*$15,887*	*$29,031*	100.0	100.0	100.0
Cash	*6,397*	*8,172*	*11,881*	*80.8*	*40.9*	*26.0*
Social security	3,691	4,785	6,097	46.6	21.0	11.4
Public assistance for the aged, blind and disabled (SSI)	735	853	1,334	9.3	4.6	2.8
Aid to families with dependent children	613	1,154	2,417	7.7	8.3	8.5
Veterans' programs	823	881	1,055	10.4	3.6	1.1
Other	535	499	978	6.7	3.4	2.1
Food	218	476	3,617	2.8	12.5	16.1
Housing	116	192	848	1.5	2.9	3.5
Education	147	1,188	2,082	1.9	7.2	9.2
Health	656	3,546	6,389	8.3	22.0	27.2
Manpower	182	1,429	2,190	2.3	7.5	9.5
Community organization	–	516	721	–	2.5	3.4
Social services and other	199	368	1,303	2.5	4.5	5.2

Source: Office of Management and Budget, unpublished tabulations.

ences in emphasis between them. The noncash expenditures that contributed most to growth between fiscal 1964 and 1969 were education, health, manpower, and community organization. During the Nixon years the emphasis was on food, housing, and social services. These shifts were accomplished through expansion in new programs, rather than reallocation from one category to another. Policy makers in both the Johnson and Nixon administrations moved from one need component to another, shifting beachheads once progress had been made and the terrain secured. By the mid-1970s the advances had stalled, but substantial progress has been made over the previous decade.

The Poor

As antipoverty outlays mounted in the 1960s, there was a substantial decline in the number of poor, from 36.1 million in 1964 to 24.3 million in 1974, or from 19.0 percent to 11.6 percent of the population. Yet most of this decline was concentrated in the

Johnson years. By 1969 poverty had fallen to 24.1 million and it changed little during the Nixon and Ford stewardship (Figure 10-2).

These changes in poverty are, of course, dependent on its definition. The Johnson administration adopted an absolute standard based on the cost of providing a minimally adequate diet, adjusted annually for changes in the cost of living. With society's generally rising real income, it is to be expected that the number of poor would decline; on the other hand, those remaining in poverty would fall further behind average real income. In 1963 the poverty threshold for a nonfarm family of four was $3,130; by 1974 it had risen 61 percent, to $5,040. But median family income rose by 106 percent, so that the threshold fell from half to two fifths of median family income.

Given the stationary poverty benchmarks, the rate of growth in real income affects the rate of decline in poverty. From 1964 to 1969 real median family income rose by over a fifth. In the next five years it rose by 1 percent. To the extent the poor shared in

Figure 10–2. Federal antipoverty outlays and persons in poverty, 1960–1974

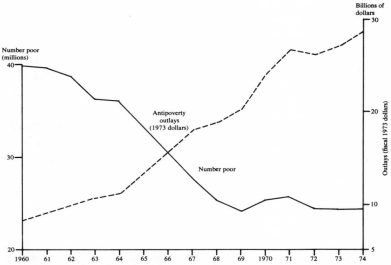

Source: Office of Management and Budget, unpublished tabulations; U.S. Bureau of the Census, *Characteristics of the Low-Income Population,* P–60, No. 99, July 1975, p. 15.

these trends rapid advances over the fixed poverty thresholds would be expected in the first period but slower progress subsequently. This, of course, is what occurred. The number of poor declined 34 percent in the first five years and stabilized thereafter.

Changes in the labor market also affect the number in poverty, since more than half of poor families are headed by persons with some work experience in the previous year. For these and other low-income workers the rate of entry and exit from poverty is largely dependent on the availability and adequacy of jobs. Between 1964 and 1969 the number of unemployed fell by nearly a fourth, but then rose four fifths by 1974. In the latter year there were 5.1 million poor families, an increase of 100,000 over 1969. Those headed by persons with part-year work experience resulting from unemployment increased from 355,000 to 643,000.

These data suggest that changing macroeconomic conditions, not the failure of antipoverty programs, were largely responsible for the lack of progress in eliminating poverty in the first half of the 1970s. Rising poverty outlays had to counteract these adverse developments. Their effect cannot be negated by the absence of progress, any more than the gains in the Johnson years are, by themselves, proof of their success. Moreover, the growth of outlays did not level off until after 1972, so the Nixon administration's poverty (though not its macroeconomic) policies cannot be blamed for the stalemate in the antipoverty effort.

Changes in the poverty population also affected the rate of progress. In 1964 a fifth of all poor lived in female-headed families, compared to over a third a decade later (Table 10-2). This change was especially marked between 1969 and 1974. Since the proportion of female-headed families who were poor remained constant over this latter period and declined during the preceding five years, the greater incidence of women heading families, rather than of poverty among female heads, explained the poverty growth.

Family changes were most notable among nonwhites. From 1964 to 1974 the number of persons in poor nonwhite female-headed families rose by 1.5 million (while the number in those with white heads of family fell by 0.3 million). Since the incidence of poverty among all nonwhite female-headed families actually declined over this period, the increase in poverty is explained by the deterioration of the black husband-wife family.

Table 10-2. Characteristics of the poor, 1964–74

Category	(thousands of dollars)			Percent Change 1964–69	Percent Change 1969–74
	1964	1969	1974		
Total	*36,055*	*24,147*	*24,260*	−33	0
White	24,957	16,659	16,290	−33	− 2
Nonwhite	11,098	7,488	7,970	−33	+ 6
65 years and over	5,550	4,491	3,299	−19	−27
Related children under 18 years	15,736	9,501	10,196	−40	+ 7
Persons in families	*30,912*	*19,175*	*19,440*	−38	+ 1
Male headed	23,615	12,296	10,877	−48	+12
Female headed	7,297	6,879	8,563	− 6	+24
Nonwhite	3,386	3,302	4,923	− 2	+49
Unrelated individuals	5,143	4,972	4,820	−33	− 3
Number of families	7,160	5,005	5,104	−30	+ 2
Head worked in previous year	4,612	2,711	2,691	−41	− 1
Head worked full-time full year	2,314	1,295	1,180	−44	− 9

Source: U.S. Bureau of the Census, *Characteristics of the Low-Income Population, 1974,* P-60, No. 99, July 1975, pp. 17–22, and *Poverty in the United States 1959 to 1966.* P-60, No. 68, December 1969, pp. 1–65.

The number of poor unrelated individuals—persons not residing with their families—declined slightly while poverty among the elderly fell precipitously. These trends continued between 1969 and 1974 despite the general rise in poverty, reflecting the improvements in social security, veterans' pensions, and public assistance for the aged.

While the number of poor is perhaps the most telling statistic, the average income deficits—the dollar amounts by which the poor fall below the poverty thresholds—are also important. Measured by this yardstick, the poor were no better off in terms of their ability to purchase vital goods and services in 1974 than in 1964.

The Impact of Federal Aid

What is the relationship between federal antipoverty efforts and changes in the size and status of the poverty population? Since poverty is defined in terms of money income, only cash transfer programs have a directly measurable impact. Service and human investment programs may have transfer components and may also raise income over the long run by increasing self-sufficiency, but these effects are difficult to measure. In-kind aid is not counted, though in cases such as food stamps it is a very close substitute to cash income. Housing, medical care, school lunches, and other goods and services may cost more than their reported value to recipients, but when these essentials are provided, money is left over for other necessities.

The rapid increase in antipoverty outlays, accompanied by a decline in the number of poor, resulted in more than tripling real per capita aid from 1964 to 1974. The federal government spent almost $1,200 per person in poverty in 1974, only slightly less than the per capita poverty threshold for a family of four.

	1964	1974
Total antipoverty outlays per poor person (1974 dollars)	$329	$1,197
Cash	266	490
Health, housing, and food	41	447
Education, manpower, and other	22	260

Income Transfers

Income support programs have played a major role in reducing poverty. In 1965 there were an estimated 16.0 million households with an income below the poverty level before government transfer payments (Table 10-3). Two thirds of these received cash from one or more programs, and 4.7 million of the recipients were raised above the official poverty thresholds. In the following six years the number of households with poverty incomes before receipt of any transfers fell by only 900,000. But support programs had expanded to reach 80 percent of the otherwise poor and raised 53 percent of these transfer recipients above the poverty thresholds. The number of poor households after transfers declined by 2.6 million between 1965 and 1971, or nearly three times the drop in the number of poor before receiving aid.

Income programs were most significant in reducing poverty among the aged. In 1971, 57 percent of the households with an

Table 10-3. Impact of income support programs

Category	1965	1971
Households (thousands)	60,402	72,046
Poor without government transfers (thousands)	15,950	15,059
Poor receiving transfers (thousands)	10,760	12,095
Percent poor receiving transfers	67	80
Lifted out of poverty by transfers (thousands)	4,730	6,432
Percent of otherwise poor made nonpoor by transfers	30	43
Percent of otherwise poor transfer recipients made nonpoor	44	53

Source: Mollie Orshansky, "Counting the Poor: Before and After Federal Income Support Programs," *Old-Age Income Assurance, Part II,* U.S. Congress, Joint Economic Committee (Washington: Government Printing Office, December 1971), pp. 218–223; and Michael Barth, George J. Carcagno, and John L. Palmer, *Toward An Effective Income Support System: Problems, Prospects and Choices* (Madison, Wisconsin: Institute for Research on Poverty, 1974), pp. 25–30.

aged head which would have been poor in the absence of transfer payments were raised out of poverty compared with 30 percent of those with a nonaged head. The aged were much more likely to receive transfers—97 percent compared to 66 percent for those with a nonaged head—and these transfers were more effective in eliminating poverty—making 59 percent of otherwise poor aged recipients nonpoor compared with only 46 percent of the nonaged.

The expansion of income support programs from 1965 to 1971 raised, however, greater numbers of the nonaged from poverty. If the poverty elimination rate had remained at the 1965 level for the elderly, there would have been 811,000 more households in 1971; if the percentage for the nonaged had remained constant, there would have been 1.2 million more in 1971. Since nonaged households are larger, the improvements in income support for families with a nonaged head were of greater importance in reducing the number of poor than the improvements in aid to the aged, at least from 1965 to 1971. Increases in social security and SSI, and the stabilization of AFDC, may have reversed this trend in more recent years.

Still, by far the most important program in eliminating poverty is social security. In 1971 social security checks lifted 4.4 million households above the poverty threshold, accounting for three fourths of all those made nonpoor by transfer programs.[1]

Transfer programs were also increasingly important in ameliorating the deprivation of those who remained below poverty thresholds. In 1964, 64 percent of the aggregate income of poor families came from earnings, but by 1972 the proportion had fallen to 47 percent. The big change between the two years was the increased importance of public assistance income, which combined with unemployment insurance provided 13 percent of the income of poor families in 1964, but 33 percent in 1973. In part, there may have been some substitution of welfare for workfare, but for the most part it was related to the changing composition of the poverty population; persons with earnings were raised above poverty thresholds and were replaced by the increased numbers of female family heads having less potential for self-support.[2]

With earnings among the poor declining, the income support programs were vital in reducing the aggregate poverty deficit in the 1960s and stopping it from rising substantially in the 1970s. In 1964 the poor required $20.8 billion (1974 dollars) to raise them to the poverty threshold, and federal cash payments made up for nearly half the deficit. A decade later, when income transfers to the poor rose to an estimated $11.9 billion, the aggregate deficit had been reduced to $14.2 billion.[3]

In-Kind Aid: The Hidden Antipoverty Weapon

The status of those who remain poor has been dramatically improved by in-kind aid. Outlays for food, housing, and medical care, which totaled $1.5 billion in 1964 increased to $10.9 billion a decade later (both in 1974 dollars). Where in-kind aid represented a tenth of the aggregate poverty deficit in 1964, it rose to more than three fourths by 1974. If such aid had been converted to cash payments and distributed according to need among the poor, it would have almost eliminated poverty. Further, since this form of aid grew so dramatically between 1969 and 1974, the recent antipoverty progress would be much more noticeable if in-kind income were counted along with cash.

While food, shelter, and health care are clearly vital, the investment in manpower, education, community organization, and social

	Outlays (1974 dollars in millions)	
	1964	1974
Food	$326	$3,617
Housing	174	848
Health	982	6,389

services should also not be ignored. Aside from the long-run and
short-run payoffs for participants, most of the human investment
programs have significant maintenance components. Food and
health and child care are provided by Head Start. Likewise, community organizations use their funds to provide food, housing,
health care, and other needed goods and services. Probably half of
the $6.3 billion outlays for human investment programs in 1974
was allocated for tangible maintenance purposes. If that amount
were cashed out and added to in-kind aid, the income deficit of the
poor would be wiped out.

In-kind assistance, human development programs, and cash aid
have gone far toward providing the basic necessities of life for the
poor. There is no doubt that this antipoverty system is occasionally
inequitable and sometimes inefficient, or that reform may be necessary. Moreover, the basic needs standards adopted more than a
decade ago to measure poverty are less applicable today as the
living standards of the population have risen substantially. But if
the war on poverty has not been won, nor executed with precision,
substantial victories have been achieved. It is largely because of
the federal government's intervention that there are fewer poor
people today than a decade ago; and it is mostly because of these
efforts that the poor are better off. Poverty persists, not just as
defined by an arbitrary index, but in terms of misery, stunted
opportunity, and deprivation. We can claim to have improved on
society because of the government antipoverty efforts. Samuel
Johnson said, "A decent provision for the poor is the true test of
civilization." This is a test that an affluent and compassionate
society must not fail.

11 Lifting the Black Man's Burden

Changing Status of Blacks

The fundamental aims of the Great Society were to help the less fortunate to secure the fundamental necessities of life and to provide equality of opportunity for all citizens. While blacks accounted for only one in nine of the population, they included a vastly disproportionate share of the unemployed, the poor, and the disenfranchised. Blacks were, therefore, a major target group for the Johnson administration's efforts.

The most visible accomplishments were the passage of the civil rights, voting rights, and fair housing acts. But even more important in terms of improving the well-being of blacks was their increased priority under expanding social welfare programs. President Johnson said:

> . . . Freedom is not enough. You do not wipe away the scars of centuries by saying: Now you are free to go where you want, and do as you desire and choose the leaders you please . . .
>
> It is not enough just to open the gates of opportunity. All our citizens must have the ability to walk through those

Note: This chapter relies upon *Still a Dream: The Changing Status of Blacks* by Sar A. Levitan, William B. Johnston, and Robert Taggart (Harvard University Press, 1975).

gates . . . We seek not just freedom but opportunity. We seek not just legal equity but human ability, not just equality as a right and a theory but equality as a fact and equality as a result.

This commitment to help blacks and other minorities realize opportunities was the hallmark of the Great Society. Because of the greater severity of their problems, blacks benefited disproportionately from the expanding needs-based programs, such as public assistance, welfare, and Medicaid. They also became the primary targets of the human investment and community organization programs.

By the end of the Johnson administration, the equity and efficacy of these policies were being questioned. Much was made of the blue collar backlash—the resentment of middle- and lower-middle income workers to the rapid relative gains of blacks. There were those who felt that blacks had reached a "take-off point" from which they could make it on their own, justifying inaction. Others doubted that the Great Society's "helping hand" was truly helpful. Focusing on rising crime, family deterioration, urban unrest, declining labor force participation of males, and other negative developments, some asserted that government intervention was responsible for as much harm as good. Critics of community action and manpower programs questioned the efficacy of these efforts in the first place. The attackers included more than a few blacks who had got their start in compensatory programs or the war on poverty and who adopted middle-class views once they had it made. The critics tended to ignore evidence demonstrating that blacks dramatically improved their socioeconomic status during the 1960s and that government aid was a key factor. Progress was slowed on most fronts when government pressures abated.

The Parameters of Progress

Income is the primary determinant of well-being, and over the 1960s the real median for nonwhite families rose more than half in real terms compared with a third for whites (Figure 11-1). The ratio of nonwhite to white median family income, which had been stable between 1950 and 1965, rose appreciably from 55 to 64 percent in the subsequent five years. But progress toward equality reversed in the first half of the 1970s, with the real median non-

Figure 11–1. Median family income of nonwhites and whites, 1955–1974

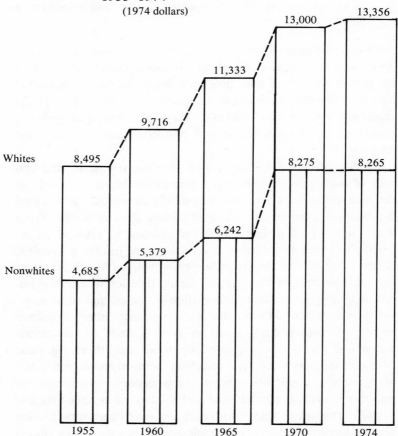

(1974 dollars)

Whites

Nonwhites

8,495	9,716	11,333	13,000	13,356
			8,275	8,265
		6,242		
4,685	5,379			
1955	1960	1965	1970	1974

Source: U.S. Bureau of the Census, *Money Income and Poverty Status of Families and Persons in the United States: 1974,* P–60, No. 99, July 1975, Table 3.

white family income declining slightly between 1970 and 1974 and the ratio of nonwhite to white median income falling to 62 percent. Poverty data tell a similar story. The number of blacks in poverty declined from 9.9 million in 1959 to 7.1 million in 1969 but rose to 7.5 million by 1974.

Since the income of most people comes from work, labor market changes were central to the income patterns. During the 1960s improvements in earnings accounted for nine tenths of the aggregate income gain of nonwhites.[1] In the slack labor markets prevailing during the first half of the 1970s, gains in real earnings slowed while needs increased for income transfers. As a result, earnings accounted for only two thirds of the more modest gains in the early 1970s.

Income of nonwhites (1973 dollars in billions)

	Total	Earnings	Other income
1959	$29.4	$26.0	$ 3.4
1969	57.3	51.3	6.0
1973	70.3	59.9	10.4

Despite the slowing gains, blacks made major labor market advances during the past decade. They got into better paying and higher status jobs; the proportion employed as managers and administrators, professional and technical workers, and craftsmen and kindred workers doubled between 1958 and 1974, while the proportion employed in service work and as nonfarm and farm labor fell a third. These changes outpaced those of whites.

Earnings improved absolutely and relatively. In 1959 the average nonwhite male earned 56 percent of the average white compared with 69 percent in 1973. Nonwhite females doubled their earnings increasing from 62 to 92 percent of the mean for whites.[2]

Blacks have traditionally been the last to be hired and the first to be fired. While they benefited from the tight labor markets in the middle 1960s, they lost ground in the subsequent recessions. In 1974 their unemployment rate was twice that of whites, the same ratio as in 1960. Joblessness among nonwhite males aged 20 years and over declined from 2.3 to 2.1 times that of whites, but this was offset by rapidly rising teenage unemployment.

Declining labor force participation rates of black males are considered by some to reflect an alienation from work. In 1960, 83 percent of all nonwhite males over 16 were labor force participants, the same proportion as for whites. By 1974 the rate for whites had fallen to 79 percent, but for nonwhites it had declined to 73 percent. Rising school attendance by the young, earlier retirement by the elderly, and greater access to disability benefits or discouragement over limited job prospects explain some but not all of the decline. Illegal activities and dependency may also have been factors.

Black gains in the classroom were substantial over the last decade and were a major factor in the labor market improvements.
Between 1960 and 1972, median years of black education rose
from 8.2 to 10.3, narrowing the lead of whites from 2.7 to 2.0
years. The proportion of nonwhites with fewer than five years of
education fell from 24 to 13 percent; those with high school diplo-
mas increased from 22 to 39 percent; and college graduates increased from 4 to 7 percent. Achievement gaps between the
average white and black student have been narrowed slightly if at
all, and blacks continue to lag behind their modal grade more
often than whites. Still, an increasing number are attaining high
school and college credentials.

Positive Manifestations

With improved income, employment, and education, blacks
have been able to improve their living conditions and socioeconomic status though relative gains have in some cases been marginal. Blacks improved their housing in the 1960s. The number of
nonwhite households in substandard units declined from 2.3 million to 1.6 million between 1960 and 1968. The proportion of
black-occupied units without adequate plumbing dropped from 41
to 10 percent between 1960 and 1973, while the proportion over-
crowded (more than one person per room) fell from 29 to 16
percent.[3] Single family homeownership also increased. In 1973,
43 percent of black households were homeowners, compared with
38 percent in 1960, and the median value of blacks' homes increased more rapidly than for whites.

Because of lower income, a different culture, a greater incidence
of social problems, and poorer medical care, blacks are, on balance, less healthy than whites, but there has been some recent
improvement. Blacks of both sexes can expect fewer years of life
at every age, and life expectancy in 1973 for nonwhites was 7
years less than for whites. Infant deaths were two thirds more
likely among nonwhites. Yet between 1960 and 1973 infant mortality declined 40 percent among nonwhites and 32 percent for
whites. Maternal death rates are declining rapidly though the racial
gap has not narrowed. Medically treatable diseases have declined
significantly in importance. For instance, blacks have one sixteenth
the chance of dying from tuberculosis than their parents had.

Other less tangible factors are essential in determining the quality of life—a sense of dignity resulting from individual responsibility and self-determination, and security resulting from stabilty and influence over the future. The past decade witnessed substantial increases in black power as blacks more frequently occupied decision-making jobs in the public and private sectors and increased their voice in political affairs.

Registration and concentration combined with cohesive voting resulted in substantial gains in Congress, state houses, and city halls. In 1975 there were 281 black legislators and executives at the state level, compared with only 94 in 1964, and 17 members of Congress compared with 5 a decade earlier. The 135 black mayors in 1975 was double the number of four years earlier. Sixteen states had at least 100 black elected officials at all levels of government, led by Illinois with 246, Louisiana with 237, Michigan with 223, and North Carolina with 194.[4]

While black representation in managerial and administrative positions is limited, it is of recent vintage. An Equal Employment Opportunity Commission study of a large matched sample of firms in 1966 and 1970 found that the proportion of black men with managerial jobs increased only from 0.8 to 1.8 percent; for women, the increase was from 0.6 to 0.9 percent.[5] Blacks have attained relatively more responsible positions in the public sector, though remain still grossly under-represented.

Membership in unions and influence on union policies are important factors affecting black employment status. In 1970 nonwhites constituted 11.7 percent of the labor force, 12 percent of all union members, and an estimated one third of all new union members.[6] Unions have proved an upward mobility route and in 1969 nonwhite male union members earned an average of 31 percent more than those outside unions.

The Negative Developments

These improvements were offset to some extent by some disturbing developments. One concern was the deterioration of the black family, which continued throughout the 1960s and accelerated in the 1970s. In 1965, 23 percent of black women age 14 years and over were single compared with 20 percent of whites; by 1973 the proportion had risen to 30 percent for blacks, but only to 21 percent for whites. Where 35 percent of black ever-married women were separated, widowed, or divorced in 1965, the proportion rose to 42 percent eight years later while remaining constant at 23 percent for white women. While illegitimacy rates declined, birth rates fell even more in husband-wife families so that the proportion of all live births born out of wedlock rose among nonwhite from 22 percent in 1960 to 37 percent in 1971. The proportion of black families headed by women rose from 23.7 to 35.3 between 1965 and 1975. While the full implications of these trends are debatable, on balance they are certainly not positive developments.

Residential segregation was another problem that became worse in the 1960s and significantly intensified in the 1970s. Continued migration increased the black share of central city populations from 16 to 22 percent. At the same time, the black share in suburbia remained relatively constant. Census tract data reveal that in 20 large cities, the average percent of blacks in neighborhoods where they represented at least three fourths of the population increased from 36 to 50 percent, while the proportion in mixed neighborhoods with 25 percent or less blacks declined from 25 to 16 percent between 1960 and 1970. In the first four years of the 1970s more whites fled the central cities than in the entire preceding decade.

Rising crime rates are another concern. In 1960 blacks were arrested five times more often than whites for robbery. By 1972 blacks in urban areas were 20 times more likely than whites to be charged with this offense. From 1964 to 1972 black arrest rates for rape, murder, robbery, and homicide increased 73 percent, while the rates for whites rose 63 percent. In 1972 the urban arrest rate for these violent crimes was 1,350 (per 100,000 population) for blacks compared with 109 for whites.[7]

In most dimensions of socioeconomic status, blacks made dramatic gains during the 1960s. They doubled their real income; they moved into preferred status occupations and higher paying jobs; they graduated from high school more frequently and went on to college more often; their health improved in areas clearly related to deficient care; substandard housing declined and ownership increased; and gains were made in union halls and legislative houses. On the other hand, some problems intensified. Buffeted by change, the black family deteriorated. Residential polarization intensified as white flight accelerated. Perhaps as one consequence of the above two developments, black crime rates increased alarmingly.

Income Support

At the beginning of the 1960s the unearned income of blacks (almost all of which was transfer payments rather than dividends, interest or private pension benefits) represented 11.4 percent of aggregate black income. By 1968 it had risen to 12.4 percent and by 1973 to 14.8 percent (Table 11-1). Among low-income families the changes were even more dramatic. In 1959 a fourth of the income of families with less than $3,000 annually came from non-

Table 11-1. Sources of income, 1968 and 1973

Income source	Blacks		Whites	
	1968	1973	1968	1973
	(billions)			
Total	$35.4	$57.9	$506.6	$785.6
Earnings	31.0	48.8	444.3	669.6
Wages and salaries	30.0	47.5	394.5	600.5
Nonfarm self-employment	0.9	1.3	42.3	53.6
Farm self-employment	0.1	0.1	7.6	15.5
Nonearnings	4.4	9.1	62.3	116.0
Social security and railroad retirement	1.5	3.3	20.0	41.1
Dividends and interest	0.2	0.4	22.5	36.1
Public assistance	1.6	3.2	2.7	4.8
Public pensions and other	0.7	1.2	8.7	18.3
Private pensions and other annuities	0.4	1.0	8.4	15.7
	(percent)			
Earnings	87.6	84.2	87.7	85.2
Wages	84.7	82.0	77.9	76.4
Nonfarm self-employment	2.6	2.2	8.3	6.8
Farm self-employment	0.3	0.1	1.5	2.0
Nonearnings	12.4	15.7	12.3	14.8
Social security and railroad retirement	4.2	5.7	3.9	5.2
Dividends and interest	0.6	0.7	4.4	4.6
Public assistance	4.5	5.5	0.5	0.6
Public pensions and other	1.9	2.2	1.7	2.3
Private pensions and other annuities	1.1	1.7	1.7	2.0

Source: U.S. Bureau of the Census, *Money Income of Families and Persons in the United States,* Series P-60, annual data.

earnings. By 1968 the proportion was two fifths in families with incomes of $4,000 or less. In 1973 over half the income of those living in less than $5,000 was unearned.

The explosion in transfer payments began in the late 1960s and continued into the mid-1970s. The black share of benefits under social insurance programs approached the population share, while under public assistance it exceeded the share among the poor. Nearly three fifths of black families and half of unrelated individuals had some income other than earnings in 1973, and most of this was transfer payments.

| | Percent receiving benefits | | | |
| Benefit | Families | | Unrelated individuals | |
	Black	White	Black	White
Social security and railroad retirement	21	22	25	38
Public assistance	25	4	16	6
Unemployment and workman's compensation, employee pensions, veterans' pensions	12	16	9	11

Welfare

The dramatic rise in welfare dependency was one of the most significant developments for blacks during the 1960s. In 1973 there were an estimated 1.4 million black families receiving Aid to Families with Dependent Children (AFDC), more than triple the number a decade earlier. While the AFDC caseload rose at only a slightly slower rate for whites, its base as a percentage of the white population was much lower, and the aggregate impact much less consequential. Fewer than four in every hundred white families were supported by AFDC in 1973, compared with one in four black families containing more than two fifths of black children.

In addition to the general changes which increased the availability and attractiveness of welfare, other reasons contributed to black dependence upon public assistance. The number of white children under 18 increased by 11 percent between 1960 and 1970, compared with 25 percent among nonwhites. More crucially, the number in poverty declined by one third for whites, compared with less than a fourth for blacks. The propensity of blacks to accept welfare also increased. In 1961, 21 percent of poor black families with children under 18 years were on AFDC rolls; white recipients represented only 11 percent of the white poor. By 1971 the comparable proportions had increased to 87 and 51 percent.

Another factor was the increase in female-headed families. The proportion of all black families headed by women rose from 22 to 35 percent between 1960 and 1975. The number of black mothers on welfare rose by 690,000 between 1961 and 1971; 30 percent of these net additions had been separated from or deserted by their husband, 9 percent divorced or legally separated; and 46 percent had never been married.[8] Obviously, the expansion of welfare rolls was caused mainly by those with marital and family problems.

Welfare was one of the factors causing family disruption, but as discussed previously its role was clearly exaggerated by those seeking a cause and effect relationship between rising welfare rolls and numbers of female-headed families. In cases in which individuals with a low earnings potential have elected to go on welfare rather than to enter the labor market, their higher level of income on welfare must be balanced against the negative consequences of a fatherless home.

Social Insurance

While the growth of welfare dependency among blacks has been the object of attention and concern, the rapid expansion of blacks drawing Old Age, Survivors and Disability Insurance (OASDI) has gone largely unnoticed. Welfare caseloads and payments leveled off in the early 1970s, but social security payments continued their rise, with an increasing share going to blacks.

Overall, blacks represent nearly one in ten OASDI recipients. They accounted for 7.6 percent of all retired workers receiving benefits in 1973 which was nearly equivalent to their 7.9 percent share of the elderly population (age 62 years and over). While 14.4 percent of all disability benefit recipients were black, this was less than the black share of the disabled population and less than the proportion receiving public assistance for the disabled. In all categories, recipient black familes were more likely to have children than whites. A fifth of children receiving survivors' benefits were black.[9]

Because of lower prior earnings and fewer quarters of covered employment, the $135 average monthly benefit for retired blacks in 1973 was 21 percent less than the amount received by whites. In other segments of the program, the average benefits of blacks were also less than for whites. However, since black recipients were more likely to have children and thus to receive supplements to their own benefits, the average payment per family was equalized somewhat.

The black share of benefits and beneficiaries has been increasing. Nonwhites received 8.0 percent of all benefits in 1973, compared to 7.5 percent in 1968, with their share rising in all components as a result of liberalized eligibility and the changing economic status of blacks. Formerly concentrated in irregular or uncovered agriculture and domestic service jobs, blacks currently reaching retirement age or qualifying under the disability provisions are more likely to have had steady work experience in the covered sectors. As black income and earnings increase, and as more blacks reach retirement years with extensive work in covered employment, their share of OASDI will continue to rise.

These increases largely explain the falling labor force participation rates of older black males. Because of their lower earning potential and frequent disability, retirement is an attractive option. It is a sign of the success not the failure of the system that those with the greatest needs most frequently receive assistance, and that this is an earned right rather than a handout.

Blacks receive a larger than proportional (based on population) share of public assistance for the aged, blind, and disabled, and of workmen's compensation because of more frequent death, disability, and low income. They are under-represented among beneficiaries of veterans' and unemployment compensation programs. Blacks accounted for a fifth of the unemployed, but only a seventh of unemployment compensation recipients in 1972.

Clearly, transfer programs have a massive impact on the well-being of blacks, especially the poor, more than half of whose income is from sources other than earnings. Blacks are over-represented in the needs-based programs and under-represented in the social insurance programs. Yet, the latter are growing in importance as blacks are becoming eligible under blanket coverage and are more frequently qualifying because of their improved status.

In-Kind Aid

Blacks also benefited from the massive expansion of federal in-kind aid for food, housing, and medical care. In 1972, they received an estimated $5.5 billion, an increase from less than half a billion dollars in 1960 (Table 11-2). The near poor, that is, those no more than 25 percent above poverty thresholds, had an aggregate cash income of approximately $9 billion in 1972. Since an estimated four fifths of in-kind aid went to such low-income households, it raised their real living standard by almost half. Even if part is unnecessary, overutilized, or lost in the pipelines, federal in-kind aid has clearly been important in improving the status of blacks at the bottom of the income scale.

Medicaid is by far the most important in-kind program. Blacks

Table 11-2. Estimated federal in-kind assistance to blacks, 1972

Category	Black share (percent)	Estimated value (millions)
Total	*22*	*$5,450*
Health	19	3,710
Medicaid	33	2,480
Medicare	6	510
Veterans' programs	16	390
Other	40	330
Food	*34*	*1,190*
Food stamps	41	820
Food distribution	27	100
School lunch and associated programs	24	280
Housing	*42*	*550*
Public housing	47	420
Homeownership	22	60
Rent supplements	63	50
Interest subsidies	20	20

Source: Derived from statistics compiled by the Departments of Agriculture, Health, Education, and Welfare, Housing and Urban Development and the Office of Management and Budget.

received roughly a third of all outlays, or $2.5 billion in 1972. This, however, is less than their share of public assistance payments. Nearly a quarter of all Medicaid beneficiaries are the medically indigent not on relief and this group is disproportionately white, female, and aged. Eligible blacks also tend to utilize available medical services less frequently than whites, perhaps because of access problems.

Medicare is less important. Blacks account for 8 percent of the elderly population, representing an equal proportion of those enrolled in Medicare. Again, however, they make less use of benefits, despite the fact that their health is generally worse. Only 16 percent of eligible nonwhites used health insurance in 1968, compared to 21 percent of whites; for supplementary medical insurance, the rates were 30 percent for eligible nonwhites and 40 percent for whites. As a result, only 6 percent of Medicare beneficiaries were black and they received a lower average dollar amount of care.

Lower nonwhite usage is in large part explained by inability to pay the coinsurance and deductibles under Medicare. The federal government allows the states to use Medicaid funds to pay the premium for supplementary medical insurance for the poor. Nonwhites comprised 19 percent of such "buy-ins" but only 4 percent of individual purchasers in 1969.[10]

Other health programs operated by the Veterans' Administration and the Department of Health, Education, and Welfare provide aid to blacks. Federal funds support a number of comprehensive health centers located in ghettos or rural areas remote from other facilities. These clinics, often subsidized with Medicare or Medicaid funds, usually serve blacks or Spanish-speaking clienteles.

The maternal and child health grants which subsidize states to provide clinics and visiting nurses for mothers as well as medical, dental, and diagnostic care for children are especially important. In the past unequal and inadequate health care explained much of the difference between black and white natal deaths, but this is a much less important factor today. Nearly all births now take place in hospitals and are attended by physicians.[11]

Part of the maternal and child care money goes to support

family planning assistance. Outlays for these efforts increased tenfold betweeen 1968 and 1972 as opposition nearly disappeared and birth control technology improved. A third of the 1.6 million patients who visited family planning clinics in 1972 were black.[12] These services have probably made an important contribution to the falling birth rate among poor blacks.

Federal food programs are also important. Slightly more than two fifths of food stamp recipients were black in 1972 with the nearly 4.6 million black beneficiaries receiving food aid worth approximately $900 million. The number of beneficiaries has doubled since then and black participation no doubt also expanded. In addition, blacks accounted for 27 percent of the recipients of the $350 million worth of commodities distributed in 1972. Under the school lunch program, blacks representing 14 percent of students and 37 percent of children in poor families received one fourth of free or reduced price lunches.

The subsidized housing programs expanded rapidly in the early 1970s and were of special benefit to blacks. At the end of fiscal 1972 blacks occupied about 700,000 subsidized units, over a third of all such housing, and four times the number in 1960. Roughly one in eight black families lived in a subsidized unit, and the federal housing program contributed to the decline in substandard housing among blacks of more than a million units between 1960 and 1975.

Human Resource Investments

In 1960 blacks were receiving less than 10 percent of the $1.2 billion in federal aid to education. But with the increased emphasis on compensatory programs, they were the target groups for an estimated $1.6 billion of the $8.1 billion in 1972 federal aid.

Compensatory Education

The Head Start program and related child care efforts provide educational, nutritional, and health care for three- to six-year-old children in families below the poverty level. In 1972 approximately half of the 365,000 children enrolled in the program were black. Under the Follow-Through program aimed at continuing special support for Head Start children, blacks accounted for approximately 60 percent of the persons receiving aid in 1972. Disadvantaged black youths tended to benefit even more than whites from early aid.

At the elementary and secondary level, compensatory funds were an important supplement to the resources available for educating blacks. More than a third of the students aided in 1972 were black, and those represented a third of all black students. Even if the relationship between outlays and achievement is uncertain, federal intervention has been one means of equalizing spending differentials.

Federal aid has its greatest impact at the college level. In 1973, 333,000 or nearly half of black college students received one or more types of aid. The National Defense Education Act, which provides loans to students from families with less than $15,000 annual income, assisted 81,000 black students. The college work-study program which funds part-time jobs for poor students, provided employment for 93,000 black college students in 1973. Educational opportunity grants of up to $1,500 per year to qualified high school graduates with exceptional financial need supported 88,000 blacks.[13] In addition, Upward Bound provided remedial programs and counseling to 15,000 selected tenth and eleventh grade black students from low-income backgrounds in 1972. Talent Search aided 65,000 black students by making them more aware of sources of financial assistance. In addition, approximately $30 million was spent in 1972 for Office of Education aid to black colleges. Federal programs must be given much of the credit for the marked increase in college attendance among blacks and for the success of these enrollees.

Remedial Programs

For those who have failed in or been failed by the schools, a second chance is provided by remedial education and training programs. Blacks were among the major beneficiaries of the dramatic expansion of these efforts. In fiscal 1974, of 2.1 million new enrollees in the federally supported manpower programs designed to train and employ the unskilled and poorly educated unemployed, 773,000 were members of minority races—significantly more than their share among the unemployed.[14]

The Neighborhood Youth Corps (NYC) served more blacks than any other manpower program. Its aim was to provide part-time jobs for youths to give them useful work experience and a source of income that might help them stay in or return to school. The in-school and year round out-of-school segments enrolled 115,000 blacks in fiscal 1974. An additional 300,000 were employed during the summer. While summer jobs are primarily a means of keeping youths off the streets and the cities quiet, the experience may also have had some positive longer-run impacts for blacks. A follow-up of Neighborhood Youth Corps participants found that they increased earnings an average of $831 during the 18-month follow-up period, and blacks did substantially better than whites. The probability of black youths completing high school was also increased, while for whites it remained unchanged.[15] The short-run effects are uncontestable. If participants had had the same employment patterns as all nonwhite youths, the already higher summer unemployment rate for black teenagers would have been at least a fifth higher.

The Concentrated Employment Program (CEP) was also significant. Administered initially by community action agencies, three fourths of enrollees in the first two years were minorities. When control was shifted to local employment services in 1969, minority enrollment dropped. Still, blacks constituted a majority of the 70,000 participants in 1974.

While most of the manpower programs were federal undertakings, the Opportunities Industrialization Center (OIC) was a black-initiated and black-run effort. Founded in Philadelphia by Reverend Leon Sullivan and his Zion Baptist Church, OIC was a self-help skill training program aimed at developing and supporting positive work attitudes. OIC was expanded to over 100 cities with federal support funneled through a national office in Philadelphia. In early 1972 the Department of Labor estimated that over 50,000 blacks or other minority group members had been placed by OICs at a cost of only $1,000 each, making this organization perhaps the most cost-effective of all federal manpower programs.[16]

Overall, manpower programs were profitable for blacks with clear short-run and likely long-run benefits. The community action emphasis assured them most of the benefits. During the Nixon administration, the black share of manpower programs continuously declined, reflecting conscious efforts to serve other clienteles.

Institutional Change

Cash, in-kind, and human resource development programs help individuals, but do not make up for the absence of institutions and individual leverage to protect black interests. The Great Society aimed not only at equalizing opportunity, but at shifting the balance of power so that blacks would have the leverage to realize opportunities. Labor market gains were aided by government efforts. Private sector training and apprenticeship programs helped open doors to jobs and unions. The civil rights laws were also important, not so much because of direct enforcement, but rather because of the threat of action and the publicity given to equal employment opportunity. Employers began to realize that discrimination was not only unfair but illegal, and those wanting to end discrimination for economic reasons were given a justification and impetus.

Civil rights efforts were important in overcoming *de jure* segregation in the schools and may have played some part in black education gains realized over the 1960s. Enforcement of the fair housing law was less vigorous, and white flight thwarted efforts to achieve racial balance.

The institution-building efforts of the Great Society suffered because of inflated promises and occasional excesses. It is clear, however, that they did much to augment black power. They also helped to concentrate resources on those most in need and to provide new upward mobility routes. Blacks were among the major beneficiaries of programs run by the CAAs—56 percent under the Concentrated Employment Program, 55 percent in the Neighborhood Youth Corps, and half under Head Start. In 1968, CAAs employed an estimated 83,000 full-time and summer nonprofessionals employed as social workers, counselors, day care, and outreach workers, the majority of whom were blacks. And a very large number of today's black leaders worked at one time or another in these community-based programs. Community-based groups also provided competition to existing institutions, influencing them to better serve poor and minority communities. They established some 2,500 neighborhood service centers in poverty areas, providing for a variety of needs that were not being met by existing institutions. Economic development efforts were not very effective in generating viable businesses, but they did serve as means for job creation and service delivery.

The Need for Government Action

Whatever criticism can be made of the vigor and effectiveness of government efforts, they have clearly served as the primary catalyst and engine for change over the past decade. From the initial confrontations—a governor standing on the steps of a southern university to block the entrance of blacks—to the most recent victories—the nation's largest employer agreeing to massive reparations for its past discrimination—the federal government has been the initiator of action to enforce equal rights. And the cases that made headlines were only the most visible manifestations of widespread pressure on employers, unions, local governments, and private and public institutions to assure blacks a measure of equality.

Government policies have had a massive and direct impact on the well-being of blacks. The dramatic expansion of public programs of all types provided the wherewithal to hire, train, educate, and serve more blacks. Cash transfers and in-kind services directly reached those in need, and these measures had a massive impact on the welfare of blacks. A third of all employed blacks are government workers or are employed in nongovernment jobs directly linked to government expenditures. Half of all black families receive some form of transfer income.

Substantial progress has been made by blacks, in large part as a result of governmental efforts. These have been especially important in helping to improve the status of the most disadvantaged, who lack other options. Because of the size of the initial gaps, the often inadequate commitment of resources and energies, and the problems inherent in new approaches to deep-rooted problems, there is still a long way to go before conditions are equalized.

Programs for blacks can continue to have high payoffs. Millions remain poor, ill-housed, and ill-fed, and claims that a saturation point has been reached or that further aid would have diminishing returns are without substance. Unless federal efforts on behalf of blacks are actively renewed, the rate of progress will slow as the obstacles become more formidable and as the momentum generated during the Great Society years dissipates.

12 Managing the Economy and Sharing the Wealth

Conflicting Ideologies

In his first Economic Report in 1964 President Johnson articulated the economic philosophy of his administration: "I regard achievement of the full potential of our resources—physical, human, and otherwise—to be the highest purpose of governmental policies next to the protection of those rights we regard as inalienable."[1]

Fiscal Stimulus

Picking up President Kennedy's recommendation, he proposed a massive tax cut to "provide a greater net stimulus to the economy in 1964—to jobs, production, income and profits—than in any other peacetime year in history." The underlying assumption was that this cut would increase rather than reduce governmental revenues, providing the wherewithal to "strengthen our programs to meet pressing human needs; fully satisfy our defense requirements; and respond to the demands of economic progress."[2]

The idea of cutting taxes despite budget deficits was a cornerstone of the new economics. Where the government's fiscal impact had traditionally been measured by the current balance of revenues and expenditures with a surplus assumed to be restrictive and a deficit expansionary, the Great Society economists argued that the impact was rather determined by the difference between the out-lays and revenues which would prevail at full employment. Since revenues automatically increase and expenditures decline as unemployment falls, a balanced budget under less than full em-ployment would mean a surplus if the full productive capacities were utilized. The new economists blamed the fiscal drag of such full-employment surpluses for the slow growth and unutilized capacity in the 1950s and early 1960s. This interpretation justified expanded government expenditures or tax cuts. The 1964 Eco-nomic Report stated:

> In a growing economy, periodic budget adjustments are required to maintain adequate expansion of total demand. The value of tax revenues rises as income grows if tax rates remain unchanged . . . If program needs do not require ex-penditures to grow at the same rate, tax rates must be reduced or a growing full-employment surplus will result, with in-creasingly restrictive effects on the economy.[3]

Structural Measures

Another cornerstone of the Great Society economics was the belief in structural measures to augment macroeconomic policies. Full employment brought about through monetary and fiscal stimulus without heavy inflationary pressures would still leave mil-lions without jobs or with minimal earning prospects because of discrimination, lack of training, or isolation in economically de-pressed areas. If they could be selectively helped, unemployment could be reduced overall and the equity of the economic system improved. Manpower training programs were the most direct ap-proach, equipping the unemployed with the skills needed to com-pete for jobs in occupations with labor shortages and thereby reducing both unemployment and inflationary pressures. A number of public employment programs were initiated as a supplement to or a substitute for income support. The Public Works and Eco-nomic Development Act and the Appalachian Regional Develop-ment Act provided federal aid to bolster the infrastructure of lagging economies and to help them attract new business. Mini-mum wage increases and extensions of coverage were favored as a way to help low-paid workers.

The Free Market Religion

The Nixon and Ford administrations differed markedly in economic philosophy and prescriptions. The 1970 Economic Report, the first prepared by President Nixon's administration, spelled out his priorities. The primary aim was to control inflation. High (not necessarily full) utilization of the nation's resources was a secondary goal. Other objectives included reducing government economic intervention, preserving and sustaining the free market, and bringing more credibility to government economic policies. The game plan was to permit unemployment to rise somewhat and growth to moderate in order to slow the rapid expansion of demand without severely injuring the economy.

Most structural measures were antithetical to the free market ideology. Public employment was equated with make-work and idle leaf-raking. Minimum wages were condemned for driving certain firms out of business and exacerbating the labor market problems of the unskilled, whose value to employers was less than the minimum. Subsidized economic development was regarded as an essentially useless effort that distorted market forces.

The ideological contrasts between the Johnson and Nixon-Ford administrations were substantially blurred in practice. Economic conditions more than philosophies determined policy responses. The achievement of full employment in the Johnson years was partly due to its economic policies, but the stimulus of war spending was a prime factor. On leaving office, President Johnson declared that "the immediate task is to make a decisive step toward price stability," and since the only known way of achieving this was to slow down the pace of economic growth, he essentially passed the buck. The Nixon administration, on the other hand, was forced to implement wage and price controls it abhorred. Whether its plan could have worked will never be known because of the massive economic dislocations related to international food and oil price rises. The Great Society's full employment policies cannot be given full credit for the rapid economic progress of the 1960s any more than Nixonomics alone can be blamed for the subsequent recession and price rises. A much more careful examination is required to determine the real policy differences and their implications.

Economic Conditions and Their Causes

The economic record during the Johnson administration was enviable. From 1964 through 1969 real GNP rose 25 percent compared with 13 percent over the next five years. Unemployment averaged 4.1 percent in the first period but 5.1 percent in the latter. Real weekly earnings in manufacturing rose 6.4 percent under the Great Society but stagnated thereafter. Meanwhile, the consumer price index went up 18 percent between 1964 and 1969 and then skyrocketed 35 percent by 1974.

Feast and Famine

Despite these very significant differences, there were no clearcut demarcations between the periods of feast and famine. Inflation was an increasing problem throughout the 1960s (Figure 12-1). The brief 1967 decline in the growth rate of GNP gave a glimmer of the problems that emerged more sharply two years later. A slump may have been inevitable at the end of the decade and even necessary to thwart inflationary pressures.

It was the depth of the slump that was disturbing. The growth in GNP stopped in 1969, while unemployment skyrocketed. Inflation leveled off but only after the imposition of wage and price controls. Then there was a sudden and dramatic turnaround in 1972 and 1973, followed by another cycle of recession in 1974 and 1975. Whether a longer but less severe settling down period at the end of the 1960s would have avoided subsequent problems is uncertain; but clearly the notion that rising joblessness would dissipate inflationary pressures was wrong.

Government policies were both a cause and an effect in these economic developments. The Great Society opened with a flourish. In February 1964 the President signed a tax cut of $9.1 billion for individuals and $2.4 billion for corporations, calling it "the single most important step that we have taken to strengthen our economy since World War II."[4]

The promised "uninterrupted and vigorous expansion" followed, aided by already mounting Vietnam spending in 1965. President Johnson presssed for fiscal expansion in the 1966 budget, which had an expected deficit of $6.4 billion, compared with $5.3 billion the previous year. He opposed the Federal Reserve Board when it

Figure 12–1. Year-to-year changes in unemployment, GNP, and prices, 1961–1974

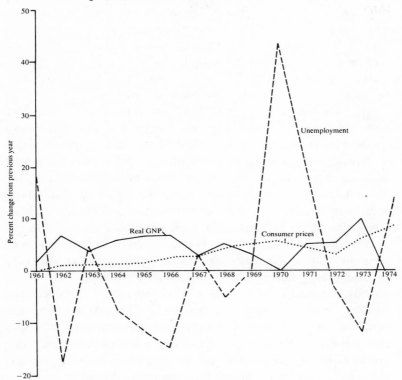

Source: Derived from *Economic Report of the President, 1975* (Washington: Government Printing Office, 1975).

adopted a restrictive monetary policy at the end of the year. His solution to rising price pressures was jawboning. Wage and price guidelines, which had been first laid down in 1962, were reintroduced. An announced aluminum price rise was countered by the government's threat to sell off stockpiled aluminum and steel increases were countered by a threat to purchase only from companies exercising price restraint. Meanwhile, measures were expanded to overcome structural problems. The Public Works and Economic Development Act of 1965 extended and broadened the 1961 Area Redevelopment Act, and the Appalachian Regional Development Act provided assistance to the 360 counties of Appalachia.

In 1966 the economy experienced general good health, but rapidly rising defense spending plus brisk private consumption and business investment inflated prices. Restrictive monetary policies were used to restrain the economy, resulting in a severe credit crunch. The Johnson administration flirted with the idea of an income tax increase but did not propose it despite a 3.3 percent increase in prices. The federal minimum wage was raised and broadened in this year to protect lower paid workers.

The economic slowdown in 1967 generated little action. The investment tax credit was reinstituted but not until the economy was already in an upswing. In the 1967 state of the union message, the President proposed a 6 percent surtax, but then delayed action because of the sluggish conditions. It was not until the next year when inflation had risen to 4 percent that restrictive fiscal measures were taken. A 10 percent surcharge was enacted in 1968, along with a congressional ceiling on federal spending.

Both Presidents Johnson and Nixon agreed on the desirability of restraint. But the Nixon administration favored greater austerity, proposing $2.4 billion in cuts to the fiscal 1970 budget which was already designed to yield a $3.4 billion surplus. The 10 percent surcharge was continued through calendar 1969, with a 5 percent surcharge the next year. The business investment tax credit was also suspended. Yet despite the threat of a presidential veto, Congress passed the Tax Reform Act of 1969, which reduced personal taxes by an estimated $2.5 billion annually, offsetting the other efforts at restraint.

President Nixon countered with the veto of spending measures, but the severe recession and continuing Vietnam expenses turned an anticipated 1971 budget surplus of $1.3 billion into $23.0 billion deficit. The unemployment rate rose to 5.9 percent, but inflation continued at 3.4 percent, and the balance of payments fell precipitously. Faced with these deteriorating conditions President Nixon launched an economic stabilization policy in August 1971. Using standby legislation, he ordered a 90-day wage-price freeze. This was followed in October by less stringent controls, which allowed annual wage boosts up to 5.5 percent and price increases up to 2.5 percent. Congress passed the Revenue Act of 1971, which provided some $11.4 billion in tax cuts to stimulate the economy. Having announced the previous year, "I am now a Keynesian in economics," President Nixon proposed a 1973 budget with a full employment deficit of $25.5 billion. By mid-year Congress had added $7 billion to the budget and was considering bills that would add much more. This was too much for the administration. Billions of dollars in spending were checked by vetoes and impoundment.

Wage and price controls were terminated except in the health, construction, and food industries in January 1973. The fiscal 1974 budget was also trimmed to an estimated deficit of $12.7 billion, with much of this coming through cutbacks in Great Society programs. By discarding controls, holding the line on taxes, and reducing government social spending, President Nixon's economic advisers hoped to achieve a low unemployment rate of 4.5 percent by the year's end, which they claimed was the new full employment equilibrium level for the economy.

By 1973 the Watergate scandals were occupying the administration full time. With a leadership vacuum, the game plan foundered as massive inflation, rising unemployment, drastically falling stock prices, and balance-of-payment deficits buffeted the economy. But the banner was picked up again by the Ford administration. Eschewing wage and price controls, resisting stimulative tax measures, and vetoing expanded public employment initiatives, President Ford returned to fighting inflation with unemployment. The administration's answer to the most extensive joblessness since the Great Depression was a continuing plea for spending restraint and a proposal for substantial tax benefits for the business sector.

A Reasonable Interpretation

The national economic experience and federal economic policies from the advent of the Great Society through mid-1975 are subject to widely varying interpretations. Some have blamed the woes of the 1970s on the shortcomings of Nixonomics and have credited the Great Society policies for the sustained economic growth and high employment during the preceding decade. Others have charged that the excesses of the Johnson years and the attempt to maintain an artificially low level of unemployment were the major causes of the subsequent problems. Causes and effects are difficult to disentangle, but any explanation would have to recognize some basic factors:

1. Fiscal policies are responsible along with the Vietnam war for generating and sustaining growth. The 1964 tax cut provided an estimated $11.5 billion stimulus, but this was augmented by the $6.1 billion Vietnam spending the next year and $20.6 billion the following one. The removal of some 800,000 draftees from the civilian labor force contributed to declining unemployment.

2. The economy was overheated in the late 1960s as much by the Vietnam war as by government economic policies. But Congress resisted cutting domestic programs and refused to raise taxes. If the surcharge had been implemented when first proposed in early 1967, some unemployment might have followed but stabler prices might have been achieved.

3. The Nixon plan might have worked in the late 1960s, if it had been pursued. The Tax Reform Act of 1969 was a major fiscal stimulus, opposed by the President because of its stimulative effect. Combined with continued war spending and the growth in domestic outlays the result was a huge deficit in fiscal 1970. Further, when the economy really needed restraint once recovery was working, the administration changed tack.

4. President Nixon accepted wage and price controls only out of necessity. An incomes policy was inconsistent with his own precepts (and with those of his predecessor who had labeled this "a dead end for economic freedom and progress"). Yet controls worked in the sense that inflation eased and unemployment declined. The claim that these measures merely postponed problems is not proven, since the real resurgence of inflation did not follow immediately after controls were dropped.

5. There were no consistent economic policies. Economic, military, and political conditions largely dictated policy responses. This was especially true during the Nixon administration, despite its promise to intervene less in the economy and to stabilize federal policies. The lesson would seem to be that the government cannot abdicate its responsibilities even if it desires to do so. The economy does not manage itself.

In the 1960s the new economics claimed that balanced budgets were outmoded and that sustained full employment could be achieved if the federal government would be sure to spend the fiscal dividend. This approach had considerable appeal following a decade of slow economic growth and limited social action. As social expenditures outpaced income and as inflation accelerated, there was a return to the old-time religion of restraint, accepting high unemployment as a necessary evil to combat inflation. Advocates of the new economics claimed that full employment in the 1960s demonstrated the validity of their thinking, but critics in the 1970s claimed that the subsequent problems were the result of past heresies. It is somewhat paradoxical that as conditions grew worse under the policy of restraint and bore less similarity to the policies of Great Society, the measures that had generated prosperity were increasingly condemned.

Given the complexity of economic matters and theories, and the lack of consistent economic policies in the Johnson and Nixon administrations it is impossible to prove or disprove the viability of new economics or the old doctrines. In this case, it is more important to recognize what we do not know than to try to defend one view or the other.

Structural Measures

The Johnson administration favored structural measures to augment macroeconomic policies. Generally, the Nixon administration opposed efforts to regulate or alter market processes claiming them to be demonstrably ineffective and a distortion of the economic system.

Assisting Lagging Areas

Area economic development programs were pushed by the Great Society. With larger numbers of unemployed stranded in depressed areas, even in a tight labor market, job creation was advocated as the best way to reduce unemployment. The Public Works and Economic Development Act and the Appalachian Regional Development Act pumped $4.3 billion into depressed areas between 1965 and 1974 for public works that would presumably bolster the infrastructure needed to attract new businesses (primarily highways in the case of Appalachia); business loans, technical assistance, and other development aids were also funded.

These programs were subsequently opposed by the Nixon administration, which tried unsuccessfully to phase EDA out.

The record of such efforts is, however, inconclusive. The primary purpose of the Public Works and Economic Development Act of 1965 (EDA) was "to alleviate conditions of sustantial and persistent unemployment and underemployment in economically distressed areas and regions." Yet while $2.5 billion was obligated through fiscal 1974, it was spread so broadly that the impact in any one area was minimal. Aid went to some 1,600 counties which contained one third of the nation's population.[5]

It is problematic how to allocate scarce resources among the many competing areas and needs, and much of the criticism of the EDA has focused on such choices. The original policy was to maximize job creation and development by choosing the most viable projects in areas with some economic development momentum. EDA then reversed itself by adopting a "worst first" strategy, distributing aid primarily according to severity of conditions. Before businesses could be attracted to the most depressed areas, substantial investments in infrastructure were required. EDA was therefore criticized for its limited immediate job creation and for focusing on public works projects. It went back, then, to a growth center strategy, putting money into rapidly growing small and medium sized cities in lagging regions. The Nixon administration favored, if anything, a revenue sharing approach which would presumably distribute funds over a broader clientele, leaving the development strategies to local officials. Any of these approaches involves trade-offs, and each change in policy has brought a new set of criticisms.

By the same token, there has been a continuing debate over development strategies. Advocates of loans and other aids to business tend to stress immediate job creation. Advocates of public works usually have a longer-run focus, aiming to provide the wherewithal for sustained growth. Advocates of technical assistance and planning view EDA as a catalyst for other activities, emphasizing the institutional change and leveraging features of governmental aid. All these groups have criticized EDA when it has departed from their favorite strategy.

Criticisms of strategy were sometimes deserved and sometimes carping, but they did not get at the more basic question of whether government aid could foster economic development. Because the funds have been widely and thinly spread, the economic effect has been marginal and therefore difficult to discern except in a few isolated cases. For example, in fiscal 1974 EDA and the Appalachian Regional Commission expended about $400 million for public works. This amount was less than 5 percent of total federal public works outlays.

When the focus shifts, there is evidence that government efforts can influence local development. A 1969 study evaluated a sample of 274 public works projects which had been in existence for more than a year. The total EDA investment was $77 million, and the total government costs were $125 million. EDA claimed that 33,000 jobs were created or saved, including direct employment and estimated employment generated by the multiplier effect from increased local spending. Of the workers who filled these jobs, an estimated 90 percent were area residents, 61 percent were heads of households, and 45 percent were previously unemployed. Analysis of the jobs led to the conclusion that "EDA-generated employment was in established firms that were economically stable, contributed to employment diversification for the area, and served to materially strengthen the area's economy."[6]

An evaluation of 84 business loans (out of 216 made through 1969) estimated that 24,000 jobs had been created or retained as a result of these loans, two thirds directly and one third indirectly. These jobs had an annual payroll of $128 million. Roughly 41 of every 100 were filled by persons previously unemployed.[7]

These studies do not prove that EDA has been a worthwhile investment of public funds and a closer analysis may raise doubts about the number of jobs created. The estimates of secondary impacts on the local economy and labor market are largely theoretical. Moreover, there is no way to know what would have happened in the absence of these investments. Yet the evidence does tentatively suggest that spending money on public works and business loans in a lagging area can attract or sustain employment.

On the other hand, there is no proof of the notion that economic development efforts can reduce aggregate unemployment (more than through their aggregate fiscal stimulus). Concentrated, large-scale aid in the areas of greatest need, focused specifically on business development as opposed to more broadly directed public works, has not been tried. It cannot be claimed either a success or failure.

Public Employment

Another structural measure to reduce unemployment is public service employment. Perhaps not surprisingly, considering his background as a New Deal administrator of public works in Texas, President Johnson favored job creation programs for the unskilled and needy. Annual outlays for these efforts rose to some $900 million by the time President Johnson left office. Ironically, the scale of the programs continued to mount during the Nixon and Ford years, despite their opposition. President Nixon vetoed the Comprehensive Manpower Act in 1970, largely because of its public service employment provision, claiming that WPA-type jobs were not an answer. Rising unemployment, intensive political pressure, and an upcoming election led to the acceptance of the Emergency Employment Act (EEA) less than a year later. This law authorized the expenditure of $2.25 billion for public service jobs over two years. When economic conditions improved, President Nixon favored the expiration of the job creation program. But Congress insisted upon its retention, albeit on a smaller scale, in the Comprehensive Employment and Training Act of 1973. In response to the 1974 recession. Congress beefed up this component in 1975, but President Ford vetoed a multibillion dollar bill.

The public employment debate goes back to the New Deal. The WPA and related agencies created jobs for an average of 3 million workers during the 1930s. Yet it was tarred with a reputation for make-work which has endured to the present even though the idle workers hired by the New Deal constructed 651,000 miles of roads, built 16,000 miles of water and sewer lines, 1,300 stadiums, and 35,000 new public buildings among other accomplishments.

The 1960s public employment efforts, while on a smaller scale, were also controversial. The ultimate objective of work relief programs, to foster self-sufficiency, was rarely achieved. As a rule, wages were pegged at or near welfare levels, the jobs were short term in nature, and rarely was much training or useful work experience provided. Work relief also provided a questionable way to reduce welfare costs, since project costs, child care, and work allowances and incentives often exceeded the value of useful work. The simple fact is that wages must be above the subsistence level with intensive training and structured work experience to provide meaningful and appealing alternatives to welfare. When these have been offered (as in some large-scale demonstration programs funded under public service employment), useful work is done with significant permanent improvements in status. But the choice in the 1960s was rather to offer (or mandate) low-level jobs for the most employable recipients to work off public assistance. While hardly praiseworthy, the programs have occasionally served this purpose.

The Neighborhood Youth Corps, created by the Economic Opportunity Act of 1964, provided jobs for youths from poor homes at the minimum wage in public and private nonprofit institutions. More than 3 million youths were employed through 1973. While the jobs were mostly menial with limited transferable work experience, they differed little in this regard from other jobs for youths. Though training and education were limited, income and constructive activity were provided, keeping youths off the street and out of trouble. The program has always been popular with the public for these reasons.

Operation Mainstream, another antipoverty program, was directed to workers too young to retire but too old to find jobs. It offered low-skill, low-wage jobs cleaning up roadsides and other public property in rural areas or providing services such as school library assistance in urban settings. The participants tended to be low-income men over 45 years with few skills or alternative employment opportunities. Projects accomplished work that was highly visible and thus tended to garner public support. Since they employed older individuals who had few options, they were not criticized for their low wages or lack of training or advancement opportunities. Their impact on income was significant.

New Careers, initiated in 1966, funded new types of paraprofessional public service aide jobs providing training and other services to those hired. The federal government paid the stipends for one year and subsidized half the wages for an additional year, after which it was hoped that participants would be transferred to regular payrolls. New Careers experienced some difficulties. Professional bureaucracies sometimes resisted job restructuring. Budget limitations and merit systems limited the opportunities for placing noncredentialed participants in regular public service jobs. Yet workers who were offered the opportunity improved their earnings and the notion of utilizing paraprofessionals gained broader acceptance.

The public employment programs initiated in the 1960s were directed primarily to the structural problems of the disadvantaged. In contrast, the Emergency Employment Act (EEA) of 1971 was primarily a countercyclical measure to employ the jobless in a recession. It succeeded admirably in this mission, quickly filling funded slots with unemployed workers. Econometric simulations indicated that a public employment program like the EEA had the greatest and most rapid job creation impact of any fiscal policy, which is not surpriring, since almost all money went directly to pay the wages of the unemployed. The EEA jobs were similar to others already funded by state and local governments and were judged to be productive. Participants benefited significantly, both in the short and long run. Approximately one fifth of the cost of the program was recovered from reduced transfer payments.

Despite these positive results, the effectiveness of public employment efforts is still debated. Many of today's unresolved issues date back to the New Deal days.

First, the effect on aggregate unemployment is uncertain. Although spending money for wages to hire the unemployed is the most direct way to stimulate employment, the effects may be blunted by reduced state and local payrolls or by trimmed federal spending for other purposes.

Second, there is a continuing debate over whom to serve. Should an expanded public employment effort focus on the needs of temporarily idled workers with an established labor market attachment or should those who experience chronic difficulties in competing for jobs receive priority?

Third, the issue of whom to serve is related to wage levels and job types. There is continuing debate between advocates of a multipurpose program that funds a wide range of jobs and proponents of work relief paying wages at, or only slightly above, welfare or unemployment compensation levels. In the first case, a broader range of public service needs can be met and upgrading opportunities can be offered; but in the second, greater numbers of more needy individuals can be hired.

Fourth, there is tug and pull between countercyclical and human resources goals. The disadvantaged will be helped most by programs which provide sustained help, relatively higher wages, and maximum services. These expensive investments in human resources are not always compatible with countercyclical aims of quickly providing the greatest number of jobs in easily expandable (and contractible) public projects.

These issues have not been resolved because of the imprecision of our theoretical understanding and the normative and political factors that are fundamentally involved. It has been demonstrated that make-work does not have to be unproductive work and that useful tasks can be found for even the most disadvantaged, but the balance of costs and benefits remains a matter of individual judgment.

Minimum Wages

President Johnson actively supported the 1966 amendments to the Fair Labor Standards Act, which raised the basic minimum wage from $1.25 to $1.60 in 1968 and extended coverage to an additional 9.1 million workers in hospitals, educational institutions, retail trade, construction, and other industries. The President claimed that the substantial increases and the first major extensions in thirty years would "bring a larger piece of this country's prosperity, and greater share of personal dignity to millions of our workers."

Seven years later, President Nixon vetoed a minimum wage bill warning that "in carrying out our good intentions, we must also be sure that we do not penalize the very people who need help most . . . [The vetoed bill] would unfortunately do more harm than good. It would cause unemployment. It is inflationary. And it hurts those who can least afford it."

These contrasting views are explained by differing philosophies more than differing facts. The proposed minimum vetoed by President Nixon was lower as a proportion of average hourly wages in the private sector than that established in 1966 and was likely to have had substantially less effect. Furthermore, with inflation more rapid in the latter period, the minimum would have been more quickly eroded.

As in the case of public employment, the impacts of the minimum wage have been debated since the 1930s. The positive effects of increases must be balanced against the negative employment effects. Yet so many factors determine the level of employment that it has proved most difficult to isolate the role of the minimum wage. Teenagers constitute a large segment of low-paid workers and employers might find them most expendable. The numerous studies that have examined the relationship between rising teenage unemployment and rising minimum wages have reached no consensus. Most seem to indicate that boosts in minimum wages do decrease teenage employment but only modestly with a 25 percent increase in the minimum wage reducing youth employment between 3.5 and 5.5 percent.[8] The wage losses due to unemployment must be balanced, however, with the wage gains due to the higher wages received by the youths who retain jobs. Minimum wage studies have failed to document any displacement effect on low-paid adult workers so that the wage gains resulting from the increases in the minimum must be viewed as a net plus.

Any wage increase in excess of improved productivity contributes to rising prices. Raising the minimum wage can be inflationary. Many low-paid workers, however, are being paid less than their productivity and raising the minimum is not inflationary if it forces more efficient and equitable use of labor. Another goal of the minimum is to use the government to protect the interests of low-wage workers in an economy where other groups are pressing for wage gains above their contribution to productivity. In this case, the inflationary consequences of the minimum wage may be justified as compensatory, and the wage gains which need to be checked are those of vested interests with market power.

In essence, then, the reluctance to utilize the minimum wage to maintain the well-being of low-paid workers, much less to improve their relative position, is not based on documentation of massive job losses or inflationary pressures. Rather it is founded on the belief that any job is better than no job, that the availability of employment is much more critical than the quality of the job, and that the labor market is perfectly competitive in allocating wages and employment opportunities according to productivity. These are arguable assumptions. There is no proof that the minimum wage causes severe problems, and there is a great deal of evidence supporting its positive contributions.

The old idea that the government should intervene as little as possible in the economic system and must accept unemployment to fight inflation rests on the notion that structural measures cannot alter fundamental economic patterns. This is nothing but an old wives' tale. Measures to correct structural imbalances were not pursued vigorously and therefore had little effect. Public employment programs during the New Deal employed as much as a third of the unemployed, while in 1975 jobs were created for less than 5 percent of the jobless. In a few experimental sites where more intensive efforts were launched under EEA, there was a noticeable reduction in area unemployment. The minimum wage increases in 1966 were followed by dramatic reductions in the number of working poor, but overall, Congress has raised the minimum wage cautiously due to the concern over subsequent layoffs. Area development programs were not of a scale to alter overall patterns of economic development and spread the limited resources thinly. It is reasonable to debate whether public employment, minimum wages, and other structural measures are warranted. Yet to argue that they cannot alter the economic system and its workings is unsupported by the evidence.

The Numbers Debate

Not only has the effectiveness of structural measures been challenged but also the feasibility of attaining full employment through macroeconomic policies. One argument is that the 4.0 percent interim unemployment target of the Kennedy and Johnson administrations is no longer realistic. The *1973 Economic Report of the President* stated:

> The 96 percent employment rate, or 4 percent unemployment rate, was considered to be an "interim" goal, which might be changed later as a result of improvement in labor markets or other developments . . . The standards are a less reliable guide to policy for the 1970's than they were for the 1960's. Large and unpredicted changes have taken place in the nature, composition, and behavior of the labor force, em-

ployment and unemployment, as well as in the length of the workweek . . . [W]e believe . . . the money value of output should rise at a rate which, with reasonably expectable price and wage behavior, would reduce the rate of unemployment to the neighborhood of 4.5 percent by the end of 1973.[9]

The 1974 *Economic Report* claimed that maximum employment was achieved in 1973, even though the unemployment rate averaged 4.9 percent. Unemployment rose precipitously in 1974 and by 1975 the Ford administration was wistfully talking of achieving a 6 percent unemployment rate within a few years.

Must More Unemployment Be Accepted?

One of the ideas underlying these less ambitious targets is the changing composition of the labor force. The proportion of young and female participants has risen, and since they have traditionally experienced more frequent joblessness, this may have made the work force more unemployment-prone. The 1974 *Economic Report* calculated that the 4.9 percent measured unemployment rate in 1973 would have been only 4.1 percent if the age and sex distribution of the labor force were the same as in 1956.[10]

Rather than standardize labor market changes back to 1956, a more reasonable approach would have been to select a base year in the mid-1960s, to determine whether the changes in the late 1960s and early 1970s were significant enough to cause a revision in the Great Society's achieved full-employment target. Weighting the 1973 age/sex cohorts by their 1966 labor force share results in a standardized unemployment rate of 4.6 percent, compared with the 4.9 percent measured rate. This suggests, according to the reasoning of the *Economic Report,* that the target had to be 0.3 percentage points of unemployment higher in 1973 than in 1966. These calculations, however, present the maximum effect of the compositional shifts. Rapid growth of certain cohorts such as teenagers raised their relative unemployment rate, while slow growth of others (25 to 54 year olds) lowered theirs. If the labor force shares had remained the same as in 1966, these relative changes would not have occurred. If 1966 age/sex unemployment rates are weighted by 1973 labor force shares, the projected 1966 rate would be 4.0 percent, compared with the measured 3.8 percent, indicating a shift of only 0.2 percentage points.

More critically, age and sex were not the only factors which might have altered the unemployment propensity of the labor force. Over the 1960s and early 1970s there was a significant upgrading in the educational qualifications of workers. Educational attainment is highly correlated with employment success, and therefore a better educated labor force is presumably a more employable one. If the educational distribution of the population had remained the same as in 1966, and if each attainment cohort had the same unemployment rate as in 1973, the standardized March unemployment rate would have been 5.4 percent instead of the measured 5.2 percent. Alternatively, if the 1966 unemployment rates for each cohort were weighted by the 1973 shares, the projected 1966 rate would be 4.5 percent, as compared with 4.7 percent. These calculations suggest that the educational upgrading of the work force balanced the age/sex shifts if it is assumed that unemployment propensities can be estimated by the same methodology for education as for age/sex differences.

The withdrawal of the least educated from the labor force also reduced the unemployment propensity. From 1966 to 1973 the participation rate of persons age 18 years and over with 1 to 3 years of high school declined from 59.5 percent to 54.7 percent, while the rate of high school graduates rose from 64.5 to 67.7 percent. If the 1966 unemployment rates from each education cohort are weighted by the 1973 participation rate, the standardized unemployment rate is 3.6 percent as compared with the 3.8 percent measured rate in 1966. The dropping out of the less educated and those more prone to unemployment reduced the average unemployment propensity of the labor force by almost one fifth of a percentage point.

There are other grounds for questioning whether we must adjust unemployment targets upward. Between 1966 and 1973 the percent of female labor force participants working full year rose from 54.3 to 58.9. Frequent entrance and exit from the labor force is usually identified as one reason women have a higher unemployment propensity, but these statistics suggest that more new female workers in the 1970s are likely to be full-year jobseekers or jobholders.

Even if the labor force composition has shifted, it does not follow that higher unemployment is inescapable. For instance, youth are much more likely to be seeking part-time or summer work. The wage bill to keep them employed is not massive. If the measured unemployment rate is claimed to be inflated by such youths with marginal job commitments, it is an easy task to simply put them to work in expanded part-time and summer public employment.

The argument that the nation must settle for higher unemployment is based on a selective focus on the facts which support this conclusion as well as a refusal to consider structural measures to solve alleged structural problems. While a 4 percent unemployment rate may be a distant prospect when unemployment is more than twice that high, this is no proof that it cannot again be achieved.

Does Full Employment Accelerate Inflation?

The new economics of the 1960s assumed a trade-off between unemployment and inflation. Monetary and fiscal measures could regulate the level of unemployment but only at the cost of a higher rate of inflation. An alternative theory, developed to explain the combination of high inflation and unemployment in the 1970s, was that the attempt to lower the rate of unemployment below an optimum equilibrium would result in an accelerating, not just higher, rate of inflation.

According to this accelerationist theory the resulting inflation from straining the nation's production capacities generates further price pressures as labor and other factors of production try to advance their real income by demanding anticipatory or catch-up increases. The cost of producing any given level of goods and services thus rises, so that less is purchased and fewer workers are needed. Government attempts to increase demand temporarily reduce unemployment but raise prices further and the whole cycle is repeated.

These alternative theories are not subject to statistical verification because low unemployment has been attained in recent years only during the 1960s, which provides an inadequate base for inferring cause and effect. The accelerationists argue that inflation and unemployment have followed a pattern which supports their theory. Over the 1950s and 1960s, the rate of unemployment was inversely related to the rate of inflation (Figure 12-2). The new

Figure 12–2. Inflation and unemployment, 1950–1975

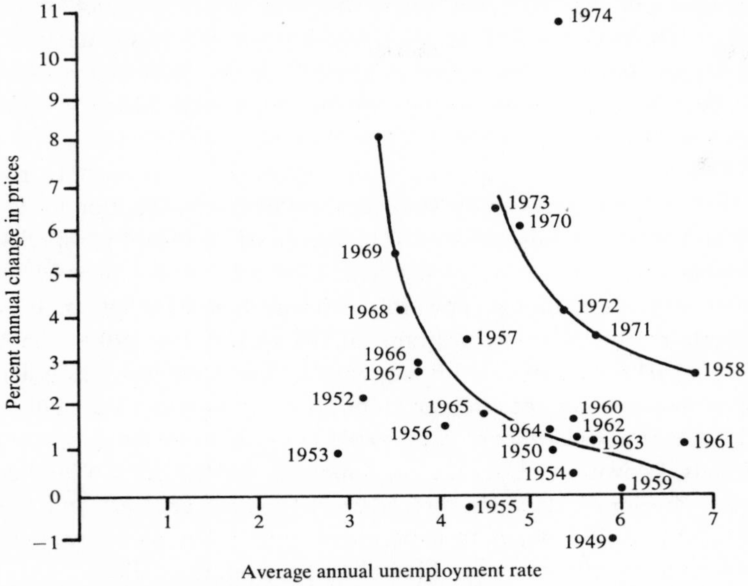

Source: U.S. Department of Labor

economics was based on the notion that unemployment could be reduced at the cost of a higher, but predictable, rate of inflation. As unemployment was reduced from 4.5 percent in 1965 to 3.6 percent in 1968, the rate of inflation rose from 1.7 to 4.9 percent. But in the 1970s there was noticeable change in the pattern of relationship between unemployment and inflation, with each level of unemployment associated with a higher rate of inflation. The accelerationists blamed the attempt to hold down unemployment in the 1960s as the cause for inflation.

Yet critical elements of the accelerationist theory do not square with the facts. By most measures of capacity utilization, the economy was less overheated in 1968 and 1969 than in 1966, and less so than in 1955 when there was actual deflation. Excess capacity developed quickly in the 1970-71 recession so that strained production capacity does not explain skyrocketing costs in 1972 and 1973. By the same token, the upward push of catch-up wage increases was not a major factor in the inflation of 1973 and 1974. In fact the increases in the hourly wage index—6.5 percent in

1973 and 9.4 percent in 1974—were well below the rises of 8.8 percent and 12.2 percent respectively in the Consumer Price Index. The major source of price pressure was from raw materials shortages, and from the cartel generated massive price increases in oil. But these developments were completely unrelated to the tight labor markets in the 1960s.

Clearly, then, there are too many unknowns at present to resolve the debate between the stable-unemployment—inflation trade-off and accelerationist theories. The record of sustained prosperity demonstrated the ability of the nation to achieve low unemployment at modest, though upwardly drifting rates of inflation. It is uncertain whether more restraint at the end of the 1960s could have checked inflation without massive unemployment if other developments had not intervened, but it is a reasonable possibility. The accelerationist theory is plausible but only in restating what is already known—that lean years followed the fat ones. Whether these developments were foreordained remains unclear, and the only way to find out is to experiment once again with sustained economic growth which would not be a hard pill to swallow.

Sharing the Plenty

Another implicit economic goal of the Great Society was the redistribution of income. The underlying assumption was that an expanding economy could afford, and government intervention could secure, a larger share of the bounty for those most in need without discomforting the more affluent or hindering the system's growth capacity. In contrast, the Nixon administration asserted that its mandate from the electorate required special attention to the needs of the middle or forgotten American, who had allegedly been denied a fair share of government assistance. A corollary claim, stressed even more by the Ford administration, was that the Great Society social welfare programs had strained the economic system, reducing the profitability and flexibility of business. The implicit assumption was that income redistribution had been pushed too far, too fast, and had to be moderated, if not reversed.

Income Shares

The rhetoric of the war on poverty and the subsequent concern with the plight of middle Americans, both exaggerated the extent of income redistribution. During the Great Society years the low income groups made gains which were partly reversed in the 1970s. Since in-kind aid more than quadrupled during the decade prior to 1973, the improvement in the real income share of those at the end of the line was greater than indicated by the census data.

Unreported income may also be a factor. The census data picked up only 45 percent of property income and 70 percent of public assistance in 1973. The first undercount is more than ten times the latter in dollar terms, so that the equality of income is much less than the reported figures indicate. On the other hand, welfare increased at a very much faster rate than dividends, interest, rentals, and royalties over the last decade, understating the relative gains of the lowest income quintile.

Social Welfare Transfers

Government policies were a major factor in income redistribution. Between 1960 and 1974 federal, state, and local income support expenditures rose from $26 to $108 billion. This represented an increase from 5.2 to 7.9 percent of GNP. Food, medical, and housing programs, providing necessary goods and services rather than money, rose from $8 to $50 billion, or from 1.5 to 3.7 percent of GNP. The total cash and in-kind transfers rose from 6.7 to 11.6 percent of GNP. Since most benefits go to those with low income and are paid by the more affluent, these expenditures significantly increased the redistribution of income.

Shifting Tax Burdens

Federal, state, and local taxes must be subtracted from cash income to determine the level of well-being. More than a third of personal income goes for taxes. Federal levies represent a declining share but still account for around two thirds of all taxes. Federal tax legislation during the Great Society and subsequently therefore had a major impact on disposable income shares. In 1964 the lowest income quintile of families received 5.1 percent of all cash income and the lowest fifth of unrelated individuals received 2.5 percent. By 1969 the share of the poorest families rose to 5.6 percent, and that of low-income unrelated individuals to 3.3 percent. Over the next five years, the income share of the lowest quintile fell back slightly, though that of low-income unrelated individuals continued to rise (Table 12-1). Put another way, the income of families at the twentieth percentile rose by 28 percent between 1963 and 1968, compared with only a 19 percent rise for families at the eightieth percentile. From 1968 through 1971, income at the lower quintile point actually declined by 1 percent in real terms, while for the upper fifth it rose 11 percent.[11]

These income data tell only part of the story. From 1963 to 1973 the mean number of children in low-quintile families fell from 1.23 to 1.05, and the number of persons per family declined from 3.25 to 2.95. The highest quintile experienced lesser declines in family size—the average number of children declined from 1.37 to 1.24 and members per family from 3.95 to 3.80.[12] The per capita redistribution was therefore greater than indicated by the family income data.

The rising number of families headed by females in the lowest quintile was another very significant development. By 1973 females headed one third of these families compared with a fourth a decade previously. To the extent this change was related to the welfare explosion, the income equalization may have been understated. If a male earning $6,000 a year left his wife because she could get, say, $4,000 annually for herself and their two children on welfare, the female-headed unit joined the ranks of the low-income quintile, and the erstwhile husband became an unrelated

Table 12-1. Income distribution by quintiles, 1964–74 (percent)

Category	1964	1969	1974
Families			
Lowest fifth	5.1	5.6	5.4
Second fifth	12.0	12.4	12.0
Third fifth	17.7	17.7	17.6
Fourth fifth	24.0	23.7	24.1
Highest fifth	41.2	40.6	41.0
Unrelated individuals			
Lowest fifth	2.5	3.3	4.0
Second fifth	7.1	7.8	8.9
Third fifth	12.8	13.8	14.5
Fourth fifth	24.4	24.3	24.2
Highest fifth	53.2	50.9	48.5

Source: U.S. Bureau of the Census, *Money Income in 1973,* January 1975, Series 60, No. 97, Tables 22 and 99, Table 4.

individual. The total income for the woman, the man, and their children had been raised from $6,000 to $10,000, but the statistical effect was to weight downward the income of the lowest fifth of all families and to add an unrelated individual with a relatively high income, making the distributions for both families and unrelated individuals more unequal.

Another important consideration is the growth of medical care, food, and housing programs, which had in fiscal 1973 a combined budget of $47.5 billion. This amount exceeded the $40 billion cash income of the lowest quintile families and unrelated individuals. If a third of the in-kind aid went to these groups, their real income would have been raised by two fifths.

The Revenue Act of 1964 reduced individual income tax rates across-the-board and added a minimum standard deduction plus some other benefits for low-income taxpayers. The aggregate impact was an estimated $9.1 billion reduction in individual taxes and $2.4 billion in corporate taxes.[13] The Revenue Act of 1969 raised the personal income tax exemption, lowered tax rates for single persons, and increased the maximum standard deduction. The oil depletion allowance was reduced, and the investment tax credit eliminated. Individual income tax payments were reduced an estimated $1.9 billion and corporate income taxes raised $3.5 billion.[14]

The Revenue Act of 1971 raised exemptions and the standard and minimum deductions. It repealed the excise tax on automobiles, reinstated the 7 percent investment tax credit, allowed accelerated depreciation, and contained other aids to business. The total impact was to reduce corporate taxes by an estimated $6.5 billion and individual taxes by $1.1 billion.[15]

Social security payroll taxes are more significant for low-income workers than income taxes. Throughout the decade there were also a number of changes in the social security tax base and rate. The base rose from $4,800 in 1965 to $14,100 in 1975, and the tax rate from 3.625 to 5.85 percent, with the base changes the major factor in providing increased revenues.[16]

On balance, the federal government's tax policy over the 1960s and early 1970s was to reduce individual income tax rates, making them more progressive, while raising social insurance revenues primarily by increasing the taxable base, thus minimizing the regressive aspects. The progressive income tax changes more than offset the regressive payroll tax increases over the 1960s. The total effective federal tax rate for a four-person family with $5,000 earnings declined from 15.4 to 13.7 percent between 1963 and 1973, while for a family with $10,000 earnings the tax bite rose from 17.2 to 20.8 percent (Figure 12-3).

The reduced federal tax burden on low-income families supplemented rising transfer payments. The lowest quintile of all families in 1972 received 1.7 percent of total income before taxes and transfers; the next quintile received 6.6 percent. After federal income and payroll taxes, the shares were increased to 1.8 to 7.0 percent, respectively. After transfers and taxes the shares were an estimated 6.3 and 9.1 percent, respectively (Table 12-2).

The incidence of other federal, state, and local taxes is not so easily calculated. The burdens of corporate taxes may ultimately be shifted to consumers, but their primary incidence is on affluent stockholders. Corporate taxes were lowered to stimulate output in 1964 and 1971 and raised to retard it in 1969. The priorities differed somewhat between the Johnson and Nixon years, with four fifths of the 1964 reductions going to individuals but 86 percent of the 1971 reductions going to corporations. The Ford administration advocated further cuts for both individuals and corporations in 1975.

Sales and property taxes place a greater burden on the less affluent. These regressive taxes declined from 62 to 59 percent of all government tax revenues (not counting social insurance collec-

Figure 12–3. Payroll and income tax rates for family of four with one earner, 1963–1973

Source: Edward R. Fried, Alice M. Rivlin, Charles L. Schultze, and Nancy H. Teeters, *Setting National Priorities, the 1974 Budget* (Washington: The Brookings Institution, 1973), p. 47.

Table 12-2. Combined effect of federal individual income and payroll taxes and transfer payments on the distribution of income, 1972 (percent)

Family income quintile	Income share before taxes and transfers	Share of individual income and payroll taxes	Income share after income and payroll taxes	Share of cash transfers received	Income share after taxes and transfers
Lowest fifth	1.7	1.1	1.8	40.2	6.3
Second fifth	6.6	5.0	7.0	26.8	9.1
Third fifth	14.5	13.3	14.8	13.1	14.6
Fourth fifth	24.1	22.8	24.4	10.3	22.8
Highest fifth	53.1	57.9	51.9	9.6	47.1

Source: Edward R. Fried, Alice M. Rivlin, Charles L. Schultze, and Nancy H. Teeters, *Setting National Priorities: The 1974 Budget* (Washington: The Brookings Institution, 1973), p. 50.

tions) between 1960 and 1972, and this should have increased the progressivity of the tax system. There was an increased reliance on the income tax at the state and local level. Moreover, the federal government's expanded responsibilities resulted in a substitution of federally raised revenues for those which would have been collected from more regressive property and sales taxes at the state and local level.

It may be assumed, then, that tax changes during and since the Great Society have probably helped to redistribute disposable income. Though the money income shares of the lowest quintiles have not risen substantially, consideration of tax incidence, in-kind aid, and changes in the composition of the low-income groups yields a more favorable picture.

Full Employment Redistribution

Full employment and rapid economic growth facilitate and contribute to the redistribution of income. In the lowest income quintile in 1973, three fifths of families had at least one earner and a fifth had two or more earners. These earners were frequently handicapped by age, race, distance from jobs, or limited education. Seven out of ten family heads in the lowest income quintile were high school dropouts; three of five were 45 years of age or over; 23 percent were nonwhites. Disadvantaged workers such as these are affected by economic fluctuations more than others. From 1967 through 1969, when the national unemployment rate averaged 3.6 percent, the difference between the unemployment rate for high school dropouts and graduates aged 25 to 34 years averaged 2.7 percentage points; from 1970 through 1972, when the national unemployment rate rose to 5.4 percent, the unemployment rate differential between the two groups widened to 4.1 percentage points. In the tight labor market of 1968, two thirds of high school dropouts aged 25 to 34 years were in the labor force, a slightly higher percentage than among high school graduates. By 1971 the participation rate of dropouts fell to 64.7 percent while rising among graduates to 68.9 percent. This was purely a cyclical phenomenon since the rates equalized when unemployment declined in 1973 and widened again in 1974.[17]

There is a trade-off between unemployment and inflation. But the result differs among groups. From 1960 to 1967 the price of the "market basket" of goods and services consumed by the poor rose an estimated 11.5 percent or less than the 12.8 percent rise in the overall consumer price index.[18] Since then the rapid rise in the price of food has hurt the poor more than the nonpoor, but government subsidies for food, housing, and medical care have reduced the cost of these necessities to the poor. No income group is immune to inflation, but for low-income quintiles mild inflation and tight labor markets are clearly preferable to price stability and high unemployment.

Was the Middle American Forgotten?

There was a good deal of political and academic debate focused in the late 1960s and early 1970s over the lot of blue-collar workers and the presumed alienation among middle-income groups. The common theme was that the gains of the poor during the Great Society years had been purchased at the expense of blue-collar workers, ethnics, and other middle Americans.

This contention was not supported by evidence. When the income share of the lowest quintile rose from 5.0 to 5.6 percent between 1963 and 1968, that of the second fifth rose from 12.1 to 12.4 percent, and that of the third fifth remained constant at 17.7 percent. The redistribution was achieved by taking 0.3 percentage points from the fourth quintile, and 0.7 percentage points from the highest income group. Subsequently, when the lowest fifth suffered a decline in their share from 5.6 to 5.4 percent through 1974, the second fifth also declined from 12.4 to 12.0. The share of the middle fifth remained virtually constant throughout both periods. Alternatively, median real income of all families grew 4.0 percent annually between 1963 and 1968, when that of the lowest quintile grew at a 5.5 percent rate. The real median of the second quintile was stable while it actually fell for the lowest quintile between 1969 and 1974. The aggregate statistics suggest that middle and lower middle income families benefited from the Great Society in relative and absolute terms and lost out subsequently.

Earnings data provide little evidence of a squeeze on blue-collar workers during the 1960s. The real median earnings of white married male blue-collar workers rose only 9 percent between 1959 and 1965, but 15 percent between 1965 and 1969, or at a faster rate than for any other occupational category of married white males. Nonwhite male blue-collar workers gained only slightly faster and certainly not so fast as to threaten the relative status of whites. Between 1960 and 1970 the mean family income of white male craftsmen and operatives rose by 30 percent, compared with 31 percent for professional and managerial workers, 31 percent for clerical and sales workers, and 34 percent for service workers and laborers.[19]

There is, therefore, no evidence that middle- or lower-middle-income families paid for the income gains of the lowest quintile. The redistribution was mainly from the affluent to the poor. There are other possible explanations for the presumed discontent of the middle American, but the redistribution of income was not a contributing factor. Massive improvements for the poor and near poor would, of course, require some sacrifice from the middle income groups, but such steps have not been undertaken, and, indeed, were not proposed by the Great Society.

Did Redistribution Kill the Goose?

Even the modest income redistribution measures of the Great Society have been charged with undermining the economic system. Increased income transfers or increased taxes to pay for them are claimed to reduce work incentives and dry up the capital needed to finance investment. Artificially tight labor markets were blamed for declining profits and increased per unit labor costs. Such assertions were fundamental to the Ford administration's call for major changes in taxing and spending policies. Again, however, these assertions are based more on ideology than fact.

The relationship between tax rates and worker productivity has never been demonstrated. In the late 1950s and early 1960s individual income tax rates for the upper-income cohorts were higher than they are today, but there is no evidence that high earners were any less committed or productive workers. The effect of greater taxes on private investment is also unclear. During the 1960s an increasing portion of investment was financed by pension funds and insurance companies, which were not directly affected by individual income tax rates. A booming stock market resulting from a steadily growing economy and rising affluence fed private investment needs.

A thesis of the Nixon and Ford administrations has been, however, that Great Society efforts had reduced the profitability of business gradually, leaving the engine of the economic system sputtering, which contributed to the economic difficulties of the 1970s. The proposed long-run solution was massive corporate tax cuts. While a number of sophisticated arguments may be marshaled to document the massive capital needs of American industry, the case for major corporate tax relief raises some questions. Profits are related to output, which in turn is related to employment. Profits rise fastest in periods of low unemployment, and they rose during each of the Great Society years except 1967. The rate of return on equity and return on sales was higher on the average in the Great Society than in the Nixon years. Profits rose rapidly in 1973 as the 1971 tax benefits were felt and inventories were revalued with inflation, but this also reflected the obvious fact that corporations do best in an expanding economy when unemployment is falling.[20]

Another dimension of the argument is that tight labor markets must rely on less skilled workers, which results in reduced productivity and slower economic growth. Over the second half of the 1960s, the rate of increase in output per man-hour declined to 2.1 percent from the 3.8 percent rate of the first half. A productivity crisis was perceived. The labor queue theory suggests that as the least employable are hired in tight labor markets, output per man-hour will decline. The real issue, however, is the change in unit labor costs, which depends on whether the marginal workers are paid more or less than their contribution to output. Suppose that because of minimum wages or other pressures, disadvantaged workers are paid the same as other entry personnel even though they are 10 percent less productive. If employment expands by 5 percent in the face of a high level of demand and all of the added workers are disadvantaged, labor cost will rise by only 0.5 percent, assuming that the extra workers are paid the same as all others. More realistically, however, entry workers will be paid less, and their wages as a proportion of all payrolls will be much smaller than their numbers as a proportion of all employees. A large increase in marginal employees will not produce any drastic decline in average per unit cost unless there is a very large differential between productivity and pay. Also, it may be assumed that with experience the less productive workers will improve their performance. Moreover, those hired in tight labor markets may also be previous victims of discrimination and their productivity may be, or become, higher than that of other workers. There are too many variables among the causes of the rise in unit labor costs in the 1960s, but there is no evidence that the employment gains of the disadvantaged have caused these cost increases.

The tenable hypothesis is that profits would improve if the economy picked up, and if the economy gained more redistribution could be financed. Certainly, the modest income redistribution achieved during the Great Society cannot be blamed for the economic problems of the 1970s.

The choice faced by the American society is not between a welfare state in which there is no incentive for productivity and a healthy and vigorous economy with inherent but unavoidable inequities. If the growth of real gross national product were to slow to 2 percent over the long-run and only half of the gain of the highest quintile were redistributed to the lowest 20 percent, this would double the latter's income share in six years. The nation did not collapse when the real GNP remained unchanged between 1969 and 1970 and declined between 1973 and 1974, nor was the highest quintile severely strained by the decline in its share in the 1960s, since its real income still improved.

The choice can be posed in other ways. Each year expenditures for leisure vehicles, home appliances, fine wines, quadrophonic sound systems, and thousands of other luxury goods expand by billions of dollars. Would foregoing some of them cause more hardship than could be alleviated by improving health, housing, and medical care for those who continue to live in penury?

Few would admit this to be the case, but they would argue instead that transfer programs are ineffective, that the recipients are ungrateful or undeserving, or that the economy could not continue to produce more goods and services at such a rapid rate if the distribution system were changed. Granted that transfer programs present problems, their benefits are unquestionable in terms of improving the overall welfare of recipients who have demonstrable needs. Arguments that further redistribution would lead to capital shortages are spurious. Experience in the 1960s showed that economic growth and redistribution are compatible rather than mutually exclusive goals.

Part Four To Promote the General Welfare

13 Fulfilling the Promise

Reassessing the Past

Historical perspective is gained only with the passage of years and successive interpretations and reinterpretations of events. Some recent chronicles of the 1960s have been biased by the needs and concerns of the early 1970s. The exponential growth of social welfare efforts had strained the social and economic fabric. Reforms were badly needed after an extended period of activism and experimentation. A stagnant economy constrained further progress. Dialectically, the negative consequences of developments in the 1960s were emphasized rather than their positive products; deficiencies and needed reforms were stressed rather than the progress which had been made; past actions were blamed for current problems.

The conventional wisdom of the first half of the 1970s is becoming in turn less and less appropriate. The momentum of governmental action has slowed, while social welfare problems have intensified. Many reforms have been made, and belts have been tightened. Consequently, it has become far-fetched to blame the continuing economic slump of the 1970s on events that occurred during the past decade.

Income Support

As transfer payments continued to expand, income support efforts have been severely criticized by friends as well as foes of the welfare state. The so-called welfare mess was a focus of attack in the early 1970s, and by the middle of the decade questions were also being raised about the viability and effectiveness of social insurance programs.

Doubts about the soundness of the social security system, if not groundless, are certainly exaggerated. During the 1965 to 1975 decade benefits were raised substantially in real terms, and the system matured to the point where coverage of workers and benefits to the elderly became nearly universal. The redistributive features of the programs were expanded while social security remained a good insurance buy for most workers.

Despite problems, social security remains secure. Declining birth rates mean fewer workers per beneficiary in the future and may require increased revenues. But this problem is more than a quarter century away, during which time productivity gains should provide the wherewithal for the needed transfers. Government contributions from general revenues are a likely possibility to finance the redistributive aspects of the system. And as a result of past improvements, benefits now meet basic needs and will not have to be raised in real terms as rapidly as in the past.

The veterans' pension and compensation system is an important complement to social security. As World War II veterans age, the proportion of the elderly receiving veterans' benefits will rise. Needs-based pensions do not carry the stigma of welfare, so their growth should increase the acceptability of transfers to the aged and raise the standards of support for many.

Unemployment compensation grew at an incredible pace during the mid-1970s recession. Benefits and coverage extensions financed out of general revenues increased the transfer, as opposed to the insurance features of the program. With such rapid growth and change, problems are imminent and reexamination is needed; nonetheless, the overall consequences have been positive. Besides protecting the jobless, unemployment compensation has evolved into a form of aid for male-headed families who, according to critics of the welfare system, were previously being short-changed. While it helps many nonpoor who only face temporary difficulties, the system also reaches the structurally unemployed. Welfare transfers, hidden in an insurance system, are apparently more acceptable than what is conceived as open charity.

Public assistance benefits for the aged, blind, and disabled were markedly improved over the last decade as the growth of social security and private pensions held down the case load and made reform possible. The Supplemental Security Income program established a federal floor under benefits and reduced geographic eligibility differences. The changes did not achieve the perfection desired by reformers—neither cashing out food stamps nor assuring equal benefits to all states despite substantial additions to outlays. The experience with SSI illustrates the constraints on reforms without denying their necessity or the significance of the progress that has been made.

Aid to Families with Dependent Children has been the center of controversy. The tripling of caseloads and the quadrupling of costs between 1965 and 1972 was alarming to some, just as the subsequent failure of welfare reform and the resort to "hard-line" measures was disturbing to others in the opposite camp. In retrospect, however, the process was neither incomprehensible nor inimical. AFDC benefits were raised substantially in real terms to provide most recipients, in combination with in-kind aid, a standard of living approaching the poverty threshold. With liberalized eligibility rules and more attractive benefits, most low-income female-headed families were covered by the welfare umbrella in the early 1970s. Once this had occurred, the momentum of growth slowed.

The welfare explosion did have side-effects. No doubt some recipients chose welfare over workfare as benefits rose above potential earnings. In part, welfare freed mothers from low-paid drudgery to take care of their families. Moreover, the difficulties of placing even the most employable and motivated recipients in jobs paying adequate wages suggested the limited options for the majority of clients. As benefits stabilized in the 1970s, the increase in real wages promised to reduce the attractiveness of welfare to unskilled workers.

The welfare system's bias against families with a male head offered some inducement for nonmarriage or desertion. In cases where AFDC provided a higher or steadier income than male family heads could earn, the costs of broken families had to be balanced against the benefits of improved living standards. Further, the stabilization of real benefits and the rise in real wages should, over time, diminish the inducement to break up homes.

The income support system, including social security, veterans' programs, unemployment insurance, workman's compensation, public assistance for the aged, blind, and disabled, AFDC, and near-cash programs such as food stamps, is incredibly complex. Yet "messiness" is inevitable where needs are multifaceted and goals contradictory. Concentrating aid on female-headed families yields high target efficiency, since these families have the most severe needs and fewest options, but there are unavoidable results, for example, the effect on family stability. Ratchets and high marginal tax rates may discourage work, but they also tend to keep down costs and to make sure benefits go to the most needy. Benefits may be too high in some areas and too low in others, but on the average they are close to poverty levels and geographic differentials are declining. Most families receiving multiple benefits have severe or special needs.

The income maintenance system is thus functioning reasonably well. The developments that seemed chaotic and dysfunctional have created a system within sight of assuring at least a poverty threshold standard of living for all citizens through a combination of cash and in-kind aid.

Health Care
The Great Society went far toward eliminating the main concern of the aged and a major problem of the poor—health care. Medicare and Medicaid have generally fulfilled their promise of assuring the "availability of and accessibility to the best health care for all Americans regardless of age, geography or economic status."

Medicare experienced early difficulties in striving for a balance between assuring adequate services and avoiding overutilization. Problems were associated most frequently with innovations. For instance, extended care was initiated as an alternative to longer hospital stays but became a subsidy for nursing home care until corrective measures were taken. Overly extended hospital stays were shortened through a variety of utilization review methods. Perhaps to quell fears that government intervention would mean government control, Medicare may have displayed excessive generosity in considering the desires of doctors and other vested interests. After problems emerged, reasonable steps were taken to cut the fat from the system.

Medicaid was an object of much criticism because of its rapid and unexpected growth. The scapegoats were overutilization and inefficiency, but quite clearly the basic cause was the explosion of AFDC. By the early 1970s the momentum of growth had already subsided as the eligible universe was reached and measures were taken to discourage overutilization and waste. Being tied to AFDC, Medicaid shared the geographic inequalities of that system, with even greater disparities resulting from the extension of aid to the medically indigent not on welfare in only some of the states. Yet there have been substantial improvements over the years as more open-handed states have cut back on frills while the tight-fisted ones have become more generous.

Medicare and Medicaid contributed to the rapid inflation of health care prices in the late 1960s. But supply did expand and reallocation occurred. The price rises pinched middle-income families and those at the margin of eligibility, and significant inequities were created, providing cogent arguments for a more comprehensive health care system. But with limited resources, those most in need (as defined by individual states) are generally being helped. Attempts to blame Medicare and Medicaid for the alleged (and very questionably documented) failure of our health care system are misplaced and even critics must admit their effectiveness in performing their basic missions.

Housing

Low-income housing programs provide obvious benefits to participants, despite the undeniable difficulties which have resulted from concentration of poor residents beset by multiple problems. Subsidies reduce the strain on limited budgets, and the shelter is far superior to what participants could otherwise afford. The long waiting lists and low vacancy rates argue that poor people value these programs, notwithstanding the drawbacks associated with project housing.

There are secondary benefits. Publicly-assisted units have helped to suburbanize low-income minority families. The courts have used these subsidy programs as a lever for countering residential segregation. Other lesser accomplishments of the programs include increasing the stability and long-term economic status of some families, organizing and delivering services using housing as the nexus, and experimenting with new industrialized construction methods.

Most significantly, however, the housing programs have built new homes for the poor. Construction yields a tangible, lasting product, permitting some control over location and quality. Building specifically for the needy tends to soften the low rent and low cost housing market, rather than wait for the trickle-down of increased production resulting from aid to the more affluent. Housing is as good an investment for the government as it is for private individuals in the present inflationary environment; and in a construction slump, increased assisted housing production can provide a needed stimulus to the economy.

The real issue is not the benefits—but rather the costs. Assistance programs are expensive because they house large numbers of people who cannot afford to contribute much to their maintenance. Subsidized units are more expensive when they are built in high cost areas or according to high standards, or when they are subject to union wage or minority contracting requirements. The government has been bilked at times like any other buyer, but the exposés of the early 1970s exaggerated the extent of such violations. The new housing programs introduced in 1965 and 1968 needed to be refined and administered more carefully. A housing allowance is certainly worth considering, but the payoffs of direct production should not be ignored in deciding on the best course.

Education

Learning is difficult to define or measure and the relationship between educational inputs and outputs is uncertain. Hence, there is little conclusive evidence that intensified efforts on behalf of disadvantaged students have improved their cognitive and social development or that educational gains yield long-run benefits.

The limited and very early evaluations of Head Start indicated that statistically significant improvements in achievement were washed out later when students returned to an "unenriched" environment. Evaluations of Follow-Through suggested that the gains could be sustained, and even more optimistically, that the programs improved with experience. Though these conclusions are all very tenuous, early childhood education is a society-wide phenomenon. Given the underlying societal premise that school is worthwhile for younger children, it is sound public policy to concentrate resources on those most in need.

The effectiveness of elementary and secondary education programs for the disadvantaged is equally uncertain. Early studies were not encouraging but more recent findings suggest notable success cases. This may reflect the fact that the programs have improved substantially. Compensatory education resources were initially diverted for noneducational purposes and for nondisadvantaged students, but tightened controls have reduced waste and misallocation. Until proven otherwise, there is reason for guarded optimism about the current overall impact of the effort.

Federal aid for higher education can stand on its demonstrated merits. The value of the sheepskin has been documented. The test of success is whether resources are concentrated on those most in need, whether their college attendance has increased, and whether they are able to continue until graduation. By these standards, there has been a high measure of success.

Manpower Services

Training, education, counseling, placement, work experience, and other manpower services can improve the attractiveness of disadvantaged workers to employers and can help open doors to better jobs. Evidence suggests that participants improved their wages and job stability. Further, the value of projected future earnings increments exceeded the average cost of the programs. Society's investment in human resources has been profitable.

Institutional vocational training has been most carefully studied, and the findings indicate beneficial effects despite the usually short duration and a frequent absence of linkages to subsequent jobs. On-the-job training has an even greater payoff as measured by benefit/cost studies, because the participant is able to earn while learning and is usually guaranteed employment upon completion. More intensive remedial efforts such as the Job Corps have had mixed success. The Job Corps has not demonstrated that the average street-hardened youth can be rehabilitated by six or nine months of intensive aid in a specially structured center; the program has shown, however, that at least some will seize the opportunity and benefit substantially.

The assertion that the disadvantaged are trapped by their backgrounds or by labor market realities is subject to all-important exceptions and modifications. Many can be helped, and even if the improvements are only moderate, on the average, they are well worth the effort.

Civil Rights

One of the primary aims of the Great Society was finally to secure the fundamental rights of blacks. Along with its impressive legislative record, the administration exerted its leverage in the marketplace and its power as a rule setter while the courts expanded the government's responsibilities and prerogatives. The Nixon administration was less forceful, some critics argue. Nevertheless, the stalling points such as employment quotas or busing to end *de facto* segregation were far different from those of the early 1960s when the rights rather than the corrective measures were being debated.

The salutary effects of these civil rights advances were not difficult to ascertain. Black registration and voting increased, with a visible payoff in office holding. Equal employment opportunity efforts had little direct effect in the 1960s, but the screws were tightened considerably in the 1970s. *De jure* school segregation was largely eliminated and busing to achieve racial balance became widespread despite fervent opposition in some cases and repeated efforts by Congress with the administration prodding to proscribe busing as a weapon in combating segregation. Fair housing machinery provided legal resources for some victims of discrimination, but little leverage to overcome patterns and practices was included in housing acts or administration decisions.

While attention was focused on racial issues, there were other areas of advancement. At the beginning of the 1960s, recipients or potential recipients of governmental aid were dependent on the whim and caprice of government bureaucracies. Antipoverty legal efforts established the principle of due process under social welfare programs and pressed the notions of equal protection and welfare as a right, chalking up some noteworthy victories in overturning the man-in-the-house and state residency restrictions.

The neighborhood legal services program was a vital tool in combating poverty, establishing new rights through law reform as well as providing traditional legal aid. Suits on behalf of clients against state and local governments got the program into political hot water. However, since the courts decided most cases in favor of the poor, the program was criticized for its effectiveness and not for its shortcomings.

Community Action

Maximum feasible participation—an ill-defined and much maligned goal—was a basic approach of the Great Society. In the community action programs, as well as in model cities, concentrated employment programs, neighborhood health centers, and community development corporations, the aim was to give minorities and the poor a degree of organizational power in order to change institutions, to protect their interests, and to design innovative strategies to serve themselves. Community-based organizations, though no more participatory or democratic than other groups in our society, had the express purpose of representing the needs of the poor. In doing so, it was necessary to step on firmly entrenched toes, and this generated antagonism, as did efforts to bring about institutional change. Friction was a necessary ingredient in the process, and though new community leaders sometimes made a virtue of antagonizing the establishment, conflict was mainly rhetorical. Community groups initiated a number of innovative approaches and were condemned for the waste and high failure rate implicit in experimentation. Yet many of the seeds bore fruit locally and nationally.

The community action and model cities programs defy rigorous assessment because of their diversity, but the more narrowly focused community-based efforts can be compared with alternative approaches. Neighborhood health centers, for instance, provided care at roughly the same cost as established institutions even though there were high start-up expenses. The quality of care was equal, but accessibility and amenability were greater. Health centers used paraprofessionals and took other steps to reach out to those in need, increasing the level of usage. Community development corporations were no more successful in establishing viable businesses in poverty areas than other establishment-run efforts, but the CDCs helped organize the neighborhood and generated short-term employment and income for the poor.

The Broader Developments

More basic than the indictment of individual programs was the charge that together they did not significantly alter the problems to which they were addressed. Racial equality was not achieved; poverty was not eliminated; income and wealth shares were not equalized; and full employment was not sustained. These charges are correct. The Great Society was not the millennium. But it was a period of very substantial improvement. Its greatest fault was not what it failed to do but overselling its initiatives and promising unrealized expectations. Relative to any realistic standards, its accomplishments were significant. Minorities achieved greater equality; unemployment was lowered and maintained for years at levels which now seem wishful thinking; income was modestly redistributed with beneficial results for the needy; and the rights and powers of those at the bottom of the heap were augmented.

Improving the Status of Blacks

Blacks made very substantial gains on a number of fronts during the 1960s and into the 1970s when progress began to falter. Income is a measure of well-being and during the 1960s the purchasing power of the average black family rose by half. The ratio of black to white income increased noticeably. The Great Society's efforts were instrumental in generating advancement. But relative black income gains did not recover following the 1971 recession and continued downward in the subsequent recession.

Earnings were the primary factor in the income gains made by blacks, although income support and in-kind aid also rose. Blacks moved into more prestigious professional, technical, craft, and secretarial jobs previously closed to them. Earnings rose absolutely and relatively as discrimination declined. Sustained tight labor markets, improved education, manpower programs, and equal employment opportunity efforts all played a role.

The improvements in schooling were dramatic and consequential. Black preschoolers were more likely to enroll than whites, largely because of government financed early education programs. High school completion increased significantly and compensatory programs provided vital resources to the schools where black youths were concentrated. At the college level absolute and relative enrollment gains were dramatic, the direct result of government aid programs.

Economic and social progress was not without serious drawbacks. Dependency increased, the black family was buffeted, and already high crime rates accelerated. Without minimizing the negative spillover, there is clear proof that in terms of opportunity or condition, measured relatively and in most cases absolutely, blacks were far better off before the advent of the economic slump than a decade earlier. There is a long way to go to equality and progress has been uneven, but advances have been made.

Fighting Poverty

While the war on poverty was not unconditional, it was more than a brief skirmish. The Economic Opportunity Act programs were only one—and not the primary—front in this assault. The Great Society's economic policies, which combined tight labor markets with structural measures such as minimum wages and manpower programs, helped the employable poor. Welfare, social security, and in-kind aid focused on persons with limited labor market attachment.

The number of poor declined sharply in the 1960s then leveled off. While these trends have been used both to praise the Great Society and to attack the subsequent administrations, an analysis of the facts does not justify such conclusions. The early declines were achieved by raising the income of the working poor, and their place was taken by female heads with little opportunity for self-support. The combination of deteriorating labor markets, declining numbers of working poor, and accelerating family breakups caused poverty to level off despite the fact that the government's anti-poverty expenditures continued to rise.

The continuance of poverty does not mean government efforts are useless. In 1971, 43 percent of the otherwise poor were lifted out of poverty by income transfers compared with 30 percent in

1965. In-kind aid and services going to the poor are not included as income in the poverty measurements, yet they cost more than the cash poverty deficit. If victory in the war on poverty means providing the minimal standard of living, then the war has very nearly been won, though many battles remain to be fought.

Achieving Full Employment

The economic setting is a crucial determinant of social welfare policy. The Great Society's expanding efforts could be afforded, despite the drain of the Vietnam war, because of the healthy growth dividend. Manpower development, equal employment opportunity, and economic development efforts worked best in a tight labor market. Inflation and rising unemployment in the 1970s increased needs and at the same time reduced society's ability to pay. A fundamental question is whether economic growth and full employment can be achieved through governmental action.

It is ironic that in the economically troubled 1970s the successes of the 1960s were quickly forgotten and even condemned. The Johnson administration placed highest priority on achieving rapid growth and low unemployment. It succeeded, and prices rose slowly (at least by mid-1970s standards). The Nixon administration acted on the premise that added joblessness was necessary to combat inflation and to provide a foundation for measured growth. Unemployment rose precipitously and growth declined, but prices continued to accelerate. Common sense would suggest that something was being done right in the 1960s, which was not in the 1970s, and prudence would caution against accepting the claims of policy makers and economists anxious to pass the buck for their own dismal record. Common sense would also question the effectiveness of the strategy of combating inflation by increasing unemployment.

The charge that the Great Society's excesses were the primary cause of the mid-1970s economic difficulties does not square with the facts. Needed restraint was not exercised during the last few years of the Johnson administration and inflationary pressures built up. It is entirely possible that the end-of-the-decade recession could have been moderated or even avoided with more timely action. The Nixon game plan was to let the recession run its course and clamp down on spending. But as the 1972 elections approached, a choice was made to spur the economy. Excessive stimulation and the decontrol of wages and prices led to inflation. The international oil and food crises then continued to push up prices while a combination of governmental restraint and international recession dramatically increased unemployment. The Great Society might be blamed for contributing to the 1969-71 slump, but subsequent policies have missed the mark far more and, together with international events, must bear the blame for the deepening malaise.

The theoretical basis for shifting blame has always been suspect, suggesting a sophisticated witch hunt more than sound analysis. Apologists for the 1970s recessions have argued that there is a natural rate of unemployment. Pushing the aggregate rate below this level in the 1960s allegedly set off a price explosion, and demographic changes in the labor market have allegedly raised the potential equilibrium so that unemployment of 5 percent or higher must be accepted. The statistical evidence for this claim is rather shaky at best, and it certainly cannot justify the massive joblessness that prevailed in the mid-1970s. To dismiss structural measures such as manpower training, public employment, and economic development as if the public policy trade-offs were set in concrete is merely to insure that they will be. The Great Society's structural programs were not of a scale to change things dramatically, but they were certainly steps forward.

Defeatism about reducing unemployment goes back to the 1950s when similar arguments led to a lengthy period of stagnation. The Great Society demonstrated that a tight labor market could be achieved and maintained for many years. The nation has paid dearly for continuing to ignore this lesson.

Redistributing Income

The money income shares of the highest and lowest quintiles are not much different now than at the outset of the Great Society. The aim of the Great Society was not a large-scale redistribution of income, but rather the opening of opportunities for those at the end of the line so that they could gradually pull themselves up. Meanwhile it attempted to provide minimal income, goods, and services for all citizens. From 1960 to 1973, total government social welfare spending rose by 5 percentage points of GNP and needs-based aid less than 2 percentage points. This was certainly a modest effort at redistribution through direct transfers.

Yet there were some important changes. Federal taxes have become more progressive, leaving the poor a larger proportion of income. The continuing expansion of payroll taxes has been detrimental to the working poor, but the burden was alleviated by raising the tax base more than the tax rate and by altering the benefit formula to make it more redistributive. Tight labor markets are unquestionably the most effective redistributive mechanism. Low unemployment in the 1960s, combined with boosts in the minimum wage, helped those at the end of the labor queue. Conversely, the subsequent recession hurt them most.

Much was made in the late 1960s of the squeeze on middle income families. The real culprit was the slowed growth of real earnings and not redistribution of income. During the Great Society the gains of the poor were achieved by reducing the share of the rich, but the rich were still better off in absolute terms as aggregate GNP grew rapidly. The Nixon administration claimed to champion the forgotten American, but its tax and transfer policies did little to improve his status.

Limits and Potentials

These diverse experiences suggest the limits and potentials of government activities and intervention. The Great Society succeeded most clearly where its actions were long-debated and the decisions the result of general consensus. Measures had much less success when they were pushed ahead of public sentiment. Equal voting rights were strongly supported and generally achieved. Equal housing efforts, opposed by a majority of Americans, were largely unsuccessful. In a broader sense the activism of the Johnson administration and the restraint of the Nixon administration were less the result of presidential leadership than a response to sweeping public mandates. In the 1960s the country sought action after more than a decade of inactivity. It then desired a respite after rapid change.

Certain fundamental social relationships have proved resistant to government intervention. One of these is stratification—the desire of the rich to live with the rich, and of whites to live predominantly with whites. Where based on exclusionary laws or open discrimination, it can be successfully, albeit painfully, challenged. Where it is based on the advantaged individual's decisions and the exercise of basic rights, governmental intervention is of no avail. Restrictive zoning practices which contributed to residential polarization were attacked legally, but the law could not restrict white flight from central cities.

The same basic constraints were present in the economic realm. The most successful economic measures were those that gained popular support. In tight labor markets, manpower programs which provided trained individuals or subsidized the costs of on-site training helped employers do "good" by doing what came naturally. On the other hand, in a recession, when relatively skilled workers were readily available, employers were reluctant to hire the disadvantaged. Similarly, when the working poor were improving their income in tight labor markets, government transfers helped reduce the poverty population. With the recession and accelerated family deterioration, the transfer system was swamped and could only hold poverty in check. Again, the government programs of the past decade did not have the leverage to reverse general social and economic trends.

The Imperfections of Public Policy

Within these broad constraints, intervention and action are limited in a number of ways:

First, in a free society, individuals are not putty who can be molded by Big Brother. The Great Society's human resource investment programs promised to remake individuals with a short-term injection of attention and aid. Those failing in or being failed by the schools and the labor market proved resistant. A few participants benefited greatly, many somewhat, but large numbers also dropped out or simply marked time while accepting allowances. The government opened doors, but many potential clients did not seek entry.

Second, government intervention can rarely succeed as a one-shot proposition. The Great Society promised to eliminate the causes of poverty rather than treat symptoms and to serve as a catalyst for needed or desired changes. In fact, however, government efforts were neither intensive nor broad enough to cure social problems. Preschool education did not eliminate problems at the elementary and secondary level. Remedial manpower programs did not eliminate hard-core unemployment. Social services and antipoverty measures did not lead the poor into the promised land.

Third, the government must be responsive to many pressures, so that its actions are rarely simple and direct. Dilution is one problem. Resources adequate to substantially improve the welfare of some clients are usually watered down to reach large numbers. Consensus building requires compromises with interest groups, which may lead to later complications whereas pressing ahead uncompromisingly may spell immediate failure. The government must also set models in its wage and hiring patterns, its competitive bid procedures, its environmental and consumer planning, and these complicate action.

Fourth, the sticks and carrots available to the government are not especially selective or efficient. Those who might have acted without aid are likely to take advantage of incentives and it is impossible to completely prevent them from gaining windfalls. Punitive measures also have limits. Human suffering is a possible result when aid is restricted or denied, so that action is only taken in the most extreme cases. This leaves a large gray area in which threats are meaningless.

Fifth, there are no panaceas. The Great Society shared with the Nixon administration a penchant for overselling remedies for existing problems. While the former advocated new initiatives which increased the federal role, the latter favored structural reforms—cash over in-kind aid, comprehensive programs over categorical funding, revenue sharing over federal implementation. Whatever the merits of the Nixon–Ford reforms, the proposed changes could at best have only marginally affected the quality or cost of services. Perfection remains an elusive goal, and no new design or change seems to increase drastically the effectiveness of government activities.

Sixth, the federal government cannot call all the shots. The principle of subsidiarity still holds, that a higher unit of society should not undertake those tasks which can be performed as well or almost as well by a lower unit. There is no doubt that in stressing immediate and visible action, the Great Society placed too much emphasis on federal initiatives.

The Art of the Possible

In an imperfect world, the existence of such constraints does not prove the failure of government intervention. The Holy Grails of public policy may remain elusive, but the quest itself may be constructive.

If government action rests ultimately on national consensus, there is still room for leadership, which may either advance the boundaries of activity or impose restraints on change until the inevitable occurs. Public opinion also tends to evolve and change continuously. Social welfare measures at the margin of acceptability in one year may become commonplace a few years later. Social security in the 1930s and Medicare more recently are prime examples. Welfare was a major domestic issue in the 1970s, but when the growth of AFDC slowed, the public was willing to accept its greater scale and scope. Where action exceeded the bounds of public acceptability, as was apparently the case in court-ordered busing, fair housing, or early community action, some retreat was necessary; but holding ground permitted a gradual filling in of support, as witnessed by the acceptance in the early 1970s of previously controversial community action programs.

If it is not possible to reverse the ebb and flow of socioeconomic developments, the current can be directed to useful purposes. In some cases the government can navigate upstream to protect or promote the interests of a particular group, at least for the short run. The case of blacks is perhaps most illustrative. When labor markets were tight and job openings plentiful, the Great Society moved ahead vigorously to maximize the gains for minorities and to break down the barriers of discrimination. When the recession came, blacks were, as always, hurt more than others, but government efforts minimized the slippage relative to previous recessions.

Where efforts to counter socioeconomic trends did not succeed, they may still have been warranted, helping target groups while they lasted. This was the case, for instance, with rural cooperatives; though not always achieving viability, they raised the income of participants much more effectively and economically than transfers. Some potentially effective endeavors are not undertaken because the private sector cannot afford the risks. The social welfare benefits do not enter economic calculations but must be central to public decision making.

If the government's efforts did not dramatically alter our society's distribution of income, wealth, and power, the changes were significant in improving the welfare of those at the end of the line. For instance, the lowest quintile of families receives roughly 5 percent of income. Increasing their share by 1 percentage point improves their welfare by a fifth while lowering that of the rest of society only marginally. Relative changes did occur in the Great Society although the statistician's idea of significance is likely to be very different from that of the poverty stricken. Certainly, there can be no doubt of the government's capacity to improve the absolute living standards of the poor.

The existence of operational constraints does not imply the ineffectiveness of governmental action. The war on poverty and its aftermath are a prime example. Federal initiatives were required at the outset because most state and local governments had demonstrated their incapacity or disinclination to act. The direct ties between the federal government and community-based groups were, in fact, consistent with the principle of subsidiarity; the assumption was that poverty neighborhoods and the poor could make better decisions about the programs affecting their lives than locally elected officials representing a more diversified electorate.

The war on poverty was not a precision attack. Spillovers were a problem. Activism contributed to the racial friction of the late 1960s, yet the traumas changed public and private attitudes and the problems of minorities and the poor were thrust to the forefront of national attention. The Economic Opportunity Act was an amalgam of programs directed haphazardly at an ill-defined nexus of problems. Not all the antipoverty efforts hit their mark, but the beneficial and lasting effects of the new approaches developed by the antipoverty agency demonstrated its effectiveness.

The Great Society did not eliminate poverty, but the number of poor was reduced and their deprivation significantly alleviated. The Great Society did not equalize the status of blacks and other minorities, but substantial gains were made which have not been completely eroded. Significant redistribution of income was not achieved or sought, but the disadvantaged and disenfranchised were helped. The Great Society did not have any magic formula for prosperity but its policies contributed to the longest period of

sustained growth in the nation's history. It did not revamp education, or assure health care for everyone, or feed all the hungry, but
as a result of its efforts, the disadvantaged were considerably better
educated, fed, and cared for.

Reasonable Standards

Why, then, has the Great Society been so severely criticized not
only by its opponents, but also by many of its former champions
and even its beneficiaries. A combination of shifting fashions
among opinion makers and limited analysis of the facts seems to
be responsible for these misimpressions. On any given issue, there
is a range of reasonable opinion, with policy makers selecting the
inputs which will be emphasized. In the dialectical swing away
from 1960s social thinking every effort was made to discredit the
past. The facts were selectively analyzed with limited rebuttal from
more knowledgeable observers. The Great Society's failings were
presumably demonstrated by a wealth of factual material. Yet
consideration of the complete range of data and studies, with
emphasis on the good as well as the bad, raises serious questions
about the factual underpinnings of negative arguments and, even
more critically, about the reasoning and the standards of judgment
implicit in these arguments.

Null Hypotheses

To assess the effectiveness and value of diverse and complex
social welfare endeavors, a judgmental framework is needed. De-
terminations of statistical significance begin with the articulation of
a null hypothesis. This is a statement asserting a relationship
which is then tested against the evidence using some standard of
proof to ascertain whether contradictions are too frequent to allow
acceptance. In assessing the performance of some efforts, one hypothesis would be that it works, demanding contrary evidence of
failure. The converse would be to assume failure and require proof
of effectiveness. Different results can be obtained from these different null hypotheses requiring different standards of proof, especially when measurements are imprecise and proof equivocal. If
clear evidence of success is demanded to discount an assumption

of failure, then a positive verdict is unlikely; while if absolute failure must be demonstrated to alter the assumption of success, a more positive judgment is inevitable.

What is the most reasonable null hypothesis? A primary consideration must be the danger of drawing the wrong conclusion. Almost all social welfare efforts provide benefits to those who would be worse off without them—extra nutrients, a roof that does not leak, more cash, or preventive health care. To conclude that these goods and services are unnecessary, less important than others which could have been acquired with the same funds, or ineffectively delivered, runs the risk of seriously affecting the welfare of recipients if conclusions are wrong. It may also become the basis for retrenchment or counterproductive change. In our criminal system, we assume that an accused person is innocent until proven guilty on the assumption that the consequences to the individual are more serious if the person is wrongly sentenced than the danger to society if a guilty individual is freed. In evaluating social welfare efforts, the small monetary costs to each citizen must be weighed against the possibly severe losses to particular individuals in need. In considering programs with altruistic goals, the compassionate approach is to assume success until failure is reasonably demonstrated.

The Canons of Gainsayers

Besides basing judgments on negative hypotheses, critics have applied a number of other questionable standards supportive of their gainsaying. One sure way to support a negative case is to measure the real against the ideal. In support of revenue sharing, for instance, the ideal of a politically accountable and locally adaptable decentralized and decategorized system was compared with the realities of categorical efforts with their inherent administrative complexities. Yet where revenue sharing was tried, it did not significantly alter either adaptability or accountability, while the loss of federal control had some negative consequences.

New and experimental efforts will usually come up wanting when compared to longstanding programs. Most Great Society endeavors got underway in 1965 or later, yet their failure was being trumpeted by the late 1960s on the basis of evidence drawn from the first few years of operation. A longer time period encompassing the evolution of the more successful approaches, the retrenchment of the less successful, as well as the implementation of needed reforms, is required to get an adequate perspective.

Secondary and nonquantifiable goals are frequently ignored, biasing judgments against multipurpose programs. The Great Society efforts usually had many aims—to deliver goods and services but also to achieve institutional change, to maximize help for the disadvantaged, and to improve the status of minorities. These were not usually as efficient as programs whose sole purpose was service delivery, but they had more positive spillovers. Categorical programs suffered in comparison with comprehensive ones. It was easy to identify gaps and overlaps, and to argue about relative priorities where the goals, target groups, and approaches were specified separately and funds distributed through different channels. Putting all the money in one basket and decentralizing decision making eliminated second-guessing by hiding the choices without necessarily resolving the issues.

While the positive secondary effects of programs were frequently ignored, the negative secondary effects were often in the spotlight. Opponents and threatened interests were quick to seize on incidents of gross failure. Side effects were sometimes taken as proof of failure even when these were part and parcel of achieving the primary aims. For instance, programs redistributing resources by paying for the needs of the poor were blamed for raising prices, while efforts to supply goods and services directly were blamed for competing with alternative sources of supply which had demonstrably failed to provide for the same clients.

Critics applied contradictory standards to social welfare activities. Opponents railed against large or mounting costs as if these inherently demonstrated failure or else stressed the inefficiencies and exaggerated potential savings. Critics of the opposite persuasion focused on what was not being done—target groups who were not being served and benefits which were not adequate to meet minimal standards. The result was a discordant critical chorus of complaints against excessive spending and demands for expanded aid.

Dynamic processes were often ignored in the focus on the problems of the day. Few approaches are right for all seasons and many Great Society initiatives were dependent on rapid economic growth and low unemployment, becoming less effective in subsequent slack labor markets. Some approaches suitable in the early stages of development were inappropriate or unnecessary later. For example, categorical programs staked out new areas and after expansion set the stage for comprehensive reform. These reforms were pushed by emphasizing previous failures when, in fact, they were only feasible because of the successes in building up a foundation through categorical efforts.

Critics tended to use the tools and perspectives of economists, examining the equity and efficiency of existing arrangements, focusing on the pluses and minuses at the margin and implicitly accepting the status quo. Such emphasis and methods, presumed to be purely objective and completely rational, were inherently biased. One of the most frequent charges against the Great Society's social welfare programs was their inequity. Geographic disparities and uneven treatment of client groups were inherent in building a system from the ground up. Variations in living conditions and values permitted only gradual standardization. Analysts frequently assumed that inequalities were necessarily inequitable and reprehensible, when in fact they stemmed from a decentralized approach to determining what was equitable.

Great Society programs were also criticized for inefficiencies. If a program aims to change institutions, to experiment with new approaches, or to let a hundred flowers bloom, then it is bound to be inefficient. Change is not an efficient process.

During the Great Society, social analysts and humanists balanced the views of the economists. The latter triumphed in the subsequent years (despite their dismal record in their own area of expertise) because they provided apparent rigorousness and raised the hard-nosed questions consistent with the Nixon and Ford administration philosophies. The result was a deemphasis of nonquantifiable ends, of social and economic change, and of dynamic rather than static analysis.

Unreasonable Arguments

The critical assessments of the Great Society's social welfare efforts were based on a number of underlying fallacies, perhaps best illustrated in the critique of the income support system. The performance of welfare programs tended to be measured against an idealized comprehensive system devoid of inequities or inefficiencies, a system in which all those in need would be given cash aid without work disincentives and without any negative spillovers on family stability. Advocates of guaranteed income schemes tended to brush aside fundamental questions of work disincentives, the role of in-kind aid, the difficulties of altering disparities, and many other critical issues. The existing system was contrasted with and found deficient relative to an alternative which was unrealistic and unattainable, as the difficulties of reforming aid for the aged, blind, and disabled demonstrated.

Critics usually ignored constructive processes in their efforts to find fault. Over the late 1960s and early 1970s variations among areas were significantly reduced, standards were raised to near the poverty level, and most of the defined universe of need was reached, yet there was little recognition of these achievements in the debate over the welfare mess.

Critics overemphasized the negative spillovers on work and the family. As welfare standards approached or exceeded wages available to potential clients, some chose to stop or reduce work. While some potential job competitors left the labor market, the supply of workers was still excessive and unemployment rates for the unskilled remained at high levels. Although paid labor may have been reduced, it is still a presumption in our society that children are better off with a mother's care and supervision.

The income support programs have been judged by contradictory standards, criticized simultaneously for costing too much and doing too little. Conservative critics focused on in-kind and cash packages which exceeded prevailing wages in some states. Liberal critics focused on the benefits in other states which fell below subsistence levels. These groups joined hands briefly under the banner of welfare reform when conservatives were convinced that the extension of benefits to male heads was the only way to check the growth of AFDC. When the costs became apparent and growth slowed on its own account, there was a parting of company.

The influence of economists was predominant in the welfare reform debate. The work disincentives issue was argued in terms of trade-offs between lower marginal tax rates, income guarantees, and costs, glossing over the evidence that the 1967 changes which made work more profitable for those on welfare had resulted in almost no increase in work and that training and employment programs for mothers on AFDC accomplished little because jobs were not available. Focusing on the margin where work and welfare overlap, broader realities such as the saturation of the universe of need and consequently slowing growth were ignored.

The critique of health care programs was based on equally weak foundations. Medicare and Medicaid tried to assuage fears of socialized medicine by giving doctors, hospitals, insurance carriers, and other interest groups a voice in decision making and by imposing on them minimal controls. That the freedom was abused in some cases should have come as no surprise, and that regulations had to be gradually established to curb excesses was hardly a sign of failure. Being a totally new system, a lengthy shakedown period should have been expected. Noticeable improvements were achieved as the system matured. Professional review bodies and prepaid group health practices were sold as solutions to spiraling costs when, in fact, they could make only marginal contributions at best.

Relying upon the price system, the government gave the needy the power to bid for scarce resources and rejected the alternative of controlling and restructuring the delivery system. Inevitably, prices went up as a result. More important, however, supplies were reallocated and augmented. The poor got more care, health resources grew, and major price pressures from Medicare and Medicaid declined by the early 1970s.

The critique of low-income housing programs was much more ideological in orientation. Posited on the belief that in-kind aid was inherently ineffective and inefficient, a quite sophisticated case was constructed seeking to prove that residents in subsidized units valued their benefits less than they cost; and that the government's direct intervention had negative rather than positive consequences in the marketplace. Consumers tend to believe everything is overpriced, so it was not surprising that subsidized residents undervalued federal aid. And contrary to claims of official critics, most evidence suggested that production of low-income units substantially increased the supply of housing for low-income families and therefore helped soften the market for all those in need. While economic and racial integration was not achieved in subsidized units, mixing was significantly better in assisted housing than in the free market.

As an alternative to the existing subsidy programs the administration favored housing allowances. In support of its case, administration spokesmen overemphasized start-up problems encountered by the new subsidy approaches introduced in 1965 and 1968. The assumption that unsubsidized housing was immune to difficulties was naive. High costs and shoddy quality did occur in some projects, but most of these problems were eliminated with more adequate administration. More than shelter was expected under government programs, and cost comparisons with the private market frequently ignored the many secondary missions assigned to public sector efforts. Many in Congress were unprepared when the rent came due under interest subsidy programs with low front-end spending requirements. But this technique was adopted expressly to get production underway and to postpone costs, and it succeeded in these aims.

The critics of education and manpower programs took different roads to reach similar conclusions. Manpower efforts were more rigorously assessed than any other social welfare undertaking. Performance was measured in terms of increased employment and earnings of participants, and to calculate the rate of returns on costs. Most initial studies indicated a positive impact on participants and concluded that gains exceeded costs.

These studies were based on a number of assumptions, and the positive results were initially accepted without adequate recognition of the qualifications. Later, when negativism was in fashion, the validity of these studies was questioned, while a lengthy, though clearly fallacious, evaluation was leaked to the press to support the administration's view that manpower programs failed. This view reflected a shift in the null hypothesis and its standard of proof, from one demanding reasonable proof of failure to one demanding unequivocal proof of success.

In contrast, compensatory education programs were subjected to little rigorous evaluation. The measures of ability and attainment as well as the ingredients in learning are highly uncertain, so that efforts to assess the effectiveness of compensatory programs are undermined. Preschool education seemed to give disadvantaged children a head start, but the gains were subsequently eroded. Following through with continued aid seemed to sustain gains, but no one could say with any certainty. Elementary and secondary school programs added only marginally to available resources, and whatever improvements resulted were difficult to discern. Ultimately, judgments must rest on suppositions about the value of education and faith in the effectiveness of the education establishment.

Community action efforts were symbolic of the Great Society approach to social problems, and the subsequent critiques were equally characteristic of the gainsaying perspective. Community action was essentially a decision making process, with the fundamental aim of concentrating resources on the disadvantaged and giving them control over their use. Yet the program was subsequently judged by its tangible products, its efficiency in delivering goods and services being compared with that of long established alternatives. Community-run programs reached those most in need who were ignored by established institutions; they hired community residents and located in poverty areas; they competed with other agencies and acted as advocates for their clients. This was all ignored when the cost per unit of service was adopted as the controlling performance criterion.

There were excesses in the early days of the war on poverty, but friction was not necessarily dysfunctional. It is naive to think that there could be redistributions of power without generating controversy or that a few billion dollars spent over a decade and spread over thousands of neighborhoods with millions of poor could remake poverty areas. The model cities and community action programs were blamed for dribbling away money, but there was no other option given the myriad needs and clients. Because so many activities were funded, the impact could not be measured and many analysts, therefore, assumed that there was none. Lacking proof that community action did work, it was assumed that it did not. The inability to measure benefits did not deter the critics in the Nixon administration from advocating revenue sharing, even though the allocation of funds to state and local governments for distribution among a variety of functions would make it equally impossible to assess the results. It was assumed that mayors, governors, and county officials would make decisions best suited to their constituents. However, in connection with community-based groups the assumption was that they were not serving the best interests of their clients unless there was evidence of widespread democratic participation.

The Fundamental Issues

The case against the Great Society's social welfare efforts is based on selective use of the facts and a set of biased standards. This analysis has tried to demonstrate the effectiveness of the Great Society's initiatives as well as to counter the arguments of its critics. Negative judgments have been rebutted by an analysis of their limitations, contradictions, and biases. Reasonable achievement has been demonstrated relative to realistic goals, without the supposition of failure.

This positive verdict might be reversed on appeal. The facts are subject to differing interpretations and the prosecution's case was not prepared carefully and comprehensively because of the misconception that guilt was self-evident. It might be possible, therefore, for a skilled critic of the Great Society to reinterpret the facts again, to hone down the arguments to a level of greater sophistication and to present a more convincing case that will again cast reasonable doubt on these favorable conclusions.

The fundamental issue is the choice of the null hypothesis. Are we as a nation to assume that efforts meeting recognized and critical needs are worthwhile unless proven otherwise, or must there be unimpeachable evidence that they are successful before they can be accepted? The choice of perspectives is fundamentally political and normative. It has been demonstrated that social welfare programs substantially improve the well-being of most beneficiaries and that retrenchment does have serious repercussions. It has been demonstrated also that the negative spillovers and costs of the Great Society's initiatives have been overrated. It remains, however, a matter of judgment whether the consequences of erring on the side of generosity are considered more serious than results of erring on the side of parsimony.

Underlying this judgment are a number of basic uncertainties about where our nation is moving and what the consequences will be. Public social welfare spending rose from 11.6 percent of GNP in fiscal 1965 to 17.7 percent in 1974, absorbing nearly a fourth of the economic growth dividend over the period. Critics of government intervention contend that the nation has been pushed and pulled down the road to a welfare state, with the ultimate destination a society in which individual liberties are curtailed in the search for equality, where a massive and growing underclass parasitically thrives off overburdened workers, where Big Brother is watching over every shoulder, and where economic and social stagnation prevail. If this vision is valid, then there is indeed reason to tighten purse strings and to retrench the social welfare efforts of the last decade.

The Consequences of Government Intervention

Social welfare efforts have been blamed not only for the unemployment and inflation of the 1970s but also for the longer term erosion of the economic system. Good times were followed by bad times, but the *post hoc ergo propter hoc* reasoning blaming the lean years on the fat ones does not hold up under close scrutiny. The economic policies which produced tight labor markets and rapid growth in the 1960s generated some inflationary pressures and perhaps an inflationary psychology. The recession at the end of the decade might have been alleviated with earlier restraint. But other events and policies were responsible for the drastic deterioration of economic conditions. The idea of an unavoidable tradeoff between low unemployment and rapid price increase was contradicted by the continuation of both high joblessness and inflation. Forced to downplay the presumed tradeoff of unemployment and inflation, economists turned to an even less testable notion that full employment caused accelerating price pressures. The policy response was to cool the economy by combatting inflation with joblessness. The result has been the highest unemployment since the Great Depression and persisting inflation.

The Ford and Nixon administrations charged that burgeoning social welfare programs absorbed resources that would otherwise have financed the expansion of the economy. The underlying idea was that when money was transferred from the rich to the poor, it was taken out of the hands of those with the greatest propensity to save and invest and put in the hands of persons who consumed resources needed for maintaining an efficient economy. The depressed conditions of the mid-1970s were not, however, a reflection of a shortage of capital, but rather of inadequate consumer demand. Investment was depressed because productive capacity was already idle. Projections that future investment needs would exceed resources were hypothetical, and there was no proof that these needs would not be met.

Even if more saving and investment had been necessary, the expansion of the welfare state could not explain any capital shortage. The income distribution was not significantly changed over the 1965–75 decade, so that redistribution was not a major factor in savings and investment patterns. In the absence of social welfare efforts, inequality of income might have increased; and if this had occurred, there might have been somewhat greater saving by the affluent. But the differences would have been marginal. If transfers had remained a constant portion of income from 1964 to 1974, $55 billion less would have been taken from taxpayers and given to transfer recipients in 1974. Personal savings equaled 8 percent of disposable personal income, and if it is assumed that transfers went from those who would have saved 8 percent to those who would have saved none, personal savings would have been reduced by $4.4 billion, all else being equal. In 1974 gross private domestic investment was $209.4 billion. Therefore, increased transfers over the decade could have had only a minor impact on investment even if all those savings were channeled into investments. To blame transfer programs for any loss in the dynamism of the economy is an unsupportable exaggeration.

The notion that the welfare state has sapped the nation's human resources by sustaining a vast underclass in idleness is equally fallacious. Most of those who withdrew from the work force prior to normal retirement age because they were attracted by improved social welfare benefits were adult males with physical disabilities, teenagers who had not yet planted roots in the labor market, and unskilled women. They became expendable when millions of more skilled workers lost their jobs. There is surely a tradeoff between higher welfare standards and the number of persons who work. But considering the low productivity of the workers, their difficulty in finding employment and the number of workers they would displace if they found employment, the drag on the economy from their being on welfare is quite small. It is proper to resent hand-outs to those who can find work but it is wrong to view most recipients of social welfare benefits as loafers. As long as the policy of fighting inflation with unemployment continues, the majority of beneficiaries do not have any choice between work and welfare. The loss in output due to withdrawal from the work force because of the availability of welfare payments is dwarfed by involuntary unemployment.

The social welfare efforts of the Great Society have been blamed for almost every social ill. The urban riots and the presumed alienation of middle Americans were blamed on the too rapid pace of social change. Family deterioration and increasing dependency were viewed as the products of expanding welfare. Forced school integration was linked with accelerating white flight from central cities.

These charges are yet to be proved, may be overblown and even misplaced. The urban riots came after a century of pent-up black frustration, and the fact that they occurred when progress began to be achieved only means that improvements put the underprivileged in a position to see their severe disadvantage. Yet, whether gains occurred despite or because of the riots, our nation is closer to achieving the goals of a democratic society by advancing the rights and opportunities of minorities. The plight of the middle American was more a political invention than a documented national problem. The average working-class white was victimized in the 1970s not because of the gains of blacks but because of a stagnant economy. Dependency increased partly because it became a more attractive option to work and also because declining demand for agricultural, domestic, and other unskilled workers forced the disadvantaged out of the labor market. Despite the withdrawal allegedly induced by relief, unemployment rates remained high among those with limited education and skills and suggest that the welfare system was absorbing workers rejected by the economy. Family deterioration was a society-wide phenomenon, not just a result of social welfare policies. Finally, the flight of millions of whites from central cities began years before school integration was even an issue. While it was occurring, blacks were also migrating to cities. As whites preferred suburban living, the ratio of whites to blacks in central cities declined. More information is needed about the direct effect of imposed school integration. Economic, social, and racial separation were not primarily created or caused by social legislation, and could not be overcome by attempts to develop central cities. In brief, the deleterious effects of expanding social welfare programs have been exaggerated, and the negative is far outweighed by the positive improvements in the welfare of those in need.

Are We Going to the Poorhouse?

Critics of the welfare state have charged that the nation is being driven to the poorhouse by increasing social welfare outlays. Yet between 1965 and 1975, real disposable income rose by two fifths, and real disposable income excluding transfers rose by a third. While government efforts absorbed a fourth of the GNP growth dividend, a large portion of this was merely a substitution of public for private provision of goods and services. With Medicare and social security, people could spend less of their income supporting parents. Improved retirement benefits substituted for or complemented private retirement plans. Over the long-run the nation was able to provide adequately for private as well as public needs.

In the severe recession of 1974, millions of idled workers turned to unemployment compensation, food stamps, and other aids. The result was a sharp rise in social welfare expenditures as a proportion of declining GNP. Critics of the welfare state were quick to project these trends into the future, predicting a long-term slowing of economic growth and a continuing rapid rise in social welfare spending unless Draconian measures were adopted.

The projections of penury was based on a number of considerations. The rise in the price of oil focused attention on the critical importance of raw materials, raising the possibility that shortages would depress economic growth below previous rates. The rapid development of the Common Market, Japan, and the communist bloc countries put them in competition not only for scarce resources but also for markets. Declines in measured productivity nurtured fears that the American worker had grown fat and lazy. There were assertions that the large corporations which had grown dominant lacked initiative and innovation. Government regulation was blamed for sapping the private sector's dynamism.

Clearly these dismal forecasts were biased by adverse current circumstances. During the booming 1960s the horizon looked bright for continued growth; in a recessionary trough, it is hard to be optimistic. Yet for each of the arguments of despair there are countervailing reasons to believe that things may not be so bad over the long run. While it is true that other nations have grown more rapidly, much of this was a catching up process and they are not likely to continue to outstrip the United States, especially when they are forced to invest heavily in social overhead capital. Competition is a stimulus, and world trade can help improve all economies if a stable international system can be developed. In retrospect, the dependence on foreign oil was not nearly as critical as was thought when the oil cartel boosted prices. Rising oil prices did lead to painful readjustments, but there is no *a priori* reason why the price system should be any less responsive now than in the past to new needs or that the scientific establishment, spurred by market incentives, should be any less fertile in developing alternatives. It is also doubtful whether the oil cartel will be able to exact rising prices over the long run, and in any period of economic warfare it is the economically strong rather than weak nations who will tend to do best.

Domestic productivity should be enhanced by the maturing of well-educated postwar children into their prime working years. Broader distribution of opportunity should tap underutilized human resources. Zero population growth is not likely to be detrimental to gains in per capita GNP. While ecology measures may reduce profits of some corporations, there is no reason why this must have a negative effect on the economy. Money spent on nitrogen scrubbers or sewage treatment has no less job creation potential than defense spending; vital needs are filled by both.

Whether the 2.6 percent annual real per capital growth rate of the 1960s will be attained in the next decade is a matter of conjecture. Even growth of 1.5 to 2.0 percent per year will allow measured expansion of social welfare efforts. Two percent of a $1.5 trillion economy is $30 billion, providing, in a single year, a growth dividend double the cash income needed to raise all the poor above the poverty threshold. As people enjoy more luxuries, they can presumably afford to devote more of any real increments to other ends. It may prove necessary to weigh the alternatives more carefully than in the past, and to move ahead in a more measured fashion, but continued progress should be possible.

Beyond the Welfare State

However affluent, the nation cannot afford a continuous expansion of social welfare efforts at the rate of the previous decade. The misleading extrapolation of the 1965–75 trends leads quickly to an absolute welfare state. Fears of this eventuality led the Nixon administration to try to halt the growth of domestic programs and the Ford administration to go even further to propose substantial retrenchment.

The social welfare explosion during the previous decade resulted from rapidly raising benefit levels and expanding the eligible populations. There were millions of deprived persons who qualified for aid. Once they had been helped, the growth momentum slowed. By the mid-1970s, public assistance was reaching almost all the low-income aged, blind, and disabled, as well as most needy female-headed families. Health programs also treated most of the indigent. The food stamp program expanded rapidly to serve an increasing share of the eligible population once standards were liberalized in the early 1970s. After this rapid saturation process, the pressure for expansion eased. There was a distinct leveling-off in 1973 and 1974.

Spending accelerated thereafter not because of expanding responsibilities and commitments, but rather because of the severe economic troubles. The combination of rapid inflation and the highest unemployment since the Great Depression forced millions to rely on their social insurance and swelled the number qualifying on the basis of need for in-kind and cash aid. There were no new initiatives on the order of Medicare and Medicaid, assisted housing construction, the war on poverty, or even an old-fashioned WPA-type program. Social welfare expenditures grew because social problems intensified, not because policy makers were openhanded.

Real social welfare spending will in all likelihood recede or at least stabilize when the economy recovers. Retrenchment could boost this process by reducing levels of aid below poverty thresholds or restricting the number of eligibles. This would set the stage for a similar explosion some time in the future when a more generous society decided, once again, to mitigate deprivation.

If critics exaggerated the negative long-run consequences of the welfare state's expansion, those responsible for the process were naive about its short-run effects. The Johnson administration did not act prudently to choke off inflationary pressures, and it did not perceive the impact of its social welfare policies on the labor force participation of the disadvantaged. Neither did it fully comprehend the structural changes occurring in the labor market which were pushing many out of work.

Similarly, the designers and administrators of the Great Society did not fully understand the consequences of their actions. The trends toward family deterioration, especially among blacks, were noted but were not given full consideration in the formulation of welfare policies. The reactions to change, the riots and later backlash, were underestimated. There was an ill-founded notion that deep-seated trends such as white flight from central cities could be reversed by governmental intervention.

Advocates of expanded social programs tended to assume that there would be a continuing fiscal dividend. Later events laid to rest the claims of the new economists developed in the 1960s that they had mastered the secrets of achieving rapid economic growth with stable prices. The bold social welfare thrusts affordable in an expanding economy became increasingly burdensome when growth slowed while needs increased.

The most pervasive shortcoming of the Great Society was its underestimation of the scale of domestic problems and the distance to be covered in providing even minimally for the welfare of all citizens. More was promised than could be delivered, and failure to achieve overly ambitious goals obscured the substantial progress which was being made.

These shortcomings, though real and serious, were the result of farsightedness not shortsightedness. Critics of the welfare state have charged the Great Society with myopia, but, in fact, they were more often suffering from this affliction. Over the long run, the economy, as the Johnson administration believed, was able to generate the resources to expand social welfare commitments. The stresses and strains of social change were weathered. A basic system was established which served the majority of those in need, providing most with at least a rudimentary subsistence.

Social welfare efforts were a means rather than an end for the Great Society. It was not seeking the continuous expansion of public responsibilities nor a completely equalitarian welfare state. Instead, it strove for the equalization of opportunity and the eradication of poverty as defined by an absolute standard. These were fixed and attainable, rather than ever elusive, goals. But this was forgotten in the critical backlash of the 1970s. The policy makers of the subsequent decade discounted the Great Society's longer-run vision assuming erroneously that the welfare state's growth was accelerating and endless.

The most critical domestic issue, then, is whether to move forward to complete and rationalize the social welfare system or to try to halt or reverse the developments of the previous decade. Arguments for the latter course have been based on the false but nonetheless pervasive notions that past expansion has wreaked havoc with the social and economic system, and that new initiatives will inevitably lead to an absolute welfare state. In truth, however, the Great Society programs have promoted the general welfare, and they have brought the nation to the mountain top from where it is possible to envision the terrain beyond the welfare state.

The Promise of a Better Society

Once a minimally adequate social welfare system is established, many of the problems which now seem so insurmountable will dissipate. As in any building process, most of the spillovers occur during early construction and these have already occurred. Many female family heads and disabled males withdrew from the labor force when offered alternative income options, and other low-income families split when welfare provided support for female-headed units. But once welfare levels stabilized in real terms and began to decline relative to earnings, caseload growth slowed and the impact upon work and family diminished. Over the long run, rising real earnings and stable or slowly growing welfare standards will increase the attractiveness of work and stable families.

Once a package of aid is provided which guarantees an income above the poverty threshold, improvements in the system should prove easier. Welfare reform floundered in the early 1970s because the costs of establishing an adequate minimum were too great and because some "reformers" were seeking retrenchment rather than improvement. Eliminating allegedly ineffective approaches proved difficult when their termination would leave former beneficiaries in greater deprivation. Once everyone in need is guaranteed a minimum, it will be easier to substitute one form of aid for another and to concentrate on program performance and effectiveness rather than on dividing too few loaves among the multitudes.

Work disincentives have been a continuing concern, but the problem cannot be attacked until a comprehensive system is in place. Aid to low-income male-headed families, even if packaged so as to maximize work incentives, will still leave some of the less motivated the means to avoid work. If unemployables are provided adequate support, some employables will find ways to qualify. But once the shock effects have been weathered, it will be possible to start improving work incentives without pushing down on the help offered to those who cannot work and to minimize the number of nonworkers by making available attractive jobs.

The choice between public or private provision of goods and services can be more easily resolved once the specter of deprivation is eliminated. As long as welfare standards are inadequate, social insurance programs are pressed into service as transfer mechanisms. Once everyone is above poverty thresholds, the scale and scope of transfer payments can be decided on relative merits rather than on the basis of pressing needs. Similarly the issue of relative versus absolute poverty standards can be addressed directly once a minimum is secured.

The nation has already moved beyond the welfare state in the provision of medical care. The aged and poor are provided for by Medicare and Medicaid. Most of those who remain unprotected are above poverty levels. The question is whether to expand insurance coverage to protect the middle and lower-middle class from sinking into poverty because of health expenses.

All this does not mean that the tasks ahead are light. Completion of a comprehensive social welfare system requires raising the benefit floor under existing programs in many areas of the nation. It involves complex decisions related to the extension of help to male-headed families. In-kind aid such as housing assistance will have to be provided more comprehensively. All this involves a multibillion dollar price tag. Further, the world beyond the welfare state is not the millennium. Societal standards will be debated. Questions about income redistribution are likely to recur. Reform of the social welfare system will always be difficult.

Yet if the challenges are formidable, they are not insuperable, as so many now believe. There is no reason to fear that modest steps which are positive and constructive in alleviating age-old problems will in some way unleash uncontrollable forces or will undermine the broader welfare of the body politic. Only dedicated pessimists and gainsayers can doubt our capacity to achieve substantial improvements. And there is no reason to abandon the aim of providing a minimal level of support for all who remain in need. Progress has been meaningful; it can and must continue. As we enter our third century as a nation, we must reevaluate the recent, as well as distant, past to get a realistic understanding of our limitations but also a greater confidence in our potential. We have the power, if we have the will, to forge a greater society and to promote the general welfare.

Notes

2. Programs and Policies

1. Alfred Skolnik and Sophie R. Dales, "Social Welfare Expenditures: Fiscal Year 1974," *Social Security Bulletin* (January 1975), pp. 7–11; and *The United States Budget in Brief, 1976* (Washington: Government Printing Office, 1975), p. 49.
2. Office of Management and Budget, unpublished data.
3. *The Budget of the United States Government, 1965* (Washington: Government Printing Office, 1964), p. 7.
4. *The Budget of the United States Government, Fiscal Year 1973* (Washington: Government Printing Office, 1972), pp. 36–37.
5. Charles Schultze et al., *Setting National Priorities: The 1973 Budget* (Washington: The Brookings Institution, 1972), p. 11.
6. *The Budget of the United States Government, Fiscal 1965–Fiscal 1974* (Washington: Government Printing Office, 1963–1973).

3. Income Support

1. Social Security Administration, *The Aged Population of the United States* (Washington: Government Printing Office, 1964), pp. 274–309.
2. *Social Security Bulletin Annual Statistical Supplement, 1972* (Washington: Government Printing Office, 1973), p. 22.
3. Peter Henle, "Trends in Retirement Benefits Related to Earnings," *Monthly Labor Review* (June 1972), pp. 14–15.
4. U.S. Bureau of Census, *Estimates of the Population of the United States, by Age, Sex and Race: April 1, 1910 to July 1, 1973* (Washington: Government Printing Office, April 1974), pp. 26 and 36.
5. *Social Security Bulletin Annual Statistical Supplement, 1972,* p. 22.
6. Henle, p. 15.
7. *Ibid.*
8. *Social Security Bulletin* (February 1975), pp. 49 and 73.
9. Estimates from data in *Social Security Bulletin Annual Statistical Supplement, 1972,* p. 64.
10. U.S. Bureau of the Census, *Statistical Abstract of the United States, 1974* (Washington: Government Printing Office, 1974), p. 468.
11. *Social Security Bulletin Annual Statistical Supplement, 1972,* p. 57.
12. Alexander Korns, "The Future of Social Security," *Issues in Financing Retirement Income,* U.S. Congress, Joint Economic Committee, 93rd Cong., 2nd Sess. (Washington: Government Printing Office, December 1974), pp. 5–6.

13. *Employee Benefits, 1971* (Washington: U.S. Chamber of Commerce, 1973), p. 11.

14. George E. Rejda and Richard J. Shepler, "The Impact of Zero Population Growth on the OASDI Program," *Journal of Risk and Insurance* (September 1973), pp. 313–325.

15. James R. Storey, *Public Income Transfer Programs: The Incidence of Multiple Benefits and the Issues Raised by Their Receipt*, U.S. Congress, Joint Economic Committee, 92nd Cong., 2nd Sess. (Washington: Government Printing Office, April 1972), p. 26.

16. "Graphic Material for the New Supplemental Security Income Program: Impact on Current Benefits and Unresolved Issues," U.S. Congress, Joint Economic Committee, 93rd Cong., 1st Sess., October 7, 1973, mimeo., p. 6.

17. Donald E. Rigby, "State Supplementation under Federal SSI Program," *Social Security Bulletin* (November 1974), p. 27.

18. John K. Iglehart, "HEW's Reform Proposal Falls Victim to Economic Problems," *National Journal Reports* (January 4, 1975), p. 11.

19. "Graphic Material for the New Supplemental Security Income Program," p. 16.

20. Department of Health, Education, and Welfare, *Findings of the 1973 AFDC Study: Demographic and Program Characteristics* (Washington: Government Printing Office, 1974), pp. 22, 56, and 58.

21. Sar Levitan, Martin Rein, and David Marwick, *Work and Welfare Go Together* (Baltimore: Johns Hopkins University Press, 1972), p. 59.

22. *Findings of the 1973 AFDC Survey*, pp. 58 and 60.

23. Comptroller General of the United States, *Report to the Congress on Problems in Accomplishing Objectives of the Work Incentive Program (WIN)* (Washington: General Accounting Office, September 1971), p. 30.

24. Vee Burke and Alair Townsend, *Public Welfare and Work Incentives: Theory and Practice*, U.S. Congress, Joint Economic Committee, 93rd Cong., 2nd Sess. (Washington: Government Printing Office, April 1974), pp. 37–38.

25. Irwin Garfinkel, "Income Transfer Programs and Work Effort: A Review," *How Income Supplements Can Affect Work Behavior*, Joint Economic Committee, 93rd Cong., 2nd Sess. (Washington: Government Printing Office, February 1974), pp. 25–26.

26. Heather L. Ross, *Poverty: Women and Children Last* (Washington: The Urban Institute, December 1973), figure 3.

27. Marjorie Honig, "The Impact of Welfare Payment Levels on Family Stability," *The Family, Poverty, and Welfare Programs: Factors Influencing Family Instability*, U.S. Congress, Joint Economic Committee, 93rd Cong., 1st Sess., November 1973, pp. 49 and 53.

28. Derived from U.S. Bureau of the Census, *Fertility Histories*

and *Birth Expectations of American Women,* June 1971, P-20, no. 263, April 1974, p. 53; and *Statistical Abstract of the United States, 1974,* p. 56.

29. Phillips Cutright, "Illegitimacy and Income Supplement," U.S. Congress, Joint Economic Committee, *The Family, Poverty and Welfare Programs,* 93rd Cong., 1st Sess. (Washington: Government Printing Office, 1973), p. 130.

30. George W. Mayeske, *A Study of the Achievement of Our Nation's Students* (Washington: Government Printing Office, 1973), p. 9.

31. James R. Storey, *Welfare in the 70s: A National Study of Benefits Available in 100 Local Areas,* U.S. Congress, Joint Economic Committee, 93 rd Cong., 2nd Sess. (Washington: Government Printing Office, 1974), p. 37.

32. Heather L. Ross, *Poverty: Women and Children Last,* statistical tables.

33. *Congressional Record* (daily edition), February 4, 1975, p. H486.

34. Calculation based on data in *National Survey of Food Stamp and Food Distribution Program Recipients: A Summary of Findings on Income Sources, Amount and Incidence of Multiple Benefits,* U.S. Congress, Joint Economic Committee, 93rd Cong., 2nd Sess. (Washington: Government Printing Office, 1974), p. 24.

35. Sar A. Levitan and Karen Cleary, *Old Wars Remain Unfinished* (Baltimore: Johns Hopkins University Press, 1973), pp. 62–66.

36. James R. Storey, Alair A. Townsend, and Irene Cox, *How Public Welfare Benefits Are Distributed in Low-Income Areas,* U.S. Congress, Joint Economic Committee, 93rd Cong., 1st Sess. (Washington: Government Printing Office, March 1973), p. 66.

37. *Ibid.,* pp. 83–84.

38. *Ibid.,* pp. 88–91.

39. *General Social and Economic Characteristics, United States Summary,* 1970 Census, PC(1)-C(1), p. 545. It should be noted that the census undercounts public assistance by a significant degree.

40. *Graphic Presentation of Public Assistance and Related Data, 1973 and 1963,* Department of Health, Education, and Welfare (Washington: Government Printing Office, 1974 and 1964).

41. *Welfare in the 70s: A National Study of Benefits Available in 100 Areas,* pp. 90, 172.

42. *General Social and Economic Characteristics,* pp. 539–548.

43. *Welfare in the 1970s,* p. 152.

44. *Ibid.,* pp. 68–267.

45. Irwin Garfinkel, "Income Transfer Programs and Work Effort: A Review," *How Income Supplement Can Affect Work Behavior,* U.S. Congress, Joint Economic Committee, 93rd Cong., 2nd Sess. (Washington: Government Printing Office, 1974), p. 10.

46. Winifred Bell and Dennis M. Bushe, *Neglecting the Many,*

Helping the Few: The Impact of the 1967 AFDC Work Incentives (New York: Center for Studies in Income Maintenance Policy, 1975), p. 44.

4. Health Care

1. Regina Lowenstein, "Early Effects of Medicare in the Health Care of the Aged," *Social Security Bulletin* (April 1971), pp. 3–20.

2. *Ibid.*, p. 16.

3. *Medicare and Medicaid: Problems, Issues and Alternatives,* Staff Report, Senate Committee on Finance, 91st Cong., 1st Sess. (Washington: Government Printing Office, February 1970), pp. 17–18.

4. *Ibid.*, pp. 60–69.

5. *Social Security Bulletin* (December 1971), table M-18; and *Social Security Bulletin* (August 1975), table M-18.

6. *Ibid.*, table M-19.

7. Barbara S. Cooper and Paula A. Piro, "Age Differences in Medical Care Spending, Fiscal Year 1973," *Social Security Bulletin* (May 1974), p. 11.

8. Karen Davis, "Lessons of Medicare and Medicaid for National Health Insurance," reprint 295 (Washington: The Brookings Institution, August 1974).

9. *Medicare and Medicaid,* pp. 42–44.

10. John Holahan, *An Economic Analysis of Medicaid* (Washington: The Urban Institute, 1974), working paper no. 976–01, p. 37.

11. *Social Security Bulletin* (December 1974), table M-29; and Dorothy P. Rice and Barbara S. Cooper, "National Health Expenditures, 1929–1970," *Social Security Bulletin* (January 1971), pp. 10–12.

12. *Medicare and Medicaid,* p. 13.

13. "Public Assistance Statistics, February 1974," DHEW, publication no. (SRS) 75-03100, July 1974, table 8; and "Public Assistance Statistics, March 1970," NCSS report P-23, March 1970, table 12.

14. Cooper and Piro, "Age Differences in Medical Care Spending," p. 13; and Barbara S. Cooper and Mary F. McGill, "Medical Care Outlays for Three Age Groups: Young, Intermediate, and Aged," *Social Scurity Bulletin* (May 1971), p. 6.

15. "Age Patterns in Medical Care, Illness and Disability, U.S., July 1933–1965," *Vital Health Statistics,* series 10, no. 32, table 2; and "Age Patterns in Medical Care, Illness and Disability, U.S., 1968–1969," *Vital Health Statistics,* series 10, no. 60.

16. Judith and Lester Lave, *The Hospital Construction Act* (Washington: The American Enterprise Institute, 1974).

17. Barbara S. Cooper, Nancy L. Worthington, and Paula A. Piro, "National Health Expenditures, 1929–1973," *Social Security Bulletin* (February 1974), p. 4.

18. Saul Waldman, *The Effect of Changing Technology on Hospital Costs,* Research and Statistics Note 4 (Washington: Social Security Administration, 1972).

19. *Congressional Record* (daily edition), August 27, 1970, p. S. 14399.

20. *Statistical Abstract of the United States, 1973* (Washington: Government Printing Office, 1974), p. 61.

21. J. D. Beasky, "Presidential Proposals for Revisions of the Social Security System," Hearings, U.S. Congress, Committee on Ways and Means, 88th Cong., 1st Sess. (Washington: Government Printing Office, March–April 1967), part 3, p. 1512; and E. W. Page, "Pathologies and Prophylaxis of Low Birth Weights," *Chronical of Obstetrics and Gynecology* (March 1970), p. 85.

22. *Statistical Abstract of the United States, 1973* (Washington: Government Printing Office, 1974), p. 59.

5. Low-Income Housing

1. Department of Housing and Urban Development, *Housing in the Seventies* (Washington: Government Printing Office, 1973), p. 4–39.

2. Department of Housing and Urban Development, *1972 HUD Statistical Yearbook* (Washington: Government Printing Office, 1974), p. 324.

3. Comptroller General of the United States, *Opportunities to Improve Effectiveness and Reduce Costs of Homeownership Assistance Programs,* B-171630 (Washington: General Accounting Office, December 1972), p. 24.

4. *Ibid.*

5. *Housing in the Seventies,* p. 4–66.

6. *Ibid.,* pp. 4–17 and 4–20.

7. "National Housing Conference Legislative Program," *Congressional Record* (daily edition), April 29, 1974, p. S6453.

8. *1972 HUD Statistical Yearbook* (Washington: Government Printing Office, 1974), pp. 203–204.

9. *Housing in the Seventies,* p. 4–30.

10. *Ibid.,* pp. 4–22 and 4–24.

11. *Ibid.,* p. 4–19.

12. *Ibid.*

13. *Ibid.,* p. 4–106.

14. Frank de Leeuw, "Market Effect of Moderate Income Construction Subsidies," report prepared for the Department of Housing and Urban Development, 1973, mimeo.

15. Harrison G. Wehner, Jr., *Sections 235 and 236: An Economic Evaluation of HUD's Principal Housing Subsidy Programs* (Washington: American Enterprise Institute, 1973), p. 29.

16. *Housing in the Seventies*, p. 4–21.

17. U.S. Congress, Senate, Committee on Banking, Housing and Urban Affairs, *Critique of "Housing in the Seventies,"* 93rd Cong., 2nd Sess. (Washington: Government Printing Office, February 1974), p. vii.

18. U.S. Congress, Joint Economic Subcommittee on Priorities and Economy, *Housing Subsidies and Housing Policies,* 92nd Cong., 2nd Sess. (Washington: Government Printing Office, December 1972), pp. 287 and 292.

6. Compensatory Education

1. George W. Mayeske et al., *A Study of the Achievement of Our Nation's Students* (Washington: Government Printing Office, 1973), p. 11.

2. *Statistical Abstract of the United States, 1974* (Washington: Government Printing Office, 1974), pp. 107–147.

3. Sar A. Levitan and Karen Cleary Alderman, *Child Care and ABCs Too* (Baltimore: Johns Hopkins University Press, 1975), pp. 83–105.

4. Westinghouse Learning Corporation, "Evaluation of the Head Start Program," *The Effectiveness of Compensatory Education* (Washington: Government Printing Office, 1972), pp. 110–113.

5. Stanford Research Institute, *Selected Outcomes of the Longitudinal Evaluation of Follow-Through* (Menlo Park, Calif.: The Institute, March 1973), p. 1.

6. Michael J. Wargo et al., *ESEA Title I: A Reanalysis and Synthesis of Evaluation Data from Fiscal Year 1965 through 1970* (Palo Alto, Calif.: American Institute for Research in the Behavioral Sciences, 1972), p. 121.

7. Department of Health, Education, and Welfare, *The Effectiveness of Compensatory Education* (Washington: Government Printing Office, 1972), pp. 11–13.

8. Peter G. Briggs, *A Perspective on Change: The Administration of Title I of the Elementary and Secondary Education Act* (Washington: The Planar Corporation, 1973), p. 78.

9. *Ibid.*

10. *Digest of Educational Statistics, 1974* (Washington: Government Printing Office, 1974), p. 78.

11. Wargo et al., *ESEA Title I,* pp. 67–96.

12. *The Effectiveness of Compensatory Education,* p. 96.

13. Wargo et al., *ESEA Title I,* pp. 170–174.

14. *Ibid.,* p. 112.

15. *The Effectiveness of Compensatory Education,* p. 2.

16. The Planar Corporation, *Title I—Reading and Mathematics Programs: A Compilation and Synthesis of Available Achievement, Expenditure, and Model Project Information* (Washington: The Planar Corporation, 1973), pp. 39–53.

17. U.S. Bureau of the Census, *Social and Economic Characteristics of Students, October 1972,* P-20, no. 260 (Washington: Government Printing Office, February 1974), p. 5.

18. Office of Management and Budget, *Social Indicators, 1973* (Washington: Government Printing Office, 1973), p. 88.

19. U.S. Department of Health, Education, and Welfare, Bureau of Post-Secondary Education, *Summary of Program Information through Fiscal Year 1974* (Washington: Government Printing Office, 1974), pp. 42–43.

20. U.S. Department of Health, Education, and Welfare, "Summary —The Federal College Work-Study Program: A Status Report, Fiscal Year 1971," p. 2, mimeo.

21. *Summary of Program Information through Fiscal Year 1974,* pp. 20–22.

22. Nathalie Friedman, *The Federal Educational Opportunity Grant Program: A Status Report, Fiscal Year 1970* (New York: Bureau of Applied Social Research, Columbia University, May 1971), mimeo.

23. U.S Department of Health, Education, and Welfare, Bureau of Higher Education, *Summary of Program Information through Fiscal 1974* (Washington: Health, Education, and Welfare, 1974), mimeo., pp. 23–25.

24. Office of Education, unpublished tabulations.

25. *Statistical Abstract of the United States, 1974* (Washington: Government Printing Office, 1974), p. 143.

26. *Ibid.,* pp. 113–114.

27. Ivar Berg, *Education and Jobs: The Great Training Robbery* (New York: Praeger, 1970).

28. U.S. Bureau of the Census, *Annual Mean Income, Lifetime Income, and Educational Attainment of Men in the United States, For Selected Years 1956 and 1972,* P-60, no. 92 (Washington: Government Printing Office, 1974), p. 24.

29. John S. Akin and Irwin Garfinkel, *Economic Returns to Educational Quality: An Empirical Analysis for Whites, Blacks, Poor Whites and Poor Blacks* (Madison: Institute for Research on Poverty, University of Wisconsin, September 1974), pp. 27–29.

7. Manpower Programs

1. Garth L. Mangum, *The Emergence of Manpower Policy* (New York: Holt, Rinehart and Winston, Inc., 1969), pp. 35–68.

2. Joe N. Nay, John W. Scanlon, and Joseph Wholey, *Benefits and Costs of Manpower Training Programs* (Washington: Urban Institute, 1973), p. 11.

3. Jon H. Goldstein, *The Effectiveness of Manpower Training Programs: A Review of Research on the Impact of the Poor,* U.S. Congress, Joint Economic Committee (Washington: Government Printing Office, November 1972), p. 29.

4. Garth L. Mangum and John Walsh, *A Decade of Manpower Development and Training* (Salt Lake City: Olympus Publishing Co., 1973), p. 46.

5. Nay, *Benefits and Costs,* p. 11.

6. Goldstein, *Effectiveness of Manpower Training Programs,* p. 30.

7. David J. Farber, "Changes in the Duration of the Post Training Period in Relative Earnings Credits of Trainees," Manpower Administration, U.S. Department of Labor, August 1971, mimeo.

8. Orley Ashenfelter, "Progress on the Development of Continuous Performance Information of the Impact of the Manpower Development and Training Act, " Manpower Administration, U.S. Department of Labor, Oct. 1973, p. 12, mimeo.

9. Glen G. Cain, *Benefit/Cost Estimates for Job Corps* (Madison: Institute of Research on Poverty, University of Wisconsin, September 1967), p. 10.

10. Louis Harris and Associates, Inc., *A Survey of Ex-Job Corpsmen* (New York: Louis Harris and Associates, April 1969), pp. 25 and 75.

11. Resource Management Corporation, *The Feasibility of Benefit-Cost Analysis for Manpower Programs,* prepared for the General Accounting Office, March 1969, p. 70.

12. Norman C. Murphy, "Quarterly Gains Analysis," General Learning Corporation, report prepared for the Job Corps, U.S. Department of Labor, March 1974, p. 4, mimeo.

13. Sar A. Levitan and Benjamin H. Johnston, *The Job Corps: A Social Experiment That Works* (Baltimore: Johns Hopkins University Press, 1975), Chapter 4.

14. Harris, *A Survey of Ex-Job Corpsmen,* pp. 49–66.

8. Civil Rights Action

1. *Congressional Quarterly Almanac,* 92nd Congress (Washington: Congressional Quarterly, Inc., 1972), p. 651.

2. Office of Management and Budget, *Special Analyses: Budget of the United States Government, Fiscal Year 1976* (Washington: Government Printing Office, 1975, p. 209.

3. U.S. Bureau of the Census, *Voting and Registration in the Election of November 1972,* P-20, no. 253 (Washington: Government Printing Office, October 1973), p. 3.

4. U.S. Bureau of the Census, *Statistical Abstract of the United States, 1974* (Washington: Government Printing Office, 1975), p. 436.

5. Orley Ashenfelter and James Heckman, "Changes in Minority Employment Patterns, 1966 to 1970," prepared for the Equal Employment Opportunity Commission, January 1973, mimeo., pp. ii–vii.

6. George Burman, "The Economics of Discrimination: The Impact of Public Policy," Ph.D. diss., Graduate School of Business, University of Chicago, 1973.

7. "Busing Backfired," interview with James S. Coleman, *National Observer,* June 7, 1975.

8. "Testing Time for Busing," *Newsweek* (September 8, 1975), p. 78.

9. Thomas Pettigrew, "Attitudes on Race and Housing: A Social-Psychological View," in Amos Hawley and Vincent Rock, eds., *Segregation in Residential Areas* (Washington: National Academy of Sciences, 1973), pp. 26–27.

10. Samuel Krislov, "The OEO Lawyers Fail to Constitutionalize a Right to Welfare: A Study of the Uses and Limits of Judicial Power," *Minnesota Law Review,* 58.2 (1973), 102–104.

11. Richard M. Pious, ed., *Civil Rights and Liberties in the 1970s* (New York: Random House, 1973), p. 58.

12. *Ibid.,* p. 63.

13. Address by E. Clinton Bamberger to the National Conference of Bar Presidents, February 19, 1966, in Harry Stumpt, "Law and Poverty: A Political Perspective," *Wisconsin Law Review,* 3 (1968), 711.

14. Quoted in Richard E. Cohen, "Congress Weighs Legal Services Expansion to Benefit Low, Moderate Income Groups," *National Journal* (May 26, 1973), p. 770.

15. *Ibid.,* p. 767.

16. U.S. Congress, Senate Committee on Labor and Public Welfare, Hearings on *Legal Services Program of the Office of Economic Opportunity,* 91st Cong., 1st Sess. (Washington: Government Printing Office, November 1969), p. 84.

9. Community Organization

1. Edward J. O'Donnell and Otto M. Reid, "The Multi-Service Neighborhood Center: Preliminary Findings from a National Survey," *Welfare in Review* (May–June 1971), p. 2.

2. Office of Economic Opportunity, Office of Operations, "Utilization Test Survey Data for 591 CAAs," January 1973, mimeo.

3. Kenneth Clark and Jeannette Hopkins, *A Relevant War against Poverty* (New York: Harper and Row, 1969), pp. 60–61.

4. H. W. Hallman, "The Community Action Program: An Interpretative Analysis," in W. Bloomberg and H. Schmandt, eds., *Power,*

Poverty and Urban Policy, Urban Affairs Annual Review No. 2 (Beverly Hills, Calif.: Sage Publications, 1968), p. 289.

5. Stephen M. Rose, *The Betrayal of the Poor: The Transformation of Community Action* (Cambridge, Mass.: Schenkman, 1972).

6. David M. Austin, "Resident Participation: Political Mobilization of Organizational Cooperation?" *Public Administration Review* (September 1972, special edition), pp. 410–411.

7. Walter Grove and Herbert Costner, "Organizing the Poor: An Evaluation of a Strategy," *Social Science Quarterly* (December 1969), p. 654.

8. Peter Backrach and Martin Baraty, *Power and Poverty: Theory and Practice* (New York: Oxford University Press, 1970), p. 69.

9. Frances F. Piven and Richard A. Cloward, *Regulating the Poor: The Functions of Public Welfare* (New York: Random House, 1971), p. 289.

10. Ralph Kramer, *Participation of the Poor* (Englewood Cliffs, N.J.: Prentice-Hall, 1969), pp. 237–238.

11. Barss, Rietzel, and Associates, "Community Action and Institutional Change," unpublished report to OEO, July 1969, pp. I. 16–17.

12. National Opinion Research Center, "Community Organization Effects, Political and Institutional Change, and the Diffusion of Change Produced by Community Action Programs," unpublished report to OEO, April 1970, p. 28.

13. Office of Economic Opportunity, Office of Operations, "Utilization Test Survey Data for 591 CAAs," January 1973, mimeo.

14. George J. Washnis, *Model Cities Impact on Better Communities,* U.S. Congress, House Committee on Banking and Currency, 93rd Cong., 1st Sess. (Washington: Government Printing Office, December 1973), p. 3.

15. Daniel I. Zwick, "Some Accomplishments and Findings of Neighborhood Health Centers," in Robert M. Hollister, Bernard M. Kramer, and Seymour S. Bellin, eds., *Neighborhood Health Centers* (Lexington, Mass.: Lexington Books, 1974), pp. 69–90.

16. Gerald Sparer and Arne Anderson, "Cost of Services at Neighborhood Health Centers—A Comparative Analysis," *ibid.,* p. 183.

17. Mildred A. Morehead, Rose S. Donaldson, and Mary Seravalli, "Comparisons Between OEO Neighborhood Health Centers and Other Health Care Providers of Ratings of the Quality of Health Care," *ibid.,* pp. 262–263.

18. Bruce Hillman and Evan Charney, "A Neighborhood Health Center: What the Patients Know and Think of Its Operation," *ibid.,* p. 250.

19. Seymour S. Bellin and H. Jack Geiger, "The Impact of a Neighborhood Health Center in Patient's Behavior and Attitudes Relating to Health Care: A Study of a Low-Income Housing Project," *ibid.,* pp. 213 and 230.

20. Abt Associates, Inc., *An Evaluation of the Special Impact Program: Interim Report,* vol. 3, prepared for the Office of Economic Opportunity, March 1973, pp. 2–1 to 2–28. The following discussion is based on the three volume Abt evaluation covering activities through 1972.

21. "MESBICS," *Black Enterprise* (January 1973), pp. 19–22.

22. U.S. Department of Commerce, Office of Minority Business Enterprise, Progress Report on the Minority Business Enterprise Program 1972 (Washington: Government Printing Office, 1972), p. 6; and Jack Eisen, "Failures High among Firms Aided by SBA," *The Washington Post,* November 10, 1973.

23. Raymond Williams and Lloyd Biser, *Analysis of Emerging Cooperatives* (Washington: Department of Agriculture, Farmer Cooperative Service, 1972), pp. 15 and 21.

24. Ray Marshall and Lamond Godwin, *Cooperatives and Rural Poverty in the South* (Baltimore: Johns Hopkins University Press, 1971), pp. 85–98.

25. Abt Associates, *A Study of Rural Cooperatives: Final Report,* prepared for the Office of Economic Opportunity, 1973, pp. 62 and 130.

26. *Manpower Report of the President, 1973* (Washington: Government Printing Office, April 1974), table F-10.

27. *Cost Effectiveness Evaluation of the Urban Concentrated Employment Program* (Falls Church, Va.: Systems Development Corporation, June 1973), p. 75.

28. *Manpower Report of the President* (Washington: Government Printing Office, 1969 and 1974), table F-6 (1969) and table F-10 (1974).

29. Jonathan Spivak, "No Funeral Wreaths for OEO," *The Wall Street Journal,* July 16, 1974, p. 14.

30. Henry J. Schmandt, "Municipal Decentralization: An Overview," *Public Administration Review* (special issue, 1972), pp. 571–602.

10. Aid to the Poor

1. Mollie Orshansky, "Counting the Poor: Before and After Federal Income Support Programs," *Old-Age Income Assurance, Part II,* U.S. Congress, Joint Economic Committee (Washington: Government Printing Office, December 1971), pp. 218–223; and Michael Barth, George J. Carcagno, and John L. Palmer, *Toward an Effective Income Support System: Problems, Prospects and Choices* (Madison: Institute for Research on Poverty, 1974), pp. 25–30.

2. Mollie Orshansky, "More About the Poor in 1964," *Social Security Bulletin* (May 1966), p. 20; and U.S. Bureau of the Census, *Char-*

acteristics of the Low-Income Population, 1972, P-60, no. 91, December 1973, p. 124.

3. U.S. Bureau of the Census, *Money Income and Poverty Status of Families and Persons in the United States, 1974,* series P-60, no. 99, advance report (Washington: Government Printing Office, July 1975), p. 23.

11. Lifting the Black Man's Burden

1. U.S. Bureau of the Census, *Sources and Structure of Family Income,* series PC(2)-4C, tables 6 and 7, series PC(2)-8A, tables 4 and 5; and *Money Income in 1973 of Families and Persons in the United States,* series P-60, no. 97, January 1975, table 72.

2. U.S. Bureau of the Census, *Sources and Structure of Family Income,* series PC(2)-4C, table 23; U.S. Bureau of the Census, *Money Income in 1973 of Families and Persons in the United States,* series P-60, no. 97, January 1975, table 72.

3. U.S. Bureau of the Census, *The Social and Economic Status of the Black Population in the United States, 1974,* P-23, no. 54, July 1975, tables 87 and 91.

4. *Ibid.,* tables 99–100.

5. Orley Ashenfelter and James Heckman, "Changes in Minority Employment Patterns, 1966 to 1970," prepared for the Equal Employment Opportunity Commission, January 1973, mimeo., pp. ii–vii.

6. U.S. Bureau of the Labor Statistics, *Selected Earnings and Demographic Characteristics of Union Members, 1970,* Report 417 (Washington: Government Printing Office, 1972), table 6.

7. Derived from U.S. Department of Justice, *Uniform Crime Reports 1972* (Washington: Government Printing Office, 1973).

8. U.S. Department of Health, Education, and Welfare, Welfare Administration, *Study of Recipients of Aid to Families with Dependent Children, November–December 1971: National Cross-Tabulations,* and U.S. Department of Health, Education, and Welfare, Social and Rehabilitation Service, "Findings of the 1971 AFDC Study," unpublished table.

9. *Social Security Bulletin, Annual Statistical Supplement, 1973,* table 66.

10. U.S. Department of Health, Education, and Welfare, *Medicare: Public Assistance Recipients in the Supplementary Medical Insurance Program, 1969,* publication no. SSA73–11702 (Washington, HEW, July 5, 1973), p. 6.

11. 1970 White House Conference on Children, U.S. Department of Health, Education, and Welfare, *Profiles of Children* (Washington: Government Printing Office, 1971), tables 25 and 26.

12. Office of Economic Opportunity, "Number of Patients by Pa-

tient Characteristics According to Sex and Age in the United States," mimeo., 1973.

13. *The Social and Economic Status of Blacks in the United States, 1974,* table 71.

14. U.S. Office of Management and Budget, *Special Analyses, Budget of the United States Government, 1976* (Washington: Government Printing Office, 1975), p. 166.

15. Gerald G. Somers and Ernst Stromsdorfer, *A Cost Effectiveness Analysis of the In-School and Summer Neighborhood Youth Corps* (Washington: The Urban Institute, November 1970), working paper no. 350–22, table 3.

16. U.S. Department of Labor, Employment and Training Administration, unpublished tabulations.

12. Managing the Economy and Sharing the Wealth

1. *Economic Report of the President, 1964* (Washington: Government Printing Office, January 1964), p. 3.

2. *Ibid.,* p. 8.

3. *Ibid.,* p. 42.

4. *Federal Economic Policy* (Washington: Congressional Quarterly, Inc., 1969), p. 70.

5. U.S. Department of Commerce, *1973 Annual Report of the Economic Development Administration* (Washington: Government Printing Office, 1973), pp. 4–6.

6. Raymond Milkman, Christopher Bladen, Beverly Lyford, and Howard Walton, *Alleviating Economic Distress* (Lexington, Mass.: D.C. Heath and Co., 1972), p. 109.

7. *Ibid.,* pp. 111–113.

8. Robert S. Goldfarb, "The Policy Content of Quantitative Minimum Wage Research," *Proceedings of the Twenty-Seventh Annual Meeting* (Madison: Industrial Relations Research Association, 1974), p. 266.

9. *Economic Report of the President, 1973* (Washington: Government Printing Office, 1973), pp. 72–73.

10. *Economic Report of the President, 1974* (Washington: Government Printing Office, 1974), p. 60.

11. Murray S. Weitzman, *Family (Money) Income 1947 to 1971: Summarizing Twenty-Five Years of Summary Statistics* (Washington: Government Printing Office, July 1974), technical paper no. 35.

12. U.S. Bureau of the Census, *Money Income in 1973 of Families and Persons in the United States,* series 60, no. 97, January 1975, table 17.

13. *Congress and the Nation 1945–1964* (Washington: Congressional Quarterly, Inc., 1965), pp. 437–440.

14. *Congressional Quarterly Almanac, 91st Congress, 1st Session, 1969* (Washington: Congressional Quarterly, Inc., 1970), pp. 589–590.

15. *Congressional Quarterly Almanac, 92nd Congress, 1st Session, 1971* (Washington: Congressional Quarterly, Inc., 1972), pp. 430–440.

16. *A Review of Government and Politics during Nixon's First Term* (Washington: Congressional Quarterly, Inc., 1973), p. 95.

17. U.S. Bureau of Labor Statistics, *Educational Attainment of the Work Force*, Special Labor Force Reports, annual issues (Washington: Government Printing Office, 1968–1974).

18. Robinson G. Hollister and John L. Palmer, "The Impact of Inflation on the Poor" and "The Implicit Tax of Inflation and Unemployment since Policy Implications," in Kenneth Boulding and Martin Pfaff, eds., *Redistribution to the Rich and Poor: The Grants Economics of Income Redistribution* (Belmont, Calif.: Wadsworth Publishing Co., 1972), p. 247.

19. Herman P. Miller, "A Profile of the Blue-Collar American," in Sar A. Levitan, ed., *Blue-Collar Workers* (New York: McGraw-Hill, 1971), pp. 72–73.

20. Lawrence A. Mayer, "The Clouded Prospect for Corporate Profits," *Fortune* (May 1973), p. 184.

Tables

Figures

Index